THE ABRAHAM CONNECTION

A Jew, Christian and Muslim in Dialogue

**George B. Grose and Benjamin J. Hubbard,
Editors**

D1417148

THE ABRAHAM CONNECTION

A Jew, Christian and Muslim in Dialogue

An Encounter between Dr. David Gordis,
Dr. George Grose and Dr. Muzammil Siddiqi
Moderated by Dr. Benjamin Hubbard

George B. Grose and Benjamin J. Hubbard
Editors

Volume VI
THE CHURCH AND THE WORLD SERIES
Cyriac K. Pullapilly, Saint Mary's College, General Editor
George H. Williams, Harvard University, Consulting Editor

Cross Cultural Publications, Inc.
CrossRoads Books

A Book of The

ACADEMY FOR JUDAIC, CHRISTIAN AND ISLAMIC
STUDIES

The University Religious Conference at UCLA
900 Hilgard Avenue
Los Angeles, California 90024
Phone: (310) 208-0863
FAX: (310) 209-5535

Published by CROSS CULTURAL PUBLICATIONS, INC.
CROSS ROADS BOOKS
Post Office Box 506
Notre Dame, Indiana, 46556, U.S.A.
Phone: (219) 272-0889
FAX: (219) 273-5973

Cover Design by Judy Hubbard

To the Memory
of our Colleagues in the Academy

Sterling Wortman   **1923-1981**

Abdelmuhsin El-Biali **1931-1983**

Jacob Bernard Agus   **1911-1986**

Cynthia Clark Wedel   **1908-1986**

Henri Elias Front   **1928-1989**

Don Alan Schweitzer   **1941-1993**

Dr. Wortman was vice president of the Rockefeller Foundation. Dr. El-Biali was director of the Islamic Foundation of Southern California and vice president of The Academy for Judaic, Christian, and Islamic Studies. Dr. Agus was rabbi of Beth El Congregation, Baltimore, and an honorary president of The Academy. Dr. Wedel was a president of the World Council of Churches and an honorary president of The Academy. Dr. Front was rabbi of Temple Beth David, Westminster, California, and vice president of The Academy. Dr. Schweitzer was academic vice president of California State University, Fullerton, and chair of the Advisory Board of The Academy.

ACKNOWLEDGEMENTS

We acknowledge, first of all, our colleagues in the book, Dr. David Gordis and Dr. Muzammil Siddiqi. Their devotion to task, sense of humor and vision inspired us. Together we endeavored to be sure that we meant what we said and said what we meant in terms, God willing, understandable.

The Introduction and the Forewords are, in themselves, an intellectual feast. We thank Archbishop Edward W. Scott, Mrs. Blu Greenberg, Father Donald P. Merrifield, S.J. and Dr. Seyyed Hossein Nasr for their time and thought in preparing these gifts.

Robert McLaren, Ph.D., and Daniel Ninburg, M.D., of the Academy Board of Directors, Rayburn Dezember, the Honorable Leonard Goldstein, Maher Hathout, M.D., Nazim Karim, Sana Khan, M.D., Ph.D., Nizar Makan, M.D., Commander James Rorabaugh, Don Schweitzer, Ph.D., and Jacques Yeager of the Advisory Board gave financial and moral support at each step.

The late Dr. Don Schweitzer, while vice president for academic affairs at California State University, Fullerton, gave the encouragement of the University to this undertaking. He was a major fund raiser from private sources and generous with wise counsel and enthusiasm. We thank, as well, Mary Jo Medyn, his executive secretary, for her helpfulness.

Dr. Daniel Ninburg has shared in the project at every level and, with his mastery of grammar and syntax, gave cogent suggestions and countless hours to proof-reading this manuscript. His contribution has been magnificent.

We give a very special thank you to Nancy Willits Sattler for her unfailing encouragement and help.

The institutional enablers of this Academy book are not without significance: the Lilly Endowment; the Community Foundation of the

Jewish Federation of Orange County; the Session of the First Presbyterian Church of Fullerton, Calif.; the International Islamic Education Institute, Tustin, Calif.; and the Islamic Center of Southern California, Los Angeles.

Every Friend of the Academy who has made a financial contribution since 1991 can take satisfaction in having played a part in the crafting of this work. We thank them all.

We are grateful to the California State University Fullerton Foundation for handling all the funds for this enterprise. We could not have managed without such help.

We are indebted to Denise Schultz, a student of Dr. Hubbard at Cal State Fullerton, who read the first two chapters of the manuscript and made valuable suggestions.

We wish to thank Louise Hagan of LP Office Services, Costa Mesa, Calif. who did most of the transcriptions. This was a challenging task since it involved listening to four participants and deciphering many technical and foreign words. She also handled many word-processing matters, including the preparation of the manuscript in camera-ready form for publication.

In addition, the office staff in the Department of Religious Studies at Cal State Fullerton, especially Jo Ann Robinson and Jeanne Miner, provided invaluable assistance.

We acknowledge with gratitude the patient guidance of Dr. Cyriac Pillapully, General Editor of CrossRoads Books.

We wish to recognize artist Judy Hubbard who designed the book cover. Dr. Hubbard also wants to thank her for reading portions of the manuscript and making numerous suggestions that kept it from being too technical for the non-specialist.

Finally, Dr. Grose is grateful to God for the fortitude of his wife, Elinor Grose, who has shared in the work of the Academy since 1975.

That year, she accompanied her husband and other Academy leaders to Rome, Geneva, Cairo and, later, Jerusalem. She has been part of several overseas missions and was of immense help when leaders of the Academy addressed the Sixth Assembly of the World Council of Churches in Vancouver in 1983. The Academy has made her a Companion of the Order of Abraham. Her encouragement for the book has been great and very important.

Quotations from the Hebrew Bible and New Testament, when not translated by the dialogue participants themselves, are from the Revised Standard Version, Copyright 1952/1946, by Division of Christian Education of the National Council of Churches of Christ in the United States of America.

George B. Grose and Benjamin J. Hubbard, editors

CONTENTS

INTRODUCTION
By
The Most Reverend Edward W. Scott

Archbishop Scott was Primate of All Canada, Anglican Church of Canada (1971-86) and Moderator of the World Council of Churches (1975-84). He represents Canada in the British Commonwealth Group of Eminent Persons to advise on South Africa.

It is not unusual for developments which are little known or largely ignored as they were occurring, to be later recognized as being of tremendous significance in human history. This is particularly true in the religious realm where human beings, in the face of the challenges which confront them, seek to respond either individually or with others to a call that they are convinced comes from beyond themselves and take a further "step of faith" and become involved in something new.

Such, I believe, will be the case with the work of the Academy for Judaic, Christian, and Islamic Studies, which has now led to this publication—*The Abraham Connection.* I see it as the first major public report of work which has now been going on, quietly but steadily, for nearly 20 years. I will be doing all I can to encourage members of the religious academic community and those outside of that community who have a serious concern about religion to read this publication.

Those who do, will be challenged by the deeply held convictions and loyalties of the three persons, each representing one of the Abrahamic religions, involved in this tri-partite dialogue. Their personal authenticity is clearly evident. Readers will not only gain new and deeper insights into the three religions but also be called to reflect more deeply upon the contributions of these three monotheistic religions, which have a common connection in Abraham, to the world that is still coming to be. They will also be challenged to reassess their own religious convictions as they relate to the meaning of their own existence and the meaning of the cosmos—all that "is."

I believe many will also be stimulated by the disciplined methodology which sets the ground rules for this particular dialogue. This methodology could well be a model for many other dialogues that are coming into being. Human beings, confronted by a very troubled and troubling world, are drawn by the revolution in communication into increased awareness not only of each other's existence but of their differences. And they are seeking to maintain or discover meaning in personal existence.

I am deeply grateful to the persons involved in the dialogue and in The Academy who have made this book available at what I believe is a very opportune time in human history—a time when I believe God is calling something new into being. I believe this book is a part of that call.

Edward W. Scott, Archbishop
Toronto, Ontario

FOREWORD
By
Blu Greenberg

Blu Greenberg is an author and lecturer on subjects of contemporary Jewish interest. Her books include On Women and Judaism *and* How To Run a Traditional Jewish Household. *She has participated in many dialogue projects, including a Jewish-Palestinian women's dialogue group since 1989.*

Jews, Christians, and Muslims. Take a look at our history and who would believe that we share a common ancestor, one, no less, whom we all venerate. Had Abraham been able to look into the future and see the strife in the name of the monotheistic religions that sprang from him, he might have taken more pains to instill in his descendants a greater measure of brotherly and sisterly love. Nor can we say it was the man's fault, for Sarah and Hagar did no better.

But the religious message of all three monotheistic faiths is that we must repair the world, not simply accept it as it is. That was the greatness of Abraham in his covenant with God, and that is the task of the human partners in the covenant today. So here we stand, almost 4,000 years later in human history, painfully aware that it is up to us to find ways to bond together: for unless we do so, we shall continue to consume each other, a few hundred in this generation, a few thousand in another, a few million... The stakes grow higher and higher as science and technology are called into the service of religious and ethnic ideology.

All of this is why the work of The Academy is so important. It has created a vehicle for coming together in a spirit of amity. It has done so, not on a one-time basis, nor merely for photo opportunities, but for sustained interaction and with significant tasks to be accomplished.

In addition to its seriousness of purpose, its innovativeness in the tripartite nature of dialogue is to be celebrated. The Academy was the first, and for a long time the only, institution to enlarge the Jewish-Christian encounter to include Muslims. Years ago its founders—Dr.

George Grose, Rabbi Henri Front, Dr. Robert McLaren, Dr. Daniel Ninburg and Dr. Muzammil Siddiqi—came to a realization that is only now beginning to dawn in the Western world: that Islam is not a poor backward cousin to be ignored but rather a monotheistic faith of growing importance and presence worldwide. And while there is still a place for bipartisan dialogue of every composition, the basic principle of tripartite conversation among the children of Abraham is that the yield is greater than the mere addition of one more partner. More than that, the three are vital partners in making dialogue work in the real world.

It is instructive to take a brief look at Jewish-Christian dialogue of the past fifty years, for it points to how far along the path we have come from that time until this. In a certain sense, interfaith dialogue was born of the Holocaust. For Jews, one of the lessons to be learned was that we cannot rely wholly on God or on humanity to protect us. We must take up the task ourselves. This meant a shift in diaspora and exile mentality. It also meant that we needed to come together with persons of the majority faith so that we would never again be so isolated. For Christians, the lesson of the Holocaust was that the teachings of contempt, while not the motive of a master plan for racial annihilation, were indeed an underpinning of such a monstrous ideology. Religious doctrine that caricatures or teaches enmity is not "harmless"; on the contrary, such enmity does have consequences.

Thus, the first few years of dialogue between Christians and Jews were based on general concepts of brotherhood. We can talk to each other, share common concerns; we can be friends. Gradually, we began to talk of religious matters, primarily the commonalities between our two faiths. A major turning point in dialogue came in the 1960s, with the blessed promulgation of *Nostra Aetate* [the Second Vatican Council's 1965 Declaration on the Relationship of the Church to Non-Christian Religions] by the great Pope John XXIII. Another pivotal moment in the conversation came in the aftermath of the Six-Day War between Israel and the surrounding Arab states. In the headiness of victory over what might have been, there also came a sobering awareness. With few exceptions, the Christian community, including many who had participated in the brotherhood exchanges, had sat silently on the sidelines during the weeks preceding the war, weeks that had been filled with threats of annihilation. Many Jews who had been in dialogue were disillusioned and left; but many others began to realize that the responsibility lay in part with ourselves. Out of desire not to offend Christian theological sensibilities that interpreted the exile as permanent punishment for rejecting Jesus, Jews did not speak about that which was closest to their hearts, the return of the Jewish people to their historic homeland.

It was at that point, in the late 60s, that true dialogue got underway, for if we cannot talk about what is most sacred to us and what is most different about each of us from the other, then we are reduced to nothing more than an exchange of platitudes.

Happily, when the Academy initiated tripartite dialogue in 1977, it did not start the warm-up process all over again with the introduction of a new partner. One of the more remarkable features of *The Abraham Connection* is that even more than describing the similarities, which certainly warm the heart, the scholars tackled all of the divisive issues: the manifold parting of the ways of the children of Abraham; the sensitive theme of chosenness; the legitimacy/rejection of one faith's prophets by the others; the missionary impulse in dialogue; and the highly charged issue of land and sacred space. There is no lightly glossing over of anything here; no divisiveness is left unexamined, no provocation allowed to slide by, even in an aside.

And yet, a much larger lesson is to be learned from the discourses. For all of the tough-minded argument, there is enormous respect on all sides, a dispute, as it were, within parameters of dignity and friendliness, even of love. We see clearly that one need not blur the distinctions nor mute the quarrel in order to live side by side, in real harmony.

So an overriding question emerges, one that begets several others: Why is there so much strife and violence in the name of religious difference when we see here in microcosm that it can work in exactly the opposite manner? Could this dialogue be telling us that, contrary to the widely held stereotype, religion is not the cause of strife among peoples of the Earth but rather is used as a cover for more base instincts—greed, racism, chauvinism, xenophobia? And if so, might we presume that religious difference can be used in another way, as a healer, a bridge, a check on those base instincts? One is compelled, upon finishing this work, to ponder a moment: what would the Jewish people be like today had there been several hundred such dialogues taking place in Europe in the 1930s? What would the Palestinian people have achieved by now, had there been tripartite dialogue taking place in 1947, the year the United Nations partition plan was offered? And a decade from now, what would the young ones of Bosnia and Croatia have remembered of their childhood, had their religious leaders been talking? Can we dare to assume that religious leaders, in a spirit of mutual attachment to each other, might be a power to overcome the forces of evil that breed violence and hatred?

But it would be naive to think that a feeling of affinity or good intentions would be enough to change matters. It would take more than that; it would take a major step forward by all the parties involved, one in fact that is evident in the work at hand. In this volume, the frank and open discussion often takes a turn from how things are to how things ought to be. One of the most refreshing qualities of this dialogue—and a measure of the four men who participate in—is the occasional self criticism of one's own tradition where it is warranted. Self criticism is generally not a feature of dialogue, even at this moment in time. A healthy self criticism can flourish in a climate where two variables are present: uncompromising honesty of an individual, and an ability to hear how the things we might say internally are heard in the presence of "the other." (If I have learned anything from two decades of dialogue work, it is that one ought not say that which could not be said in the presence of the other). What ultimately flows from this, I believe, is the next and more risky step we will all have to take—the modification of our own sacred texts that are harmful to the other. Given that The Academy has achieved the state of the art in tripartite dialogue, I suspect it could be the institution to lead us in joint efforts in such a serious and delicate enterprise.

To do any or all of this, to create a climate of desire to overcome hostility, we must replicate this kind of dialogue in a thousand different places. In that sense, too, *The Abraham Connection* is a path-breaking work, not only because the reader has the opportunity to learn so much about religious faiths—including his or her own—not only because the areas of convergence and divergence between the three faiths are highlighted, but also because the model for good dialogue is right here. Thankfully these conversations were not gussied up to read like three monographs. Wisely, all the richness and flow of normal conversations have been retained, all the respectful interruptions, all the times Dr. Siddiqi says, "Now, wait a minute, David" or Dr. Hubbard waits five minutes and then says, "I'd like to go back to...", a thread the reader herself had wanted to pick up. It is precisely the "wait a minute" exchanges that give the reader not only a genuine model of how to speak, listen, learn, and even criticize the other but also a sense of empowerment with which to go forward in replicating tripartite dialogue in many places.

What emerges most powerfully from this remarkable work is the sense that there are many paths to God, that the people of each path are held in special relationship to God, each chosen, not only for a mission but for a special love, in much the same way that each child feels a parent loves him or her most specially but that all of the siblings are the objects of love. And like siblings in a healthy family, we may have great differences and squabbles and competition. But in the final analysis, we try to protect each other from danger and ill fate; we try to pull together to mend the world around us in some small way. Would that the message of *The Abraham Connection* reach into many dark corners to illuminate that way.

Blu Greenberg
Riverdale, New York

FOREWORD
By
The Reverend Donald P. Merrifield, S.J.

Fr. Merrifield is chancellor and former president of Loyola-Marymount University, Los Angeles. A physicist as well as theologian, he was a consultant to the Jet Propulsion Laboratory in Pasadena. He is the author of Hope for Tomorrow: Genuine Love Should Be the Moving Force.

Hostility and violence flare up almost daily in our world between peoples whose deep conflicts seem rooted in their religious identities: Catholics and Protestants in North Ireland; Orthodox Christians, Catholics, and Muslims in Bosnia; Jews and Muslims and Christians in Israel and its occupied territories. Many historical factors and cultural differences may add to the seemingly endless madness, but religious convictions are certainly a central element in the self-identification that sets these groups off against one another.

In Europe, the memory of the Holocaust remains as of an almost incredible slaughter rooted in centuries-old Catholic and Protestant anti-Semitism and allowed to happen by the cooperation and complicity of Christians in Germany and so many other nations. Today, the hostilities of a largely post-Christian Europe are directed at the diverse Muslim people living in its midst.

In the United States, we are far from having conquered all enmity between Protestants and Catholics, much less between Jews and Christians; and now Islam appears as an ever-growing reality on the American scene, no more welcome than the waves of foreigners of different faiths and faces that came before them. As mosques appear in suburban America, physicians named Ahmed Iqbal greet us at our hospitals and Arab-speaking taxi drivers take us to the airport, we know we are in a different world.

Certainly, strangeness is an element in the conflicts between peoples, but it seems to me that ethnic strangeness of itself—diversity of customs, foods, style of dress, dance and music—is not as alienating as diversity of religious beliefs.

In the contemporary environment both here and overseas, the contribution of The Academy for Judaic, Christian and Islamic Studies, which has commissioned this book, is extremely important. The Academy addresses the tripartite dynamic of Jewish-Christian-Islamic interaction. It is the thesis of the Academy that the communities of Judaism, Christianity and Islam are linked through the Abraham heritage, as attested by Bible and Qur'an. Hence, they will interact to the end of time; they will have intertwining destinies.

This interaction has been found to exhibit an historic dynamism from which neither Jews, Christians nor Muslims can go their separate way. Any disturbance or thwarting of this tripartite dynamism is fraught with tragedy for the human race as illustrated by the "Final Solution" of the Holocaust and "Ethnic Cleansing" in Bosnia.

It seems to me that religious beliefs are so central to our identity that when the other comes into our midst with a different belief and way of life, we are deeply threatened. This may be especially true of the Abrahamic faiths: Judaism, Christianity and Islam. With all we have in common and in spite of the genteel tone of the dialogue of this book, we definitely challenge one another's basic beliefs. The New Testament presents itself as the fulfillment and the completion of the Hebrew Bible. The Qur'an claims to be the final prophetic revelation, completing and fulfilling both the others.

It is the wonder of this dialogue between Dr. George Grose, Rabbi David Gordis and Imam Muzammil Siddiqi, that these three believers from the Abrahamic religions find it possible to demonstrate appreciation for each other's religious traditions and deep respect for one another's faith and integrity, while obviously differing on key points. This is very much in the spirit of all the work of The Academy.

It is all the more impressive because each tradition has certainly maintained a view of itself as a "chosen people" who has received a revelation of the truth from God. Of course, I must add that, within

Christianity, Catholics and Protestants have always known that they each were in possession of the truth and the other quite in error.

Indeed, today the Catholic Church no longer holds *extra ecclesiam nulla salus* [There is no salvation outside the church], but not in a way, I believe, which would make those of other faiths feel greatly respected, since we Catholics still appropriate all those of good will to our camp, even if anonymously! If I were not Christian, I might find such appropriation in Dr. Grose's belief about salvation through Christ for Muslims and Jews.

Even though Rabbi Gordis shies away from a Judaism with a special love of the Jewish people by God, I feel that all three faiths are together in a belief in God being manifested to a particular people in history in a manner that makes it certainly very hard to say we all have different paths to the same God. The question of conversion from one faith to another, which is treated very carefully in this dialogue, makes it impossible to maintain the simplistic position that Judaism is God's way for Jews, Christianity for Christians, and Islam for Muslims. Howsoever respectful of others Muslims and Christians at their best might be in spreading their faiths, they both have a mission to convert all peoples. Rabbi Gordis, once again, notes somewhat whimsically that Judaism's missionary intent shouldn't be discounted either.

So what does this book provide? It doesn't seem such scholarly and respectful discourse is for the ordinary faithful, as significant and important as it is. The masses may, however, be reached by religious leaders and educators who read this book and are themselves led into serious dialogue with those who are thus far strangers to them. Even religious leaders and educators may shy away from "the difficult areas" in conversations, formal and informal, preferring less controversial topics such as the homeless problem or teaching values in schools or health care. Hopefully, through this dialogue, they may venture into discussions of their religious beliefs and traditions. University students, as well, hopefully the leaders of tomorrow's world, would benefit greatly from the introduction to dialogue that *The Abraham Connection* provides.

The deepest encounter we can make with one another, it seems to me, is in the area of awareness of the genuine contact with God that each of us has in our particular faith. I do not have to abandon my Christian convictions to know, experientially, not just intellectually, that my Jewish brothers and sisters celebrating Passover are in awe and love before the same God as I encounter in "the breaking of the bread." So, too, as the Muslim bows in prayer before Allah, I am carried along in awe and reverence before God whom I also know as Totally Other and beyond my comprehension.

In the dialogue of this book, we find the participants showing their profound respect for each other as people of God, people indeed of the same God. Such respect can coexist with religious differences which can be explored in total authenticity, appreciated, even understood to a great extent, yet which will not be seen as parts of a whole this side of eternity. For now, it is enough if we can come to some appreciation that the other is also chosen, a beloved son and daughter of God—not only the other who is able to enter into learned dialogue, but perhaps more obviously the devout Mexican woman on her knees before the image of Our Lady of Guadalupe, the young mother lighting the candles as Shabbas begins, and the Muslim medical student leaving class on Friday to join in prayer at the mosque across the street. We all do an amazing thing, each in our own way, paying homage in our lives to that which is quite beyond our grasp but which we each believe has grasped us at the very core of our being.

In dialogue, such as is set forth in *The Abraham Connection*, our experience of being grasped by God is thus deepened and enriched by our authentic sharing of our particular faith with those of the others with a common historical origin in Abraham.

Donald P. Merrifield, S.J.
Los Angeles, California

FOREWORD
By
Dr. Seyyed Hossein Nasr

Dr. Nasr is University Professor of Islamic Studies at George Washington University, Washington, D.C. He is the first Muslim in history to give the Gifford Lectures at the University of Edinburgh, entitled "Knowledge and the Sacred" (1981). His books have been translated into many languages.

What greater tragedy for the Western and Islamic worlds than the current strife between the children of the Abrahamic family of religions, while the members of this family, namely, Judaism, Christianity and Islam, share the basic tenets of Abrahamic monotheism and the ethical principles which issue from it! The sad plight of the Palestinians and Bosnians—not to speak of Azer-baijanis and Armenians and many other victims of confrontations defined by religious identity with members of the Abrahamic family—make it an imperative necessity and even ethical duty to create better understanding among Muslims, Christians and Jews in the West whose power projects itself into the Islamic world as well.

There is so much about which there needs to be dialogue and discussion. And yet, serious dialogue is far from being an easy matter if one takes one's religion seriously, and is not willing to sacrifice one's sacred tradition at the altar of some kind of humanistic ecumenism—which would forego aspects of the Divine Message—for the sake of the attainment of some early and purely human end. Time has arrived for a serious dialogue between members of the Abrahamic family based on complete respect for sacred traditions, a dialogue which is of the utmost importance for the Western and Islamic worlds, and even, indirectly, the rest of the globe.

And yet, major obstacles need to be overcome. There are, first of all, metaphysical issues concerning the nature of God, man, creation, eschatology and other realities which have been expressed in different languages and symbols in the three religions. Still, at the highest level they all assert the unity of the Divine Principle, which is especially central to the Islamic perspective. Then there are specific theological formulations touching upon the nature of sacred scripture, the meaning of revelation, the question of redemption and salvation, incarnation, rituals and so many other facets of religion which divide the three religions, despite the remarkable resemblance of many of their metaphysical and ethical teachings.

In addition, there are the historical questions which possess a definite religious color and are even identified by some with religion itself. There is the historical experience of the Jews in Europe which stands in contrast, to a large extent, to their experience in the Islamic world where they never witnessed a 1492 nor a 1942. Then there is the millennial confrontation between two major civilizations, the Islamic and the Western, which until fairly recently was also a Christian civilization, with all that this confrontation implied: from the writing of blasphemous biographies of the Prophet in Latin; to the invasion of the heartland of the Islamic world by the Crusaders; and finally the colonial domination of that world which, although no longer driven by Christian values, nevertheless combatted Islam as if the Occident were still a Christian civilization. On the other side, there has been the ubiquitous presence of Christian minorities in many Muslim lands, with various types of friction that were bound to arise from time to time.

Finally, as far as the West is concerned, there is the great obstacle of the negative image of Islam projected by the media and propagated by vested interests of various kinds. While nearly everywhere—from Sarajevo to Hebron—it is the Muslims who are killed and are on the defensive, they are depicted as if they were about to overrun America and Europe. And even the very laudable task of creating better Jewish-Christian understanding after the colossal tragedies of the Second World War, and the use of the term "Judeo-Christian tradition" or traditions, have been used by some as an exclusionist motto to bring about further confrontation with that third member of the family not explicitly mentioned, that is, Islam.

In face of these obstacles, the important role of The Academy for Judaic, Christian, and Islamic Studies becomes clear, for here we find one of the very few centers in America seriously dedicated to the

Judeo-Christian-Islamic traditions; that is, the whole Abrahamic family without exclusion of any member. The Academy, devoted for many years to dialogue between the three Abrahamic religions, is making available in this volume much of the fruit of this labor to the public at large.

The president of the Academy, Dr. George Grose, and two of the members of the board, Dr. Muzammil Siddiqi (a Muslim) and Dr. David Gordis (a Jew), present the reader with a dialogue in depth concerning some of the most important issues in the present-day relation between the three religions. The three participants are eminently qualified for such a task, all three being men of religion with honesty and integrity, immersed in their own tradition, and not representing simply an individual opinion or a fringe group. This often happens in ecumenical efforts in the West when they also involve Islam. Also, all three men are knowledgeable in their own religious tradition, in the general questions facing a person of faith in the modern world, and in the global situation. To these qualifications must be added their sincerity as men of faith to serve the cause of peace in the context of God's injunctions and revelations to the three communities which share the world view of Abrahamic monotheism.

The result is a document of religious depth, as well as intellectual challenge, which is an important contribution to the ongoing dialogue between the children of Abraham. It is also a document which brings out some of the most crucial issues separating—as well as uniting—the three religions and their outlooks.

It must be remembered that better understanding between Judaism, Christianity and Islam is not only important for the situation in the Middle East or Europe, but that it is also of much significance for life in America itself, where Islam is now entering the religious mainstream and where the number of Muslims is fast approaching that of Jews. According to some, in fact, Islam is already the second largest religious group in America, following Christianity.

One can only pray for the success of this effort toward creating better understanding between the three inheritors of Abraham, and ask God's succor in a task in which a single step possesses enduring value far beyond the confines that one would imagine. The three religions meet ultimately in God, and every step toward better mutual understanding is consequently a step toward the One God who taught Abraham the message of unity and bequeathed, upon him and subsequent prophets in his line, a spiritual heritage which continues to dominate the lives of a major sector of humanity and will endure to the end of time.

Seyyed Hossein Nasr, Ph.D.
Washington, D.C.

GLOSSARY

B.C.E/C.E. Before the Common Era/Common Era. These designate the same time periods as **B.C./A.D.** ("Before Christ/ *Anno Domini* [In the Year of the Lord]") but in a more neutral manner. Muslims have another dating system starting with Muhammad's *hijrah* or migration from Mecca to Medina in 622 C.E.: **A.H.** (*Anno Higirae* [In the Year of the Hijrah]).

Canon. The officially accepted list of books comprising the Hebrew Bible or Old Testament for Jews and Christians, and the New Testament for Christians. "Canon" is derived from an Egyptian word for a reed used in measuring—hence, the canon is the measure or norm of the Jewish community's or Christian community's faith.

Documentary Hypothesis. The theory first proposed by German biblical scholar Julius Wellhausen (1844-1918) that the Torah is a composite of four documents written and then woven together over a lengthy period of time (about 900-400 B.C.E.)

Gospels. The four New Testament books—Matthew, Mark, Luke, John—which present the "Good News" (Old English *Godspell*) about Jesus: his birth, ministry, teaching, death and resurrection.

Hadith. Authoritative traditions concerning the words and deeds of Muhammad. After the Qur'an, this is the second most important source of Islamic faith and practice.

Halakhah. Jewish law as found in the Talmud and related literature.

Hebrew Bible. Those books, divided into three categories (Torah, Prophets, Writings), which comprise the Bible for Jews and are identical to the Old Testament for Christians.

Kaaba. The holiest shrine of Islam in Mecca which, according to the Qur'an, was first built by Abraham and Ismail (Ishmael).

Midrash. Sermonic interpretations and embellishments of biblical material by the rabbis of the Talmudic era (first century B.C.E. to seventh century C.E.).

Mishnah. A concise compilation of Jewish laws by Rabbi Judah the Patriarch in about 200 C.E., which comprises the first part of the Talmud.

New Testament. The second half of the Christian Bible (along with the Old Testament) consisting of the four gospels, the Acts of the Apostles, letters of Paul and others, and the Book of Revelation.

Qur'an (Koran). The sacred scripture of Islam revealed to Muhammad and consisting of 114 surahs or chapters of varying length.

Sharia. Muslim law derived from a study of the Qur'an and the Hadith.

Septuagint. The Greek translation of the Hebrew Bible dating from about 200 B.C.E.

Talmud. The name given to the two major compendiums of Jewish law and lore (the Babylonian Talmud and the Palestinian or Jerusalem Talmud) produced by the rabbis of the period 100 B.C.E. to 500 C.E. The Talmuds consist of the Mishnah and the Gemara, the latter a record of generations of wide-ranging discussions about the Mishnah.

Temple. The Jewish temple in Jerusalem first built by Solomon in the mid-900s B.C.E., rebuilt in 515 B.C.E. after its destruction by the Babylonians, and destroyed again by the Romans in 70 C.E.

Torah. The first five books of the Hebrew Bible (Genesis, Exodus, Leviticus, Numbers and Deuteronomy). Sometimes the term is extended to mean the entire "teaching" (Hebrew: Torah) of Judaism as contained in the Bible, the Talmud and related literature.

BIOGRAPHICAL SKETCHES
OF THE DIALOGUE PARTICIPANTS

DAVID GORDIS, Ph.D. (Jewish Theological Seminary), is president of Hebrew College, Brookline, Mass., and director of the Wilstein Institute of Jewish Policy Studies. He currently serves on the boards of the World Council of Synagogues; Interns for Peace; and the Academy for Judaic, Christian and Islamic Studies. He is chairman of the Executive Committee of the American Foundation for Polish Jewish Studies and a member of the editorial board of *Tikkun Magazine*.

GEORGE B. GROSE, D.Min. (Claremont), is founding president of The Academy for Judaic, Christian, and Islamic Studies and minister of the Word, the Presbyterian Church (USA). He pioneered the dialogue between Jews, Christians and Muslims at the Vatican; at the World Council of Churches; in Cairo and Jerusalem; and at major U.S. universities. He has published commentaries in *The Christian Science Monitor, The Los Angeles Times* and *The Toronto Star*.

MUZAMMIL SIDDIQI, Ph.D. (Harvard), is the director of the Islamic Society of Orange County, Calif.; a member of the board of the Supreme Council of Mosques, Mecca; a member of the Supreme Council for Islamic Affairs, Cairo; and an executive member of the Council on Islamic Law in North America. He is Vice President, Islamic Studies, of the Academy for Judaic, Christian, and Islamic Studies; and a lecturer in the Department of Religious Studies, California State University, Fullerton, Calif.

BENJAMIN J. HUBBARD, Ph.D. (Iowa), is professor and chair of the Department of Religious Studies, California State University, Fullerton, Calif. He is a board member and secretary of the Academy for Judaic, Christian, and Islamic Studies; and a board member of the American Jewish Committee, Orange County Chapter. He has published in the areas of Biblical studies and of studies on the interrelationship of religion and the media, including the 1990 book he edited, *Reporting Religion: Facts and Faith.*

Now the Lord said to Abram, "...by you all the families of the earth shall bless themselves. (Genesis 12: 1a, 3b)

וַיֹּאמֶר ה' אֶל־אַבְרָם...
וְנִבְרְכוּ בְךָ כֹּל מִשְׁפְּחֹת הָאֲדָמָה.

And if you are Christ's, then you are Abraham's offspring, heirs according to promise. (Galatians 3:29)

εἰ δὲ ὑμεῖς Χριστοῦ, ἄρα τοῦ Ἀβραὰμ σπέρμα
ἐστέ, κατ' ἐπαγγελίαν κληρονόμοι.

...It is the community of your father Abraham; He (God) called you Muslims before and in this revelation... (Qur'an 22:78)

...مِلَّةَ أَبِيْكُمْ اِبْرَاهِيْمَ، هُوَ سَمَّاكُمُ
الْمُسْلِمِيْنَ مِنْ قَبْلُ وَفِيْ هَذَا...(٧٨:٢٢)

PROLOGUE

We would like to think this dialogue book had its origin in the mind of God, but a more proximate beginning was in the fall of 1971. Dr. Grose, then Chaplain of Whittier College, had invited Dr. Abdelmuhsin El-Biali, director of the Islamic Foundation of Southern California, to give a convocation. Afterwards, Grose, El-Biali and John Rothmann, a Whittier alumnus and Jewish educator, had lunch together. Grose proposed that they present a dialogue-lecture at a student convocation. Little did they know that this event was the first public Jewish-Christian-Muslim dialogue in America. The response was so dramatic that further dialogue-lectures were planned for Whittier and elsewhere.

With grants from the Lilly Endowment and the Rockefeller Foundation, this work was greatly expanded with dialogue-lectures at over two hundred colleges and universities across the United States. In 1975 dialogue-lectures were given at the National Council of Churches in New York, the World Council of Churches in Geneva, and—at the invitation of the Supreme Council for Islamic Affairs in Cairo—over Radio Cairo and Cairo Television. Sergio Cardinal Pignedoli warmly welcomed us at the Vatican and Dr. W. A. Visser t' Hooft, the first Secretary General of the World Council of Churches, said to us, "What you are doing is new in the world."

1977 was a landmark year: The Academy for Judaic, Christian and Islamic Studies was founded to advance dialogue between Jews, Christians and Muslims, to conduct research and publish the results, and to teach what had been found. The three-fold dialogue continued in Rome over Vatican Radio and again in Egypt with the Grand Imam of Sunni Islam, Abdul Haleem Mahmoud, Rector of Al-Azhar University. The Egyptian participants were Drs. El-Biali and Grose, and Rabbi Dr. Harold Schulweis of Congregation Valley Beth Shalom, Encino, Calif. In 1980 the Academy co-sponsored, with Rabbi Dr. Joshua Haberman of the Washington Hebrew Congregation and with the Inter-Faith Committee of Israel, a conference in Jerusalem.

About this time teaching opportunities opened up for Dr. Grose at California State University, Fullerton, thanks to Rabbi Dr. Morton

Fierman, Chair of Religious Studies; and at the University of California, Irvine, thanks to grants from the Santa Fe International Corporation and the Ettinger Foundation. At UCI Grose developed and taught the three-quarter curriculum, "The Judeo-Christian-Islamic Interaction" with the help of Rabbi Dr. Henri Front of Temple Beth David, Westminster, and Imam Dr. Muzammil Siddiqi of the Islamic Society of Orange County (1982-85).

Through the interest of Archbishop Edward Scott, then moderator of the World Council of Churches, and Dr. John Taylor, director of the World Council Program on Peoples of Different Faiths, the Academy was approached about giving a dialogue-lecture for the Sixth Assembly of the Council convening in Vancouver (1983). Drs. Front, Grose and Siddiqi gave the dialogue-lecture titled "Foundations for Dialogue between Judaism, Christianity and Islam."

In 1989 Professor Benjamin J. Hubbard, Chair of Religious Studies at California State University, Fullerton, and Rabbi Dr. David M. Gordis, then Vice President of the University of Judaism in Los Angeles and Director of the Wilstein Institute, joined the Academy. A book had been in the wind for the past ten years, but now its time had come.

In the summer of 1991, Drs. Grose, Siddiqi, Hubbard and Gordis, and Daniel Ninburg, M.D., vice president of The Academy for Institutional Affairs, met and determined that The Academy book should not be a series of essays like ships that pass in the night nor, indeed, a collection of monologues, but a live dialogue—inspired by what The Academy had done publicly for years! Grose and Hubbard were asked to be co-editors, and Hubbard, because of special expertise, the moderator.

Between September and December, 1991, the participants met five times. Four of the meetings were at California State University, Fullerton, the other at the University of Judaism in Los Angeles. Each session lasted five to six hours, usually with a lunch break. A year later, in December, 1992—having read some of the transcriptions—we reconvened for a final morning session in which we reflected on the experience of the earlier dialogues.

As we hope you will be able to see, the experience had a profound effect on each of us. These were not polite conversations about points of theological agreement and disagreement. Instead, they were candid, lively, sometimes intense, sometimes light and always—we believe—illuminating interchanges between persons of different faith backgrounds.

Reading a dialogue book may present special challenges for some. A conventional book is a conversation between the author and reader. A dialogue, by contrast, is a conversation between the participants and runs the risk of making the reader feel left out. There is, however, an easy way of avoiding this problem. The reader needs simply to imagine that he or she is sitting at the same table with the participants and listening to them. For that, in fact, is what we had in mind as we participated in these dialogues. We want you to be caught up in the conversation so that it comes alive and you are there with us.

George B. Grose and Benjamin J. Hubbard, editors

CHAPTER ONE

HOW EACH TRADITION VIEWS ABRAHAM AND THE FOUNDING FIGURES—MOSES, JESUS, MUHAMMAD

1. ABRAHAM

DR. HUBBARD: In this first session, we want to discuss how each of you views the founders of your own and the others' traditions—Moses, Jesus and Muhammad. But let's begin with your assessments of Abraham, the common ancestor of our three religious families.

DR. GORDIS: In Jewish tradition, Abraham is the first of the three patriarchs, along with Isaac and Jacob, and he introduced monotheism. This appears in Genesis, but is orchestrated more in the Midrashic literature in the accounts of Abraham's discovery of the insight of the one God, his rejection of idolatry, and his turning away from the land of his origins and its polytheism. So he opens a new chapter in the history of the Israelites and the Jewish people, but really in the history of the world. Monotheism is a process beginning with Abraham and leading, finally, to Moses and the giving of the Torah.

DR. GROSE: In some ways there is no essential difference between Judaism, Christianity and Islam regarding Abraham. He is the primordial figure in the history of monotheism, the friend of God (2 Chronicles 20:7, James 2:23). In Abraham all the families of the earth will be blessed (Genesis 12:3). Indeed, the Qur'an affirms much the same: "God said, 'I will make thee (Abraham) an imam (spiritual leader) to the nations'" (Surah 2:124).   At the same time, Christians are children of Abraham through Christ (Galatians 3:29). That's one of Paul's major themes. He describes Abraham as a hero of faith, our father in faith; and says if we have faith like Abraham, we shall be saved (Romans 4, Galatians 3:9). So the salvation theme appears because Abraham's faith is sufficient. Certainly it was sufficient for Abraham, which raises another question. In some Christian traditions, the elect are as much the worthy people of the Old Testament as the New. So, while the patriarchs and prophets of the Bible predate the coming of Christ, they are counted among those to be saved and are part of the Church in the fullest sense. That's why Calvin said that if Abraham is not a predestined person, then all the patriarchs and prophets and the whole Church would collapse.[1]

DR. SIDDIQI: Before I say something about Abraham's position in Islamic tradition, let me note that Abraham is not called the founder of faith in Islam. He is a prophet who was chosen by God to deliver God's message. As a prophet he has a very central position. He has many names in the Qur'an. He is called *awwal al muslimin*, the prototype of the Muslim, the one who submits to God. He is also called *hanif*, a very strict monotheist who doesn't deviate from his belief. The Qur'an mentions 25 prophets by name, among them Abraham who ranks very prominently. There are about 60 different references to Abraham and different aspects of his life in the text. The Qur'an calls him *khalil*, the friend of God, and *umma*, a word which usually refers to the Muslim community. So Abraham was a community within himself because he represented the whole community of faith. God said in the Qur'an, "follow the religion of your father Abraham" (Surah 22:78). In fact, Prophet Muhammad came to reaffirm, in a sense, the message of Abraham. So this is why Abraham has an important place in Islamic tradition and why every Muslim prayer mentions his name.

DR. HUBBARD: Let me ask each of you: Is Abraham a monotheist—a believer in only one God—without qualification?

DR. GORDIS: It's very hard to answer that because it depends on the perspective one takes. When one looks at the Book of Genesis, one still clearly sees vestiges of elements of both paganism and polytheism—the so-called "giants" (Nephilim) or "sons of God" (Genesis 6:1-4, for example). In fact, the terminology used in Jewish literature for the divinity associated with Abraham, just as that used for the divinity of the other patriarchs, is specific to that person. So the God associated with Abraham is known as *magen Avraham* or shield of Abraham (Genesis 15:1). The divinity associated with Isaac was *pahad yitzhak* or "fear of Isaac," and so on. So a community which venerates Abraham in terms of all of the success he had would pray for the protection of the divinity of Abraham, *magen Avraham*, who had been responsible for all of his success.

It's clear that in the historical environment where the patriarchs functioned there were still some traces of the existence of other divinities. But the notion was that the patriarchal God was triumphant as the Divinity of divinities. Yet it's also clear that, once we move into Jewish tradition,[2] this is simply vestigial. And in Jewish tradition Abraham is looked upon as the quintessential monotheist who rejects the notion that there is any other God.

Muzammil spoke of the names given to Abraham in the Qur'an. Similarly, we should observe in Genesis the change of name from Abram to Abraham (Genesis 17:5). Adding the "H", which is symbolic of God's name, is really indicative of that insight, that connection of Abraham to the one God. The name change also indicates that he becomes the patriarch, the ancestor of peoples or of the community. It echoes the title *umma* that Muzammil mentioned as one of Abraham's names in Islam.

It's also interesting that the stories about Abraham in the Hebrew Bible oscillate between two kinds of readings: first, the symbolic or mythological interpretations of his personality which we've just talked about; but second his very human characteristics. For example, there's the story of the binding of Isaac[3] which is very personal and poignant—besides being a schematic presentation of the ultimate act of faith. Also, in the casting out of Hagar and Ishmael (Genesis 21:8-14), you have Abraham's sense of sorrow, his struggle with Sarah, the pressure she was putting on him, and his discomfort with it. So Abraham, along with the other patriarchs, is not a cardboard character.

DR. GROSE: There is no doubt that Abraham is a monotheist. But, as David has beautifully illustrated, these remnants of polytheism are in the biblical text. Still, Abraham's behavior is that of a monotheist. In the case of a polytheist, there's always a way out: if you don't like the advice of one god, you turn to another. Or you try to bend the arm of a divinity with certain ritual acts or behavior. With the Israelite God, Yahweh, it's the other way around. He's in command and the monotheist responds to the one God with this in mind.

DR. HUBBARD: Is Abraham's bargaining with God over Sodom and Gomorrah a compromise of that in any way when he says, "If I can find 50 just men, will you spare these cities?"; and then he bargains for 45, 40, and so on down to 10 (Genesis 18:22-33)?

DR. GROSE: No, I don't think so. It's part of the humanity of the great figures, as David pointed out. The final word is still with the judge, and God is depicted as judge in various settings in the Hebrew scriptures as well as the Qur'an. One pleads his case in court with a judge, but this doesn't diminish the authority of the judge (in this case, God). It may even be indicative, if we're made in the image of God, that we do have certain privileges given to us by Him.

DR. SIDDIQI: Well, the Qur'an presents Abraham as a strict monotheist, as I mentioned before. Abraham as *Hanif* is a true monotheist who has nothing to do with polytheism. In fact, the Qur'an mentions that he was born in a polytheistic home and describes his father an idol maker and idol merchant.

DR. GORDIS: This story, by the way, comes from the Midrashic literature. That's one of the stories that I was alluding to, which....

DR. SIDDIQI: It doesn't come from the Midrash, but it is parallel ....

DR. GORDIS: Parallel, okay.

DR. SIDDIQI: In the Qur'anic version, Abraham argues about idolatry with his father who gets very angry with him and expels him from the home. Abraham also goes into the temple while the people of the town are on an outing and breaks all the idols, except the biggest one, and then puts the ax on its shoulder. When the townspeople ask, "Who did this to our gods?" someone replies, "Well, we know there is a young man who was mentioning them with disrespect." So they call Abraham and ask, "Did you do this to our gods?" He replies, "Ask him (the one remaining idol with the ax on its shoulder) if he can speak." And then the people all lower their heads and say, "You know they don't speak." So he said, "How can you worship something which cannot speak?" (Surah 21:52-65). So this illustrates very well Abraham's position vis-a-vis polytheism, as far as Islam is concerned.

DR. GORDIS: So Abraham is suggesting that the large unbroken idol with the axe had destroyed the others?

DR. SIDDIQI: Yes, in a sarcastic way he says, "the big one has done that to the other idols" (Surah 21:63).

DR. GORDIS: Which pointed out to them how absurd that kind of belief would be.

DR. SIDDIQI: David just mentioned how Abraham was pleading for Sodom and Gomorrah. The Qur'an also records this incident and uses a similar word: he "argued" with God about the people of Sodom and Gomorrah—Lot's people. And two other names are given to him *awwah* and *halim* which denote a very forbearing and compassionate person. The Qur'an says his heart was *salim*, full and wholesome, so that he came to his Lord with a wholesome heart. So there are a number of motifs about Abraham's personality in the Qur'an, but he is unambiguously monotheistic.

In fact, there is another story about Abraham seeing the stars at night and saying, "Can they be my God?" But then the moon comes up, and he says, "No, the moon outshines the stars. This is God." Then the sun comes up, and he says, "This is greater, this is my Lord." But finally he says, "Until my Lord guides me, I will not find the way." And the Qur'an says, "That was Our (Allah's) argument which We gave to Abraham (to use) against his people" (Surah 6:83).

DR. HUBBARD: Against the polytheistic people?

DR. SIDDIQI: Yes, the polytheistic people can see how these objects in the heavens disappear. Each outshines the other, but God is not the phenomena; He is behind the phenomena.

DR. GORDIS: This story occurs in the Midrash, too. I wanted to pick up also on what George and Muzammil were saying about the Sodom and Gomorrah incident. I agree wholeheartedly that it does not compromise monotheism, but is one of the extraordinary texts which we have to dramatize it. The Sodom and Gomorrah story demonstrates the humaneness of God and the divinity of man because Abraham comes close to scolding God when he asks, "Can the judge of all creation not do justice?" (Genesis 18:25). Being created in God's image, human beings have the capacity to make moral judgments. They make them not simply at the whim of the divinity because God is, in fact, the source of all true values. And God can be reminded. That's the sense of partnership with God which I have spoken of before. So this is really a shocking text in that Abraham can confront God, but is only possible in a monotheistic setting. Otherwise, as George said, you could go to another god. Here we have the human being quintessentially facing God who is one and is the standard of behavior. It is a remarkable confrontation with a God who creates human beings with moral capacity and thus can be reminded by them of His own moral responsibility.

DR. SIDDIQI: And is Abraham complaining to God?

DR. GORDIS: Yes, and a similar plaint is stated by Jeremiah in bemoaning his suffering while attempting to convey God's words. Addressing God he says, "Why is my pain unending, my wounds desperate and incurable? Thou art to me like a brook that is not to be trusted, whose waters fail" (Jeremiah 15:18).

DR. GROSE: I wanted to point out something that David also said. With monotheism, you cannot pick and choose another God. But, at the same time, in the Sodom and Gomorrah episode, God wasn't going to pick another Abraham. That's an important thing to note: there was God's selection of Abraham; and His selection goes on and on in the history of the world, as He chooses persons and peoples to fulfill His will in special ways. I mention this because, in Christian thought, the patriarchs and prophets of Israel are among the elect, as are the Israelites. The problem arises after the coming of Christ, when the Church in many ways thought the continuing Jewish people were an anomaly. So the selection for a special task and special mission is very real.

DR. SIDDIQI: The question of selection is important. The Qur'an says Abraham fulfilled the commands of God, so he was selected as a leader. When God tested him, and he fulfilled the test, God said, "I'm going to make you an *imam* (leader) for the people." And then Abraham said, "But what about my children?" God replied, "My covenant does not include the wrongdoers" (Surah 2:124). Only the good are selected, not wrongdoers.

The Qur'an says that Abraham then came to Mecca and built the Kaaba, Islam's holiest shrine. When he established the city he prayed to God, "I am bringing my family here to a place which has no cultivation, no trees, no water, nothing, and I am putting them here. So feed those who are righteous." God replied, "And those who are not righteous I will also feed" (Surahs 14:37, 2:126). So God feeds the righteous and unrighteous, but the covenant applies only towards the good.

DR. GORDIS: I want to raise one additional point which I think we ought to consider, an idea that comes through already in the story we're talking about. Abraham Joshua Heschel[4] called it the notion of a pathetic God, a feeling God. One of the things our traditions hold in common is that there is nothing like the classical Greek notion of "the Unmoved Mover," the Aristotelian God. The only exception is the Medieval attempt to synthesize, to bridge Aristotle and traditional religion in the work of Moses Maimonides (1135-1204), Thomas Aquinas (1225-74) and others. But earlier, there is a parting of the ways on this point. God is pathetic in the sense of feeling, reacting and responding. There is an interdependency in that man, obviously, depends on God and obeys God who is the source of authority, creation, etc. Although whatever limits God is a product of his own will and creation, he is, in fact, also affected and changed by what human beings do. God requires human beings in this partnership. In a sense, that's also illustrated by the Sodom and Gomorrah story. You would have to say, logically, if Abraham had not reminded God of the true standard of righteous behavior, God might have gone ahead with the stated plan to destroy these cities without looking for any righteous people. So there is a kind of coming together—God and Abraham, God and man—to achieve that completeness, that wholeness. This illustrates that God actually responds to and feels what human beings do.

DR. GROSE: A qualification must be made on this idea from my perspective. In Christianity, a person does not see himself as being in a partnership with God. This is more a Judaic concept, not a characteristic of mainstream Christianity. The Divinity is sufficient unto Himself, and out of His goodness and His mystery He chose to do certain things toward human beings whom He created. But I don't think that the will of God is moved, altered or affected by what we say or do. Nevertheless, He hears and responds to our prayers. I believe this with regard to the three monotheistic faiths which are in the salvation pattern. On different occasions, I have welcomed my Jewish and Muslim colleagues praying for me, for their prayers are valid, as mine are for them. But I think there is a level of divinity which is untouched by us.

DR. GORDIS: How do you deal with the Sodom and Gomorrah story where Abraham has to remind God?

DR. GROSE: Well, he reminded him, but he didn't have to. Those are two different things.

DR. SIDDIQI: Can you say it's reminding? It's more of a pleading, like somebody who prays to God for someone else who is suffering.

DR. GORDIS: Muzammil, just listen to the words of the verse. Abraham says, "Can the ruler of all creation not act justly?" Is it pleading if Abraham says to God, "Can you act unjustly?" That's not a plea. That can be interpreted as a plea, but certainly....

DR. SIDDIQI: God doesn't need reminding. He knows everything and remembers everything. Reminding is only for those who forget.

DR. GORDIS: One can suggest that as a way of reading the story; but I would argue that, if you read it in its simplest terms in the book of Genesis, God's plan is set out. Abraham coaxes, and he has to do it step by step. The way he does it is by saying, "God, you are the *shophet kol haaretz,* the judge of all the world, can you behave unjustly?" (Genesis 18:25). While one can read into the text whatever one wants, if you simply let it speak to you, that's what it says.

DR. SIDDIQI: If you want me to give you a Muslim interpretation of this text, I'll say this is Abraham in his compassion. He is using bold language, and God—in his kindness and love for Abraham—accepts that. Still, from a theological point of view, Abraham is Abraham and God is God.

DR. GORDIS: I understand. In Jewish interpretations of this text we find the same thing said. There is a methodological question here. As a Jew, when I read a text of the Hebrew Bible, I follow a Rabbinic dictum: "Turn it over and turn it over because everything is in it," which means there is no single, definitive interpretation. But there are those in the Jewish community, and in other communities, who would say a particular text is to be interpreted according to what this expert or that expert says. I think that reduces the greatness of the text. In the Jewish tradition, as well as in Islam, God is God and man is man because there is a gap which never can be bridged. Still, what is remarkable about this text—and I would suggest it's true not simply in Jewish texts—is that there are many faces of truth, many ways the text talks. Granted, we can't fathom God in his fullness because we are human. But what this text is trying to say to us—the element of truth, of the divine—is not that Abraham is pleading. If Abraham is simply giving a plea because he is compassionate, this robs the text of its strength which is its boldness. The boldness is Abraham's confronting God and reminding him of his responsibility as "judge of all the earth." I think the dimensions of the story on its terms, explicitly stated in Genesis, are so remarkable that we would be impoverishing the account if we simply flattened it and forced it into a traditional overlay.

DR. SIDDIQI: I understand your point, but I feel you are reading too much into the text. It's true one should read it as it is, and there could be several ways of interpreting it. But one can always say someone is reading too much into the text.

DR. GORDIS: Sure, okay.

DR. SIDDIQI: Because there are so many other factors to consider: Abraham's faith, his submission and commitment to God—all of these things have to be taken into account when interpreting his statements. Of course, all of this assumes that the biblical texts are authentic, but it is also possible these are not Abraham's own words. They could be the words of scribes, redactors or interpreters of later generations. Then they represent the views of biblical writers and not those of Abraham

DR. GROSE: I need to say, from a Christological point of view, I'm

Islamic! There is an error, almost a prevailing one, in the Church today: Christ-centeredness. I see it as a problem and not as a way of relating to God for this reason: what is revealed to the Christian in Christ is all he needs in this world and the next, but it isn't *all* there is to know about God. We don't know God. He remains the supreme mystery and reaches out to us in all the ways we need, but not to disclose everything about Himself. I think that's why we worship God. We worship the living One whom we know and, at the same time, the *mysterium tremendum* or "awesome mystery"[5] who loves us.

DR. HUBBARD: So you are making a very nice distinction between what is necessary for salvation, and what is possible for a fuller understanding of the mystery of God.

DR. GROSE: We stop at the mystery and are blessed by the mystery because it captivates us and makes us human.

2. MOSES

DR. HUBBARD: On that note I'd like to suggest we turn to our second figure, Moses, and let Dr. Gordis begin by giving us a sense of how Moses fits into Jewish tradition and understanding.

DR. GORDIS: Moses is the prime, unequaled prophet. According to Jewish tradition, no prophet had the direct experience of the Divine that Moses did. And it was both the theophany on Mount Sinai (Exodus 19-20)—the personal relationship of Moses to God—and the product of that relationship—the giving of the Torah[6]—which sets Moses apart as the progenitor of the Jewish people. Sinai is the central event of the Hebrew Bible for the Jewish people, the closest we come to a central myth—myth here meaning the defining story of the Jewish people. The story begins with the descendants of Abraham going down to Egypt, continues with the Exodus from Egypt—a story of the redemption of the body, the people—and culminates in the events surrounding the revelation of God to man on Mount Sinai through

Moses. These events are reflected in the Jewish calendar, especially
Passover and Shavuot.[7] Moses is the central figure in both festivals.
He is the liberator, leader and prophet who is the instrument of giving
the Torah, which defines the Jewish people as the people of the Torah
or book. From the time it was given, the Jews became a
Torah-obsessed people, if I may use that term. The Torah is read every
sabbath in the synagogue. We just now celebrated the festival of
Simchat Torah ("rejoicing in the Torah") which marks the conclusion
of the yearly cycle of readings from the Torah and the beginning of the
new cycle. This is the central cycle of Jewish life, and Moses is pivotal
to it.

Nevertheless, care is always taken to make certain no divinity is
attributed to Moses. This is an area where both Islam and Judaism
bend over backwards to stress that divinity and humanity are not the
same thing, while Christianity approaches it differently in the figure of
Jesus. But in Judaism Moses is not to be worshiped, and the place of
his burial is not to be known. An interesting sidelight is that the story
of the Exodus, told in connection with the Passover celebration, does
not, for all intents and purposes, mention Moses. This is to avoid the
risk of venerating a human being, which could detract from the notion
of monotheism. Moses would be the closest figure to aspire to that
status, but the tradition tries to make certain he cannot be divinized.
This also relates to our discussion of Abraham—no cardboard character,
but a flawed one. Likewise, even Moses had a flaw which kept him
from being admitted to the promised land: he lacked the patience, and
even the faith, as the story of the rock and the water illustrates
(Numbers 20:2-13). But that story, like all stories, is symbolic. It was
not simply the knocking on the rock as if he had been speaking to it.
It was an indication that something was missing from this human
being. Even Moses was not perfect, even prophets are flawed.

DR. HUBBARD: Does Moses' killing of the Egyptian overseer
(Exodus 2:11-15) play into this theme as well, or is it simply a matter
of self-defense?

DR. GORDIS: Having grown up privileged in the Egyptian royal
household, returning to his people, and all of a sudden confronting

these challenges and realities—that's also part of the flesh and blood character. Also you will recall that he wanted to avoid his call to lead the Hebrews out of slavery by claiming he wasn't a good speaker, and so forth (Exodus 4:10-17). He was far from perfect.

DR. HUBBARD: Dr. Grose, how would you approach, from a Christian point of view, the figure of Moses?

DR. GROSE: Moses is prophet and lawgiver to Christians also and was present, together with Elijah at Jesus' transfiguration (Matthew 17:1-8, Mark 9:2-8, Luke 9:28-36). I have very much appreciated the paradoxical position Dr. Gordis takes regarding Moses. Humankind—and certainly prophets—are in some sense partners with God. But at the same time we have to be very careful to see that an individual doesn't get venerated because of the seeming partnership. It's an interesting paradox.

DR. SIDDIQI: You mean a partner not in divinity but in doing a task?

DR. GROSE: I can almost say yes, but does one get credit for working with God? You see, there's another element in Christianity, a very critical one, grace, which literally means gift. Just as on your birthday—and you certainly didn't earn being born—you get presents, but you didn't earn any of them. They are total gifts. Protestant Christianity has held out for salvation by faith alone as a gift of God's grace, whereas the Roman Catholic tradition speaks of salvation by faith and good works. In practice, we Protestants can't always claim that we live by grace, but we can assert that it is offered to us. And if we do, in fact, live by grace—God's gift—rather than our accomplishments, then God can indeed use flawed people to carry out his will and even be among his people.

This touches on the Christian perception of the contradictions in human nature, present in all human beings, which are sometimes called original sin. Paul described the situation this way: "I want to do the best thing, and I do the worst thing. Woe is me" (Romans 7:15-25).

The closer some Christian mystics got to God, the more they had the perception of their own frailty.

With Moses, another aspect of grace appears, a powerful one to me, in the sentence before God's recitation of the commandments. I think it reads, "I am the Lord your God who brought you out of the land of Egypt, out of the house of bondage" (Exodus 20:2). God is saying, I am the one who rescued you, that is why I have the authority to give you the commands. So the whole thing starts from grace and moves to law. This is a Christian perception of the nature of the religious life.

DR. GORDIS: A brief note on original sin. There is a shorthand which distinguishes Judaism from Christianity on this matter: In Christianity, man sins because he is a sinner; in Judaism, man is a sinner because he sins.

DR. GROSE: I think that states the differences in the anthropology of the matter very well. For Christians, Moses—in the Old Testament—is, after Abraham, the great figure. For the moral law Moses is essential to Christianity. This was made very plain in the mid-second century when the Church defeated Marcion who wanted to eliminate the Old Testament. So Paul's earlier attack on law is not an attack on law for what it is, or on Moses the law giver or law bringer. So we can mutually regard Moses for the greatness that God gave him to lead his people.

DR. SIDDIQI: The Islamic position on original sin is very close to the Judaic—that sin is not a state of being but a state of doing something. If somebody sins, then he is a sinner. One is not born a sinner.

As with Abraham, the Qur'an mentions episodes of Moses' life in various places. He is probably the second most important prophet in the Qur'an. He is *kaleem Allah*, the one who can worship God and to whom God spoke directly (Surah 4:164). His dialogue with God at Mount Sinai, the giving of the Torah and then his being unable to bear the vision of God are mentioned in the Qur'an (Surah 7:103-55).

At one point the Qur'an says we have sent a messenger among you, referring to Muhammad, as we sent a messenger to the Pharaoh (Surah 73:15). Moses and Muhammad are similar in many ways: Moses leaves Egypt and makes a migration (to Midian—Exodus 2:15); the prophet makes a migration also.[8] Moses goes to look at the burning bush and is suddenly given a revelation of God and made a prophet. Likewise, Prophet Muhammad had nothing, no knowledge, and suddenly the revelation comes to him. Was he expecting it, was he preparing for it? No, it was God who gave it to him as a gift. As a gift was given to Moses, similarly it was given to this unlettered prophet from Mecca, Muhammad. Altogether, the Qur'an frequently mentions five great prophets: Noah, Abraham, Moses, Jesus and, finally, Mohammed.

DR. HUBBARD: Are there any rejoinders or clarifications at this point on Moses?

DR. GROSE: Yes, I think so. Regarding the office of prophet, we are seeking the truth and sharing it, as it has been shared with us by the Almighty. But I see here problems for Christians over how Muhammad can be considered a prophet—not just because he came after Jesus who is the Savior. The bigger question is how he fulfilled his role as a prophet, since he was the head of a commonwealth in Medina and a commander of military forces. The Hebrew classical prophets didn't do that. But, as Muzammil has pointed out, Muhammad's exercise of leadership in Medina makes him similar to Moses who was head of the Hebrew community during the Exodus. Christians don't quite see it that way, however. They look to the other prophets, who were separate figures from rulers and were their confidants and advisors....

DR. SIDDIQI: The whole phenomenon of prophecy in the Old Testament is tied up with the monarchy. In classical Hebrew prophecy you have the king and the prophet, but in Islam the ruler and the prophet are the same. Isaiah, Jeremiah and the others, the prophets in the Jewish tradition, are not even mentioned by name in the Qur'an. The prophets mentioned are Moses, David, Solomon....

DR. GROSE: Figures of government whose work is included within their prophethood. The Christian approach to prophethood is to take the great prophets of Israel who had a working relationship with the ruler but were not themselves the ruler. There was that distinction, which I think has been played out in modern political systems....

DR. GORDIS: Is Samuel accepted as a prophet in Christianity?

DR. GROSE: Yes.

DR. GORDIS: Then Samuel is the transition point. It was through Samuel that the monarchy was established beginning with Saul (1 Samuel 8-10).

DR. GROSE: And this distinction is played out historically in the separation of church and state in the United States and, to some extent, in other English-speaking countries.

DR. SIDDIQI: The introduction of the monarchy in Israel was a later development. The earlier Israelite community had prophets who were also the leaders of the community, such as the judges.

DR. GROSE: Alright, it's late but the prototype is taken from the separation of the prophet and the king.

DR. GORDIS: I'm not certain it's as far back as the time of King Saul. In the rabbinic treatment of the Maccabees, there is an awareness that the liberation of Judea from the Syrians in 165 B. C.E.,[9] with the war and the desecration and rededication of the Temple, was a very trying period. But immediately there is a break between the Hasmonean dynasty—established by Judah Maccabee and his brothers of the House of Hasmon—and some of the religious and spiritual leaders. So the Rabbinic literature hardly mentions the Hasmonean dynasty. The rabbis were disappointed because they felt the Hasmoneans had betrayed religious principles. So I think one would find there is an awareness of the distinctiveness of roles—king, priest, teacher—a good deal earlier than modernity.

DR. SIDDIQI: There are always roles. Some play the priestly role, some are judges. But at the same time the state itself is not making a conscious separation from religion, and the two are joined in the Old Testament. That's why the Jews struggled for political freedom during the Greek and Roman periods....

DR. GORDIS: I think you're basically right; but the Torah's and the prophet Samuel's antipathy towards the monarchy is an early indication that its authority would tend to invade the religious realm. Already there was a foretaste of the need to develop a cooperative relationship but to keep the secular government of war and peace in its place and the spiritual or religious leadership in its place, rather than having them rolled into one.

DR. GROSE: We may be getting a little far afield, but I don't think so, in terms of relevancy and our readers. Americans often don't grasp, in their efforts to relate effectively with the Muslim world, that in it all political problems are at the same time religious problems, and vice-versa. There is no distinction conceptually, though they may be separated to some extent in practice.

DR. SIDDIQI: No, I don't think all political problems are religious problems, and all religious problems are political. Things are not that simple in the Muslim world. They do make distinctions between religious, political and economic issues. Yes, there are Muslims who would like to say how the state should function, but I don't think they see politics and religion in the same category.

3. JESUS

DR. HUBBARD: I want to come back to the church-state issue in a later session, but let's move on to the figure of Jesus. With Abraham and Moses there is a commonality, an acceptance by all three traditions. Now we move to a figure about whom there are going to be greater differences. And so, Dr. Gordis, how would you assess the Jewish view of Jesus?

DR. GORDIS: Here, your prefatory comment is very apt. It's hard for a Christian or a Muslim to really understand that the central figure in their faiths is not central in Judaism. In the personality of Jesus, there is a kind of familiarity because Jesus was Jewish by birth and upbringing. The dramatic discontinuity between Judaism and Christianity came after Jesus through the personality of Paul and his antipathy towards the law. But it's almost the same as asking a Christian or a Muslim to talk about the importance of Rabbi Judah the Patriarch[10] to their faiths, or Rabbis Akiba,[11] or Saadia Gaon.[12] These are the great teachers of Jewish tradition, but they are basically unknown and unimportant for Christians and Muslims. While Jews can appreciate in a sociological sense the importance of Muhammad, obviously Jews don't accept the notion of his being the last of the prophets, nor the Qur'an's being the product of revelation. We see the Qur'an as a great religious text for Muslims. Also, we don't talk of the "New Testament" and "Old Testament" but of the Hebrew Bible. The New Testament is a later work and not canonical. It's very important, we study it, are interested in it and learn about ourselves from it. We draw great religious ideas from Islam and Christianity as well, but Jesus and Muhammad themselves are neither divine nor prophetic figures. In fact, there are no prophets in the Jewish community after Malachi. The leadership of prophecy passed to the leadership of teaching and commenting on the Torah. I'm sure it's hard to fathom that there are scant references in the classical Jewish sources to Jesus. In the case of Islam, the close of the Talmudic period in 500 C.E. preceded the birth of Muhammad by 70 years. Jews have always looked on Jesus and Muhammad as important religious figures but not in terms of religious significance for them.

DR. GROSE: In Christianity, the mere mention of the name of Jesus Christ does good things, no matter who utters it. Even a curse is beneficial in the sense that God's name or Jesus' name is mentioned....

DR. SIDDIQI: I don't think a curse should be beneficial.

DR. GROSE: No, this is an extreme position. I think it's Luther's and he is quite extreme on several things. There was a prayer used in the synagogue[13] which consisted of a curse on the *minim*. This referred to certain heretics, probably including those who followed Jesus the

Nazarene. And there is a mention in the Talmud (Babylonian Talmud, *Shabbat* 104b) that Jesus was the child of Mary and a Roman soldier with a play on the word for virgin. I don't take those things seriously. What David Gordis said about Jesus is an accurate and appropriate stance, which I accept.

I rejoice in all the benefits that have come to me from Jews and Judaism in my lifetime, and also from the Jewishness of Jesus. I say this, by way of appreciation, also for an understanding of the Old Testament of the Bible. I have become, over the years, more and more grateful that Christians have it. We didn't ask for permission to use it, we just took it. But we have it and, though we interpret many places in it differently, yet we share it with Judaism.

The Apostle Paul wrote that in the fullness of time God sent forth his Son (Hebrews 1:2). This theme of the son is related to that great royal Son about whom the Almighty says, "You are my son. Today I have begotten you" (Psalm 2:7). That is one of the great proof texts from the Hebrew Bible used in Christianity about Jesus' being God's Son. His being the Son of God I call *the* profound metaphor of Christianity. In other words, it stands for reality. It is not really sonship in the way I think Islamic teachers sometimes view it. It certainly is not human descent and does not involve sexual activity. That is why I come again to admitting it is *the* profound metaphor. The Holy Spirit is not metaphorical because it is known in the Hebrew scriptures as the spirit of God (e.g., Genesis 1:2). What Jesus does, in a sense, is flesh out the Trinity. Now how did this come about? I am experiential in my understanding of Christianity, and I think the doctrine of the Trinity is an experiential reality. It did not come full cloth to the Church, but was derived from the Church's experiences.

So we have in Jesus one who fulfilled the royal son: "You are my son, today I have begotten you." He is also the one who fulfilled Isaiah 53—sometimes called the Suffering Servant passage—by bearing the transgressions of the people. By his punishment and whipping, they were healed. And it is possible to understanding certain verses in that section as alluding to a resurrection theme. Certainly, Jesus was like the lamb being led to the slaughter in that he was silent, as Isaiah 53 says (53:7). You can see how I feel moved by these passages, as a Christian.

When he advanced to death and through death, and returned, those who followed Jesus were convinced in ways not of great logic, but in the totality of their beings. They saw that he not only conquered death but evil as well by taking it upon himself on the cross. I remember a colleague of mine at a Good Friday service speaking of Jesus' agony on the cross and describing it in the fullest human terms. But I thought that fell short because it was also a divine agony that he experienced. And then the coming back, the astounding coming back, has profoundly affected and formed the Christian community.

DR. HUBBARD: Meaning the resurrection?

DR. GROSE: Yes, the resurrection. One Christian theologian describes it subjectively, such as a person losing a loved one who can still hear her foot fall in the next room. But that is not the Christian faith—it's the faith of a philosopher. He may be a Christian, but in this area he is philosophical in terms of main stream Christianity.

I want to speak briefly about three categories used to identify Jesus: prophet, priest, and king. These are very useful medieval and Protestant categories for Jesus. As the Letter to the Hebrews (7:26-28) describes it, he was the priest who sacrificed himself, and therefore made a full and sufficient sacrifice for the sins of the whole world, as expressed in Christian liturgy. His role as king refers to messiahship, because one meaning of messiah is king. So he is king, and he exercises rule, which is one function of his being the Lord. And prophethood is wonderful, not only of itself, but also because it is a tangible link to Judaism and Islam. Many Christians don't think about it, but Jesus is clearly a prophet in the traditions and doctrines of Christianity.

DR. HUBBARD: Okay, let's get Dr. Siddiqi's position.

DR. SIDDIQI: Like Abraham and Moses, Jesus has a very important place in Islam. He is called a prophet and messenger of God. He is also recognized in Islam as *Masih*, the messiah. We Muslims understand and appreciate why his noble personality has impressed the Christian community—we ourselves are impressed by him. He has a very attractive spiritual personality. The Qur'an speaks about his miracles and wonderful lifestyle. The Muslim mystics, the Sufis, call him a spiritual master. He was a religious giant, one of the greatest human beings ever to have lived, the prototype of a man of God.

We know very well how various Christian groups have spoken about Him as "Son of God." We understand that some of them use this term literally and some metaphorically. We Muslims are prohibited from using this terminology. The Qur'an has rejected the use of the term "Son of God" for any person because it confuses the very notion of divine transcendence and oneness that Islam so much emphasizes. Jesus's personality was no doubt very powerful and spiritually effective; yet, in Islamic teachings, God alone is God and Jesus only his servant and messenger. He is called in the Qur'an *Min al-muqarrabin*, one of those who are very near to God. The Qur'an also criticizes the belief in incarnation, both God becoming man or becoming something else. Also, deification is not accepted in Islam—God is God and man is man. There is a complete separation between the being of God and everything else. However, union of the will is possible. That is, the human will submits to the will of God and unites with the divine will. I think these are the major points of difference between Islam and Christianity in our understanding of Jesus.

We in Islam also take another position on Jesus which is very different from that of Christianity. According to the Qur'an, Jesus was not crucified. So Jesus' role as redeemer by suffering and dying on the cross for the sake of others is denied by Islam. Let me say, however, that the problem here is not the suffering of a prophet or the suffering and crucifixion of an innocent person.

DR. HUBBARD: So if he was crucified, he wasn't crucified for the world? He was simply executed?

DR. SIDDIQI: No, I am saying that in history many innocent persons suffered; and the Qu'ran acknowledges that there were some prophets who were killed by their people. So the crucifixion of a prophet is not a theological problem for Islam and is not the reason why Islam cannot accept the alleged crucifixion of Jesus. The Qu'ran denies it as a historical fact. The text says very clearly that this did not happen to Jesus—he was neither killed nor crucified (Surah 4:157). Furthermore, according to Islam, the death of one person does not exonerate another from sin and guilt. Only God saves and forgives sins. So even if it were the case that Jesus was crucified, this would not entail any change in Islam's theology of salvation. This is another difference between the Islamic and Christian traditions on Jesus. However, the miracles of Jesus, his virgin birth, messianic position and second coming—all these beliefs and concepts are accepted in Islam. Perhaps there is no other tradition outside of Christianity that has given Jesus such an important and prominent position as has Islam.

DR. HUBBARD: Can you tell us what the Islamic understanding of messiahship means. It was remarkable for you to call Jesus "messiah."

DR. SIDDIQI: Jesus is going to fulfill the role of messiah in his second coming.

DR. HUBBARD: But what is the nature of that role?

DR. SIDDIQI: I believe his messianic role is to prove to the world that God is the only one to be worshipped and God's rule must be established. Jesus and the Mahdi, another eschatological figure, will help establish an era of justice on this earth. Some *hadith* or sayings of Prophet Muhammad stress that Jesus will come again to break the cross, thus rejecting the crucifixion idea or the symbol of so-called redemption. He will also kill the pig to state that the Christian community erred when it renounced the rules of the Torah, especially the dietary rules. Jesus will also restate that he did not come to abolish the Torah, but to fulfill it.[14]

DR. HUBBARD: That's amazing.

DR. SIDDIQI: Also, according to the same *hadith* Jesus will remove the *Jizya*, a special tax that was imposed by Islam upon the Jewish and Christian communities living under the protection of the Islamic state. This is probably another way of saying that the three communities of faith should come together in the worship of the one God. So the Messianic role is also to bring a real union in the house of Abraham by bringing our three communities together.

DR. HUBBARD: A question for Dr. Gordis: would you say that the predominant view amongst Jews about Jesus is that he is a prophet, a rabbi—a somewhat unorthodox one—or a boogie man? Recall that there are a few Talmudic passages, to which George earlier alluded, that paint a very unflattering picture of Jesus.

DR. GORDIS: As you said, the passages are peripheral, basically non-entities, and come from a time of competition among faiths. The handful of references to Jesus are really of no significance in terms of the perception of Jesus in Jewish religion. You have many opinions among Jews on religious matters, as you have among any other people, and maybe a few more. The question is, how do you deal with the otherness of the other? There are those who are basically insular in the Jewish community, who view anyone who is not part of it as in some way out of it. Then such a person is a boogie man, as you put it, Ben. But that is not the perception as I understand it, either in the tradition or among most Jews. Thoughtful Jews realize Christianity to be a great faith, as they see Islam to be a great faith. And Jesus was certainly a figure of vast historical importance, whose origins were Jewish and who remained a Jew probably throughout his life. He was part of a group of somewhat idiosyncratic leaders, who had disciples around him. They had an anti-establishment tinge and resented certain things that went on in the Jewish establishment—but that's what the prophets did also. Recall Jeremiah standing on some great occasion in the Temple court as people came out of the Temple, all dressed up. He asks, "Are you going to steal, murder, fornicate and commit other aberrations, and then say 'I'm saved' because I've gone through these motions? You've made this place into a robber's cave, not into a temple" (Jeremiah 7:9-11). So there were precedents for figures who were very critical of the establishment.

Obviously, some of Jesus' actions are read differently by Jews, such as
the money changers in the Temple (Mark 11:15-19) which in
Christianity paints a very negative picture of the Pharisees. Pharisaic
Judaism is Judaism—the Pharisees were the rabbis. The money
changers were there because of the pilgrimage festivals, when people
came to Jerusalem from throughout the world. One of their
responsibilities was to eat of the produce they had grown in their land.
They couldn't carry the produce with them, so—according to the rules
we have in the Torah—they would sell the produce in their own
country and bring the currency to Jerusalem. The moneychangers were
just in the Temple so these pilgrims could buy more produce and eat
it to fulfill God's commandment. So this was not the kind of corruption
I'm referring to. Nevertheless, Jesus was an anti-establishment,
somewhat idiosyncratic teacher of enormous spiritual strength who had
followers and historically had an impact of immeasurable importance
on the world. He is appreciated as a teacher, but not a figure of
religious significance for Jews. Because of the interpretation of his
career, he became this human divine figure, something which removed
him from compatibility with Judaism. Jesus as a great teacher belonged
in the tradition of Jewish teachers; as man made God, he represents a
descent from the notion of pure monotheism and is a less accessible
and compatible figure for Jews.

DR. SIDDIQI: What do you say about texts the Church uses from the
Old Testament, from your Bible, which are given Christological
interpretations?

DR. GORDIS: No Jewish scholar and, I would suggest, few reputable
Christian Biblical scholars as well, would see in these Hebrew texts
anything Christological except by eisegesis, that is, reading it into the
text. It is perfectly appropriate to read something into a text, but there
is actually no reference in Isaiah to Jesus. For example, the names
Isaiah gave to his children were full of meaning (Isaiah 6:3, 8:3), so
when he gave the name "Wonderful Counselor" (Isaiah 9:6) to a future
Judean king, it was just one of the ways of putting across a message

and had nothing to do with the Jewish Christians' anticipating a divine figure. That's just simply not what the author of Isaiah intended.

DR. SIDDIQI: Is it not strange that the prophets who speak about the future events and about the end of the world would not speak about such an important event which was going to have such a lasting effect on human history, even on the history of their own people?

DR. GORDIS: What event do you mean?

DR. SIDDIQI: Jesus.

DR. GORDIS: It's not an important event to Jews.

DR. SIDDIQI: But in terms of history, sure, it is an important event.

DR. GORDIS: I'm not understanding. Are you saying that the prophets speak about it or don't speak about it?

DR. HUBBARD: He's saying they do.

DR. SIDDIQI: Shouldn't they speak of it?

DR. GORDIS: But in Jewish tradition the birth of Jesus is an event of no importance. Why should the prophets speak of it?

DR. SIDDIQI: Why is it not important? The past 2000 years show how important it is—it affected the Jewish people themselves.

DR. GORDIS: Oh, you're saying sociologically, but the classical prophets are not mantics. They don't foretell the future.

DR. SIDDIQI: But they are telling of the last days, of the end of the world.

DR. GORDIS: No, there's a very big difference between the end of the world and future events. The prophets don't talk about the Holocaust, world wars or battles. And they don't talk about the birth of one person or another person. The end of days is a vision of the direction the world is moving. There is no reason why the Hebrew Bible should talk about a personality, Jesus, who is not considered in the Jewish tradition, by the prophets or by Jews—and you're asking about Jewish interpretations. The prophets don't talk about Confucius or the Buddha. There are many things which go on in the world that are not talked about. Prophecy is not prediction or commentary. It's presenting to the world God's desires and wishes for the world and the goals towards which it should move.

DR. GROSE: That's a different interpretation. I can see where Muzammil is coming from—the declaration of Jesus' birth of the Virgin Mary. That's Qur'anic, and since the Qur'an is the final revelation, why isn't his birth foretold or indicated in the Hebrew Bible? There are two levels I work on in terms of the Hebrew scripture. One, what is it as a text that can be examined in many different ways? Now this is what I, and I think all of us, do as we teach. We don't teach our own faith but what we're assigned to teach. We do our best to present it objectively with all the available sources. So in terms of academic discipline and objectivity, certainly there is nothing in Isaiah 53, for example, that says the Suffering Servant is Jesus. It doesn't say Jesus anywhere. There is a relevant scripture in the Christian community, the Emmaus road episode (Luke 24:13-35). Two men are going to Emmaus and talking about what happened in Jerusalem to Jesus, and then a stranger joins them. As they go along, he explains to them the scriptures in light of these events. So it is through Christian faith that what happened to Jesus is found in the Hebrew Bible.

DR. HUBBARD: One begins with the conviction that Jesus is the messiah and works back into the text. Is that a fair way of putting it?

DR. GROSE: Yes, we find certain meanings as Christians. At the same time, as a scholar, I have an obligation to find what the original intention of a text is. Many Christian lay persons are not conversant with this approach. There is no contradiction in it because you are simply honoring the original intention of the author as best you can. But I also think that, although divinity is not present in the person or life of Jesus according to Judaism and Islam, to me the power of

Christianity is the idea of the divine entering human life—the distance traveled. It is the dynamism of Christianity set up by a powerful tension between the divine and human.

DR. HUBBARD: Dr. Grose, you mentioned that Jesus is seen as prophet, priest and king. The one I'm having the most trouble with is Jesus as king.

DR. GROSE: I think it is just a casting in other languages for messiah. Messiah, the anointed one, is a king and also sometimes a high priest. Am I correct on that?

DR. SIDDIQI: There is the title "King of the Jews" used somewhere in the New Testament.[15] How would you explain it, George?

DR. GROSE: Etymologically "messiah" means anointed, as does the Greek for that, *christos*. So just as King David was anointed with oil and Saul before him, it came to mean the ideal future king. The full messianic expectation, certainly in Jesus' time, was for prevailing redemption—that the messiah would usher in God's rule. Then the wolf dwells with the lamb (Isaiah 11:6), every man sits under his own fig tree and no one is greater than another—all these wonderful images from the Hebrew Bible would come into fruition. One could teach from the standpoint of Judaism that it hasn't happened; therefore, Jesus can't be the messiah. That's a Judaic reading of it; but it's not the Christian reading which says that he is even now king, in that he's the Lord of this world. Jesus shall reign until the last enemy, death, is destroyed. And then there is something which is certainly not Trinitarian: the Son himself will be subjected to God the Father (1 Corinthians 15:28). Between now and the end, the lordship of Jesus is understood as part of his kingship, and he will come as final judge. But it's all in there, that he really is the messiah.

DR. SIDDIQI: Are lordship and kingship spiritual titles?

DR. GROSE: There were those who expected Jesus to be a messiah like David, a king like David, which he wasn't, which he turned from.

So when he came into Jerusalem on Palm Sunday, riding on a donkey—a symbol not of exalted royalty but of royal humility—he wasn't coming as one who would cast off the Roman yoke. That wasn't his kind of messiahship, so Christianity has redefined messiahship. But in certain forms of Christian thought, this is the age of which Jesus is Lord. He's the Lord of this age (Philippians 2:9-11).

DR. HUBBARD: A final question for Dr. Gordis before we turn to Muhammad. There is a popular Jewish conception that Jesus was a simple Galilean rabbi, misunderstood by the power structure of Rome and by the Temple elite, and crucified. But then, according to this view, the real impetus for Christianity was given by Paul of Tarsus who took the simple message of Jesus and repackaged it into something palatable to the whole world. Is this accurate from the Jewish perspective?

DR. GORDIS: It was Paul who shaped the story of the life and death of Jesus into the central story of the Christian faith. Jesus didn't do that himself. His teachings are certainly within the spirit of Rabbinic literature and Jewish liturgy. That represents the first phase: Jesus as the Jew, and the Jewish-Christian period of early Christianity. The later development of Christianity among the Gentiles is part of the second phase. So I don't think it's just the popular view but is historically accurate. After all, the Gospels postdate, for obvious reasons, the life of Jesus. And it's from the Gospels, and their somewhat different but basically parallel telling of the story of the life and death of Jesus, that Christianity came.

DR. HUBBARD: So the proclaimer of God, Jesus, becomes the proclaimed through Paul.

DR. GORDIS: Well, remember that, not only from a Jewish viewpoint but also from an historical one, we rely on the texts of the Gospels for the evidence of Jesus' message and activity. In the same way, in relation to our earlier discussion, it wasn't simply Abraham's activity that was significant, but the recounting of the story of Abraham and the other patriarchs. The account places an event in time and space and disseminates the message from the small band of people there at the time to a larger public. Thus, the transformations their lives represented become realities and create new faiths. That's why it was important to have Torah and a Qur'an. The Qur'an not only reflects the personality of Muhammad, but was the instrument by which his message and mission were available to a larger world.

DR. GROSE: Paul was instrumental in promoting Christianity's world mission, but he was not alone. The Gospel of Matthew ends with a mandate to go to the Gentiles, baptize in the name of the Trinity, and teach all that Jesus had commanded (Matthew 28:18-20). And I don't think one can work back and say that the origins of this gospel go back to Paul. Luke also understood himself as someone who had a role in the Gentile mission, and he begins the Acts of the Apostles with Jesus' words, "You shall be my witnesses in Jerusalem...and to the end of the earth" (Acts 1: 8). So the world dimension of the mission took off quickly and, within less than a generation, it was no longer Jewish Christianity.

DR. SIDDIQI: But none of the modern New Testament scholars recognize this statement in Matthew as Jesus' actual words. It is probably a later addition and is the only place in the Gospels where a somewhat trinitarian formula is put in the mouth of Jesus.

DR. GROSE: It closes the gospel in Matthew.

DR. SIDDIQI: Yes, Go to all the world in the name of the Father, Son and Holy Spirit. But it's not Jesus' statement, or is it? I am asking this because a number of New Testament scholars have raised doubts about its authenticity.

DR. GROSE: Muzammil, the questions you raise prompt me to reflect on the Qur'an's origins. Non-Muslims can claim that the Qur'an is derived form the Hebrew Bible, the New Testament and Jewish apocryphal writings. Yet, the Muslim testimony, indeed the testimony of the Qur'an to itself, is that it came from God directly, from the "Mother of the Book." Similarly, for most Christians, Jesus' words at the close of Matthew's gospel—the "Great Commission" (Matthew

28:18-20)—are Jesus' words and are the very grounding of the Church's mission to the world. These words, together with Acts of the Apostles 1:8, have inspired the Christian community to take the gospel to the whole inhabited earth: the ecumenical vision so well described by Leslie Newbigin, first Bishop of the Church of South India.

A theological clarification is needed. Some Christian scholars have pointed out that Matthew is the only gospel which has a genuine ending. Indeed, the entire gospel builds up to the Great Commission: to go to all nations; make disciples; baptize in the name of the Father, Son and Holy Spirit; and teach all that Jesus commanded—including the celebration of Holy Communion. If the crucified Jesus is risen and has returned to his disciples, even to 500 brethren (1 Corinthians 15:6), then these are the words of the risen Christ. On the other hand, if the crucified Jesus Christ is not risen, then these words are not his. The world mission is the mission of the crucified and risen One. Christianity can only be seen for what it is when one takes into account the testimony of the Christian community to its crucified and risen Lord who was with the Church for 40 days giving instruction and guidance with the assurance of immediate and continuing fellowship "to the end of the age" (Matthew 28:20).

4. MUHAMMAD

DR. HUBBARD: May I interject that this is one of those kernel questions that we want to deal with when we get to the subject of revelation. Let's move on and see what the three of you think about the figure of Muhammad.

DR. GORDIS: When we talked about the figure of Jesus from the Jewish perspective, I commented that he was not a shared figure. The same with Muhammad—he is not a central figure, and there is no reason why Jews have had to examine and categorize him. Prophecy does not enter the picture, because there were no prophets, Jews or non-Jews, as I explained earlier, after the end of the prophetic period in the fifth century B.C.E. In the case of Muhammad there was such a long hiatus. After all the end of the Biblical period was probably the Fourth Century before the Common Era.   The completion of the Mishnah, the core Rabbinic legal text, was in approximately 198 or 200 C.E. The completion of both the Babylonian and the Palestinian Talmuds was by end of the Fifth century. Muhammad came to prominence 100 years after the Talmud was already codified and edited and is a late arrival on the scene in terms of classical Judaism. The Jewish faith is already formed.   It's almost like saying to a Muslim—and I'm pushing it to an extreme to illustrate my point—"What is the view of Islam on the Prophet Joseph Smith, the founder of the Mormon faith?"

DR. GROSE: What about the linkage we have through Abraham?

DR. GORDIS: I'm only suggesting that a figure such as Joseph Smith who comes far later is not part of the Islamic religious perception. I'm sure it's a question which has never really arisen. Obviously, none of us accepts Smith's prophecy. We understand it as a historical event which produced a scripture, but for none of us is the Book of Mormon canonical. Not to be pejorative about it, but it's not in the picture. That's the only parallel I'm drawing. So in terms of the development of Judaism, there really is no treatment of Muhammad because he doesn't fit in.

DR. GROSE: I think, in the dialogic sense, he does fit in this manner: if Muhammad fits for Christians, he fits also for Jews. We're in the same boat because he's an after-the-fact prophet with an after-the-fact scripture in an after-the-fact period. So if Christians have a way of relating to Muhammad that is religious, then it would seem Jews have a similar way of relating to him through the Abraham linkage.

DR. GORDIS: I think what you're saying is quite correct and wise. But we're talking about two different questions. What I was trying to address, I think, is the question of how does Judaism as a tradition view Muhammad?

DR. GROSE: How has it?

DR. GORDIS: How has it? Just historical.

DR. SIDDIQI: Just as he looked at Jesus, similarly he is looking at Muhammad.

DR. GROSE: I understand that.

DR. GORDIS: I think what you're opening up, George, is not only interesting but fruitful and important. I think we would be well advised to answer a second question—the first involved the historical situation—as people of three faiths linked in ways we have talked about: how ought we now, how ought a Jew, look at Jesus and Muhammad? What other possibilities are there? That's a different question.

DR. GROSE: Yes, it is. I threw out my comment in the sense that it's kind of uncooked. Even though I've tried to cook it, so to speak, it's still something to be looked at again in the dialogic sense that we're talking together about these things. I think if I can make a case for Muhammad, Judaism could, too, in some way or other. That's supposition on my part which I have no right to make, but I make it.

DR. GORDIS: I don't think it's a matter of for or against. But there was one question we talked about among ourselves which was very fruitful: how would you, Muzammil, like to see George and me relate to Muhammad—with the understanding that we are not going to accept or see him as the central figure of our faith? What are the possibilities of how we would constructively view him? How do you think we ought to be taking more seriously the religious figure of Muhammad, given the fact that we are not Muslims and would not see it the way Muslims do?

DR. GROSE: I see your questions, David, as part of the building blocks for this sort of dialogue. How can we demonstrate the place of

Muhammad in Christianity?   The Abraham line is part of the demonstration and is a very important connection which Christians need to conjure with and which I have just begun to explore. In any case, I can say several things about Muhammad. In my view, he received revelation from God, but some if it either was misunderstood by him or something else happened. In particular, I refer to the denial of the historicity of Jesus' death (Surah 4:157-58). But as to his receiving revelation, I've come to the place where I accept this. So to me he's at least an almost prophet.

DR. HUBBARD: Can you clarify what you mean by his having received revelation?

DR. SIDDIQI: And also, what do you mean by "almost a prophet"?

DR. GORDIS: Other than that, it's perfectly clear!

DR. GROSE: I would throw in the idea of a time warp, just as "Star Trek" or even going back to the "Connecticut Yankee in King Arthur's Court." With this in mind, Muhammad can appropriately be placed among the other great prophets and allowed to do what he's called to do. I see him, and this is not my only term for him, as a reformer. In fact, the Qur'an speaks of this. He wasn't called to initiate but to restore the true religion of God which had been distorted over the centuries among the Arabs and elsewhere.   There needed to be corrections in Judaism and Christianity also. So he was a reformer of Arab polytheists, but also of Christians and Jews. He attacked idolatry wherever he found it. The thrust of his critique of Christianity was to cut back on the idolatry, which I see as a creeping thing in all the great religions. Luther said the human mind is a factory for idols. People idolize things less than God all the time.

Look at how the cult of Mary had been developing. One of the early Christian creeds describes her as the "Mother of God." That's the English translation, but in Greek she's the "God-bearer."[16] That's a different sense. To be the God-bearer is one thing, but to be mother of God is something else—it's an example of how I see idolatry coming into Christianity. While my definition of idolatry would not be the same as a Muslim's or a Jew's—because of the Incarnation—yet, I see Muhammad's work as a powerful corrective world-wide to the idolatry that was certainly affecting the other monotheistic communities. I can speak about Christianity authoritatively because I'm a Christian. We had some idolatry, we still do. Muhammad, with his tremendous sense of God's transcendence, is a powerful corrective to that.

And I find that I can put the Qur'anic comment about Jesus not actually being crucified but only appearing to be (Surah 4:157) in a certain context. It is a flat contradiction of what is at the core of Christianity—no doubt about that. But, at the same time, it is completely fitting because the distinction between the divine and the human is really clear in Islam, as it is in Judaism. Muhammad was a monotheistic reformer, and therefore one doesn't even get close to the idea that God becomes man. That to me is the thrust of the passage, and it doesn't threaten me as a Christian because I know what I know. I wonder at the non-historicity of it, but I see what it is doing: maintaining the godliness of God. I'm probably unlike many Christians on this point—after all, I've worked with Jews and Muslims for a long time. So I don't fault my fellow Christians who don't see it this way, who may never see it. Overall, I see Muhammad as being a very positive figure.

DR. HUBBARD: Would you like Muhammad to be better known in America?

DR. GROSE: Institutionally, what do I say about the reality that there are about the same number of Muslims as Christians in the world?[17] If I'm taking simply an institutional position, I will want Islam as a community diminished, or at least not growing, and Christianity growing. I think there are distortions all around in our religions. There isn't any mosque that has the true view among all its members, or any church, or any synagogue. People have ideas that don't quite fit in with what the religion teaches. Yet, we all have to have religion because it's through religion that the truth addresses us. However, if we say religion is encapsulated in the churches, synagogues or mosques, then I don't think we're in a position to defend them. We're only in a position to defend the truth as we see it. That may be a radical position to take, but I'm taking it and it doesn't trouble me. I don't want America to be a Muslim country. God forbid, and far be it. It's not going to be a Muslim country, but I'm happy that Muslims are here. Muhammad is a great reformer among his people, and a great reformer is good for us.

In the West, a great deal has been made of Muhammad's several wives. Indeed, he had more wives in total than the Qur'an allows but at different times, so he didn't exceed the Qur'anic allowance of four wives. Yet, the West has attacked him not only because he was not what a prophet ought to be as a head of state, but also for being lecherous. Something has to be noted here very carefully. When Muhammad was married to Khadija, who was 15 years his senior, he had no other wives and this was the happiest time of his life. Most of his later wives were widows of friends who had died in battle. These women didn't have social security, so part of his motivation was to take care of them, give them status and recognize the memory of their husbands. So I find Muhammad highly admirable. If I can accept this time-warp idea and put aside the chronological problem, then I would say yes to his being a prophet.

Still, there are mistakes in the Qur'an; and if this is what Muhammad received, then he is a prophet misunderstood. Or somebody made some mistakes in certain sections of the Qur'an. I have to view the matter that way. How could I do else as a Christian? But I think all of this dialogue comes to the point where—as far as we can—we move toward accepting what the other says of his founder. We have to listen carefully, honor and try to understand what a Muslim says about Muhammad, what a Jew says about Moses, what a Christian says about Jesus.

DR. SIDDIQI: I appreciate very much your openness in trying to understand the prophetic claims of Prophet Muhammad. Let me state that whatever I said about Jesus, Moses and Abraham, I didn't say as my view or simply because I wanted to be open to you. I made those statements as part of my faith based on what the Qu'ran and Prophet Muhammad himself have said. Now, I do understand your difficulty as

Christians and Jews to give a religious place to Prophet Muhammad in your theological framework. You both start with the premise that the canon[18] is closed, that the door of prophecy was closed at a certain point. So you cannot recognize the religious figures who appeared after that time. You take them as mere historic figures, good persons and reformers, but not really the prophets of God. This is a much better position than the negative and derogatory terminology that was used by Christians and Jews about Prophet Muhammad in the past and is used by some people even now. So I appreciate your willingness to examine Prophet Muhammad's prophetic claims and your question, David, about how I would like to see you and George relate to Muhammad and take him seriously as a religious figure.

I want you to compare him with the other prophetic figures of the Hebrew Bible. Read about his life and work, and study his teachings. See for yourself whether he fits into the prophetic framework that the Hebrew Bible or the New Testament provide you with. My position is that he fits very well and stands tall among the great prophetic figures of the Bible. Now you say that you still cannot accept him as a prophet because the canon is closed. As I said before, in Judaism and Christianity this closing was done by the people. I do not think the people have the right to close the door of prophecy. Only God can do that. So I am afraid we have to open the door again to include Prophet Muhammad. Then why can't we Muslims also take Joseph Smith[19] or others as prophets of God? For Muslims the simple answer is that God Himself has closed that door after Prophet Muhammad. The Qu'ran said he was the last prophet and messenger of God (Surah 33:40).

However, if you don't want to take him as a prophet I don't have to force you. We can still share our basic values of faith and goodness with each other. You can see how Muhammad's teachings affect us in our own lives and what he told us concerning our relations to you, the "People of the Book"—Jews and Christians. We can still work together to seek peace and justice in the world.

George, you also raised some very important issues. I can see you have a problem accepting the Qur'anic denial of the crucifixion of

Jesus. But why do you call it a mistake? You can say that this is not what the New Testament says about Jesus and not what you and many Christians believe happened. However, you seem to be saying that Muhammad was a prophet of God who received divine revelation but that he misunderstood and misquoted the part about Jesus' crucifixion and preached a mistaken concept. This means that God who was revealing his message to Muhammad kept silent and never corrected him. I find that a strange concept of prophecy and divine revelation. Do you think that prophets sometimes misunderstand the divine message and mislead people? Are there other examples of that in the history of prophecy? Did Moses and Jesus also misunderstand God and sometimes mislead their followers? However, if you are suggesting that Prophet Muhammad gave a correct version but some alteration took place later in the reporting of the statement, then I'd like to ask you another set of questions. Who did the altering and when? Do you have another version that gives a different position? Do you have any sources from Islamic history that suggest an alternate reading? And, finally, do you have any other revelation that corrects this mistake? These issues need a good discussion among us.

As for Prophet Muhammad's marrying more than one wife and this being taken as very unprophetic of him, I would ask about many Old Testament prophets. They also had many wives but you consider them prophets![20]

DR. GROSE: That's where the time warp thing fits in.

DR. SIDDIQI: Other prophets also had more than one wife. You made a good point, George, that Khadija was Muhammad's only wife until he was 50. When she died, he married other women. However, he did not marry the widows of his friends but of leaders of the tribes he was fighting. Once he married them, the whole tribe became friendly. So these marriages were for various reasons and none of his contemporaries raised any objections. It is also true that polygamy often went along with sumptuous food and a luxurious lifestyle. But we know that Prophet Muhammad often fasted and prayed, sometimes for three or four days. He was a spiritual man not given to luxuries and sumptuousness.

DR. HUBBARD: One of Muhammad's marriages was to a woman who was very unhappy in her current marriage and ultimately divorced her husband to marry Muhammad. Can you clarify for us the circumstances behind that?

DR. SIDDIQI: That was his marriage to Zaynab, his cousin, who was married to Zayd, his adopted son. Muhammad had persuaded Zaynab to marry Zayd, but she was from the noble Quresh tribe and he was a slave, even though the adopted son of the Prophet. So she did not feel very happy about marrying him and eventually this led to a divorce. Then the revelation came to the Prophet that he should marry her. He was very reluctant to do so because she was the ex-wife of his adopted son and people would talk about it. But the Qur'an (Surah 33:37) says that God deserves to be feared, not people. So Muhammad was instructed to marry Zaynab and also abolish the practice of adoption. The Qur'an then states that Muhammad is not the father of any male among you and had no son. He was just a messenger of God, the last of the prophets (Surah 33:40).

DR. HUBBARD: Didn't he have any biological male children?

DR. SIDDIQI: He did have some sons who died as infants. Adoption was a custom in pre-Islamic Arabia but is prohibited by Islam in the sense of changing the name of a child who isn't yours biologically to your name. You may take care of a child and give him a nice home, but not change the name of his natural father.

So there are certain areas of misunderstanding that need to be discussed. But I see a problem on the point David raised: how should Jews and Christians look at Muhammad. Prophet Muhammad is not an ordinary person. He makes an absolute claim to prophethood. Either accept him as a prophet or do not. You cannot do something in between. If you say he is truly a prophet of God, you have accepted him and the Islamic position. If you say, "No, I don't accept him," I understand that also. But these are the only two positions we have and a person has to choose one of them.

DR. HUBBARD: What if I say to you that I can accept Muhammad as a prophet for Muslims, but not necessarily for other people, not for me as a Jew, or....

DR. SIDDIQI: But he did not say he was a prophet for Muslims only. He claimed he was a prophet for all mankind.

DR. GORDIS: Muzammil, I'd like to reflect on what you're saying because it fascinates me and deals with the central thrust of our whole enterprise. The notion of looking at certain historical claims—whether Jesus was crucified or Moses did go up on Mount Sinai or Muhammad did something—is interesting, but for me it's not the critical issue. We don't come here as unformed people, putting historical claims on the table. You come as a Muslim, I as a Jew, you George as a Christian. We come with certain faith attitudes shaped by our entire being. We aren't going to determine that, because the three of us agree about the claims of Jesus, we'll all become Christians. That's not what this dialogue is about.

To me there are many things in the Hebrew Bible which have emerged as historically wrong, such as the numbers of those who made the Exodus from Egypt: 600,000 men, along with women and children and "a mixed multitude" (Exodus 12:37-38). There weren't that many people, even though the numbers given were specific. So historical accuracy as such is not the issue.

What defines a person as being a Muslim or not is whether one sees Muhammad as the central prophet who came to correct certain abuses. For a Muslim that is a powerful reality, but you must understand that for a non-Muslim it's not. And it's not a question of historic claims or documentation. Of course, Muhammad claimed to be the seal of the prophets. But, since we non-Muslims don't view that Qur'anic scripture as canonical, we don't read the story the same way or credit the claim the same way. The real issue is how you would like to see a person who doesn't accept that central claim, view the prophet Muhammad. In the same way, you're not going to see the Talmud, which makes major claims on Jews, as authoritative. But I don't expect the non-Jew to do so, though I would like him or her to be interested in two things: first, what I mean when I talk about accepting the Torah, so you'll understand what makes me tick; second, the insights—the clashes of insight and truth—that are contained in the rabbinic tradition and might be enhancing to the Christian, the Muslim, the Buddhist and others.

So we are not talking conversion here. Muhammad is not the central prophet for you, George, or me. He may be a prophetic kind of figure—which is how I would translate George's earlier remarks—a great religious teacher with universal insights and ideals. But if George and I don't accept him as God's authoritative prophet, wouldn't you, Muzammil, like us to be interested in understanding what Muhammad's perspective is on the way people should relate to one another; what he says about family and the way the world is moving, how we get from where we are to the ideal state, etc.? We can be helped by all of that without assenting to the authority claim.

When we talk within our own traditions—when Muslim talks to Muslim, Jew to Jew, Christian to Christian—we have a shared sense of authority, shared assumptions, a shared language. But when Muslim talks to Jew, and Jew to Christian, then there has to be a translation. Basic to it is the notion that I'm talking to someone who views the world differently and doesn't accept the authority claim that I make internally. What do I talk to that person about? I don't think it's a question of fitting each other into schemes. George, you seem to be preoccupied with how can I put Muhammad into my scheme. That's perfectly proper and legitimate, but it's not of interest to me. My sense is we are very limited in what we can know about God. As we struggle to grasp that knowledge, each of our traditions can help us. No one of us has exclusive access to it. So I want to be helped, not by fitting you into a scheme, or your fitting me into a scheme.

I'm interested also in this great leader, Jesus. It doesn't matter if you call him a prophet, a teacher, whatever. He was a personality who changed the world with his enormous insights. They are familiar to me in certain ways because they are conditioned by Jewishness, yet they are different. The world is enriched by them, I'm enriched by them. Those are the kinds of things I most want to talk about and understand. We shouldn't be trying to level each other or put each other in some grand scheme. We should be talking to each other in our differentness and should be enriched by each other that way. We do have to communicate also within our own communities, and there's a certain kind of truth we feel in our own tradition which other traditions don't have. That's natural.. But when we talk to each other, the concerns should be these other kinds.

DR. SIDDIQI: This is a good statement, David. The point you're making has to do with figures who come after what you consider the fixing of the canon of classical Judaism in the Talmud. I think the most one can do is to look at these figures from the standpoint of how important they are for the other person who believes in them....

DR. GORDIS: But also how important they can be for me as a Jew who is not, therefore, a Muslim. It's not just a matter of the sequential order of these figures. Let me be really heretical for a moment: the Hebrew Bible intentionally distorts and misunderstands paganism. Recall that we talked about Abraham and his encounter with it. Paganism is not the story that the Qur'an tells, or that the Midrash tells when it describes Abraham mocking the silliness of those worshipping an idol, a piece of stone that cannot even talk. But that's not what paganism is all about. Pagans were sophisticated—they held a kind of pantheism in which human beings relate to gods, but in which the gods existed subject to a "meta-divine" reality, to a power beyond even them. These gods are powerful and are associated with various natural phenomena. People within paganism tried to understand this power, and how to cope with it and change the world. I'm not a pagan, I reject it. But there are things one can learn from a serious understanding of paganism as one sees it in classical Greek and Hellenistic writings. There are still pagans around, some of them Jews. Richard Rubenstein, a rabbi, calls himself a pagan. I understand what he is trying to do. Baruch Spinoza[21] rejected Judaism and was a pantheist. Yet his critique of Judaism, of classical religion, is extremely important to me as a religious person.

DR. GROSE: I think truth comes to us from many sources, and your viewpoint is interesting. But what you referred to as the "scheme" into which I want to place things is not my scheme; it's the way God has chosen to reveal himself. He sent prophets, and it's not for me to say whether someone is a prophet. God has disclosed that certain people are prophets, so it's not a scheme I originated. It's not something that I am forcing upon reality.

DR. GORDIS: This is only subjective because we disagree about those schemes. After all, the Hebrew Bible gives us criteria for distinguishing true and false prophets, right.

DR. GROSE: All right.

DR. GORDIS: Different people apply them differently.

DR. GROSE: Very well. But I'm confident there is objective truth, whether or not I understand it. Some things are true, but I may not recognize this or may be totally blind to it. To put it in terms of what we learned in Philosophy 101: when a tree falls in a forest and nobody is around to hear it, does it make a sound? My position is yes, it makes a sound. But nobody in the world ever heard the tree fall. In that sense, something may be true whether anybody believes it or not. So the question is not about a super-imposed scheme, but is simply whether or not Muhammad is a prophet similar to the other prophets or not.

DR. GORDIS: Forgive me for being so verbose, George, but that's exactly the point. You put it beautifully: there is truth, and we all struggle to find it. But even if we do, we may not know it. This is part of the human predicament and it can be baffling. The prophets and teachers, people of stature and importance and significance, no matter what label we've attached to them, can contribute to our common search for truth. We don't have to fit them into a single scheme.

DR. GROSE: We'll vary on that. But I think the question of validating Islam is important.

DR. SIDDIQI: Historically, Islam has given a lot of meaning to the lives of human beings. But what does it mean to someone who is not part of this tradition, the Jew or the Christian? That's the question David is dealing with: How can the non-Muslim appreciate or understand or even draw some lessons from Islam? Then there is the question of what the Bible says about Muhammad. Just as Christians speak about the Old Testament referring to Jesus, Muslims ask what the Old and New Testaments say about Muhammad. A third question is, what did Muhammad say about himself and about that which happened before?

DR. GROSE: The fourth question is whether or not he resembles a Hebrew prophet?

DR. SIDDIQI: That I think is part of the second question: biblical prophecy and whether Muhammad was included within it. We are people of three traditions who have certain scriptures from which we get different views. It is important to look at the scriptures to appreciate how Muslims have understood them, just as it is important for us to understand how Christians look at the Old Testament and interpret certain prophecies. You, David, as a Jew may not accept the interpretation.

DR. GROSE: I don't know how Jews feel, knowing that Christians utilize their scriptures to maintain that the Savior is Jesus. I'm not in their shoes. But we do it all the time. I know I don't feel easy having Muslims work with my New Testament to find Muhammad there when I don't. So I can infer that Jews don't feel easy about Christians reading Jesus into their Bible.

DR. HUBBARD: On that note we'll close and turn next time to the subject of linkages and core beliefs.

CHAPTER TWO

LINKAGES AND CORE BELIEFS

1. MONOTHEISM

HUBBARD: In the first session, we discussed our common ancestor Abraham and the founders of our respective traditions—Moses, Jesus and Muhammad. This time we want to explore what we have in common theologically—in our system of beliefs—and where we differ. Dr. Gordis, what can you tell us about the links between Judaism, Christianity, and Islam?

GORDIS: The most dominant parallel feature between the three traditions is that they represent monotheism, the belief in the unity of God and the ordered nature of the world. They share the sense of God as creator and source of all being who is in a continuing and caring relationship with humankind.

There is also a self-evident diachronicity or time relationship to the linkage between the three faiths. From a historical point of view, Judaism was the first great tradition to give the monotheistic insight to the world, and to do so through a scripture that became central for the other two faiths as well. However, it's a mistake to assume that because there is diachronicity—Judaism coming first, Christianity following, and Islam being the youngest—that this represents a derivation. It does not mean that all features of Christianity or Islam, or even the most important, were under the influence of Judaism.

Sometimes the nature of linkage lies precisely in the divergence between the three faiths. Perhaps it's a mistake to see Christianity and Islam as "daughter" religions, which implies a familial control by Judaism, which is not the case.

Also, we all see the world progressing towards a goal, though we formulate this notion of teleology or directedness to a goal in different ways. We see the world moving towards a state of redemption which is the product of both human efforts and the impact of divine grace within the human experience. We all have notions of messiah and salvation which are similar yet diverge in some ways. And we have the sense of human beings, as Judaism puts it, in a partnership with God. We have a responsibility to move the world towards redemption, though we know that redemption will not come exclusively on the basis of human efforts. Out of this comes a sense of an imperative for human beings. In Judaism, it's *mitzvah*, a commandment or good deed. In each of our traditions, it is expressed in different ways. We are to live life according to ethical principals which we see rooted in God. A belief in God represents a conviction that the world can become better, that there is the possibility—we might even say the inevitability—of salvation. And there is a responsibility to nurture this partnership with God.

Just to add a contemporary footnote to my remarks: the kind of shared spiritual insight I've described presents us a shared challenge. The world today is less open to accept the notion of redeemability and the need to work in partnership. We live in a world which insists on immediate gratification, and is very often unwilling to invest in the kind of long-term investment which our faiths talk about. Perhaps the fundamental inference from this historical and theological linkage is the sense of a linked responsibility to bring a message of faith to the world.

HUBBARD: Dr. Grose, how do you view the linkage between the three traditions?

GROSE: I concur in what David Gordis has just said. The resonances between the three communities are great—not the conformity but the resonances. What he said about creation, human responsibility, and God as the Lord of history is very real for all three. I'm glad he allowed for the uniqueness of each of our communities, as well as our historic connections. When I taught the course "Judeo-Christian-Islamic Interaction" at the University of California at Irvine, I spoke of the "relationship" between Judaism, Christianity and Islam. Pressed by students to clarify that, I came to realize a relationship can be close or distant. So I then described it as "linkage," a bond between the three communities and used the illustration of three mountain climbers linked to each other as they mount the precipice. Arriving at the summit they can unlink; but in the case of Judaism, Christianity, and Islam there is no unlinking to the end of time. It's all in God's hands, but historically we are bonded together and cannot escape one another. And so the moral imperative behind the dialogue is to maximize the blessings in the interaction.

I don't think anyone can understand Christianity apart from Judaism because Christianity emerged in its midst. The marvelous doctrine of creation came through Judaism and is part of Christianity. This needs to be put in perspective when so many Christian churches today are focusing on what they call a Christ-centered church.
In actuality this is the neglect of the doctrine of God the Father as creator and a pulling apart of the Holy Trinity. So I see a positive place for the Trinity: if Christians hold on to the Trinity as we should, we will not be neglecting the doctrine of creation or the doctrine of the Holy Spirit.

I want to call attention to two aspects of an early[22] Christian creed, the Apostles' Creed, that are important for our work. "God, the Father Almighty" in the Creed is really a reference to *El-Shaddai*, the Mountain God, the Mighty One mentioned in Genesis (17:1). Also, in the clause that reads "he suffered under Pontius Pilate," "suffer" includes Jesus' life, humiliation and death. There is no intimation whatsoever implicating the Jewish people in his suffering and death. That's it, as far as the central creedal affirmation of the Christian Church is concerned. The distortions came through the Church Fathers very quickly but were not lodged in the Apostles' Creed.

One matter that is very challenging for a three-fold dialogue is the Christian belief that Jesus is God as well as man. The Creed of Chalcedon dating from 451 C.E. sought to express this.

So what is a divine human? The so-called Monophysite churches were accused by the others of claiming that Jesus had one nature, which was divine, thus minimizing his humanity. Christianity at large denounced this with much un-Christian lack of charity towards the Monophysites. In fact, this was one of the reasons why—three centuries later—the Muslims met so little resistance when they conquered Egypt, the Monophysite center.

On the other hand, there is Nestorianism which holds a view of Jesus closer to the Judaic and Islamic understanding of a prophet. According to the Nestorians, Jesus is a maximized prophet, a God-intoxicated man; and mainstream Christianity likewise rejected that.

HUBBARD: What terms did the early Church use to express Jesus' divinity?

GROSE: The first creed of the Church says, "Jesus is Lord." The term "Lord" and its cognates may simply mean "Sir," a title of respect. It may also signify divinity: the Roman emperor was "Lord." It came also to be used as a special title for Jesus coming out of the Church's experience. The risen Christ came twice to the disciples in that closed room (John 20:19-29). The second time, Thomas, the great doubter, was there. Jesus invited Thomas to touch his wounds, but Thomas did not. Instead, he declared, "My Lord and my God." Now here the title "Lord" is not "Sir" but, if any parallelism exists, it means divinity. The other passage that is special in this regard, moving now from the experiential to the reflective, is Philippians 2 :5-11. Paul speaks of how the experience of the Christian community should be expressive of the mind of Christ who did not think equality with God a thing to be "grasped," "kept," or "seized," depending on how one translates the Greek word; but emptied himself, taking the form of a man, Jesus. This is the great Christian doctrine of *kenosis*, a self-emptying of the divine: "being found as a man, he was obedient unto death; therefore,

God has highly exalted him"—meaning not only to honor him but to raise him up—"and given him the name which is above every name, that Jesus Christ is Lord, to the glory of God the Father." "Lord" is found throughout the Septuagint, the Greek translation of the Hebrew Bible, to express the most holy name, Yahweh. This Greek "Old Testament" was the first scripture of the early Christians. So Paul is stating that Jesus is Yahweh, "Jesus is Lord," with the name above every name. The New Testament as a whole testifies to this. So the person of Christ, rather than scripture, is the most prominent feature of Christianity.

SIDDIQI: We are talking here about four distinct moments of divine revelation: to Abraham, Moses, Jesus and Muhammad. In the case of the last three, we have three communities of faith, all tracing their roots back to Abraham.

Let me talk about the link between our three communities in moments of revelation, as well as in history and in our existentiality. Islam recognizes that there were many prophets before Muhammad. The prophets whose names are mentioned in the Qur'an are mostly those who are recognized in Judaism and Christianity. As Muslims, we don't call them the prophets of the Old or New Testament, but the prophets of Islam. So, in a sense, Judaism and Christianity are already included in the Islamic understanding of revelation. In fact, the revelation that came to Abraham, Moses and Jesus is the same that came to Muhammad; so there is a link from the divine perspective. Islam does not claim to be a new message that came to Muhammad and was never given previously, but a reaffirmation of the earlier messages. Of course, now it is in the final form because Muhammad is the last prophet of God.

From the Muslim point of view, the many similarities in our three faiths do not cause any theological problems. All these prophets are God's prophets, so their messages ought to be similar. Problematic are the differences between us. Muslims claim that some of these are not substantial, but just a matter of particular emphasis. Some of the other differences are because the messages of earlier prophets were not recorded in their time. We question the authenticity of previous scriptures, but not the authenticity of Moses and Jesus—peace be upon them and all the prophets of God. So this is our theological link.

The second link is historical. The Jewish, Christian and Islamic communities often lived together, interacted and were influenced by each other. Sometimes this relationship was one of tension and difficulties; but often it was one of cooperation. We have to value those moments of working together. A good example is the experience in Spain[23] where Muslim, Jewish, and Christian communities had a flowering of their traditions and of cooperation. Now we have to see how we can take from our scriptural experience, theological sources, as well as our historical experience, and apply these today. On what kinds of things can we build for the future? This is the challenge the three communities have before them at this time.

HUBBARD: Dr. Gordis, I think you would like to respond to this.

GORDIS: Yes. First an observation and then two questions that emerged from the presentations. My observation is that it is fascinating that we have actually begun with *three* different questions, although they all used the same words, "What is the nature of the linkage from your own point of view?" I looked at one segment of the issue—certain theological and world-view parallels in our faiths. Basically they come down to the insight of monotheism and the implications to be drawn from that which we share, and which put us into the same world in many ways.

George, you responded to the question by sharing with us some of the characteristics involving the various transformations of the image and reality of Jesus—both main line views and what the mainliners called "schismatic" views. You suggested that this is something you as a Christian want to bring to our conversation. That's a different way of viewing linkage.

Muzammil, you were emphasizing the historical linkages, beginning with the notion of Islam's perception of the historical and theological

validity of the three fundamental revelations: the first beginning with
Abraham and culminating in Moses, the revelation to Jesus being the
second, and Islam the third. And so there was a kind of historical,
theological unity. Then you were pointing out the ambiguities and
ambivalences of historical records and suggesting that—as we look to
the future and prepare for the present—we ought to draw on positives
to try to create a working relationship. Also, in your earlier comments,
you had pointed out the fact that similarities are not a problem, but
differences are.

What you and George have said puts before us the fundamental issue:
how we deal with differences between us and among us. We come
from three different faith traditions and are natural conversational
partners—and are even more than that for reasons we have already
begun to suggest. But we are different and are obviously not intending
to transform our differences into one single identity. We are not going
to convert Judaism to Christianity, and Islam to a new
Judeo-Christian-Islamic faith, because that's both unrealistic and, from
my point of view, undesirable.

But what is it that we can bring to each other in our differences? My
view is that we are enriched, as human beings, as religious persons, by
the differences—perhaps more enriched by the differences than we are
by simply reiterating the commonalities. Because for that we don't
need interaction. If we agree on commonalities we are not going to be
adding much to them. We begin with the same fundamental insight
into the nature of the world and of God, but then we note different
orchestrations and articulations in our faith communities. This lends
richness to the human experience.

George, what is it that you expect from me as a Jew, from Muzammil
as a Muslim, in reaction to your presentation of Jesus's centrality and
the debates over his humanity and divinity in the Christian Church?
Jesus' divinity is something that Muzammil and I simply don't accept.
If you're suggesting that we're on the road to unity, to all of us
accepting Christianity, then Jesus' divinity is a stumbling block in the
way. If that's what the expectation is, then we don't have dialogue at

all. Dialogue has to be dialogue in the context of our differences. Why consider it a stumbling block if we disagree? Jews do not view Jesus as either the Messiah or the Divinity; Muslims do not view Jesus as God; Christians do. We can understand and accept that. It is certainly necessary for us to understand the debates within Christianity over the meaning of Jesus. But for me that is not central to our conversation because it doesn't resonate with Jewish tradition. But that's only my point of view. I'm interested in knowing what your expectations are of me as a Jew in response to what you're saying and of Muzammil, for whom Jesus is a different kind of figure.

GROSE: As I said before, I was surprised at myself in what I developed here. I had two things on my mind: the morning session on linkage, the afternoon on core beliefs. But I added the question of Jesus' nature as the morning discussion unfolded. David, in response to your question, my Christian particularism leads me to you all. That's the obverse of what a Unitarian Universalist might do when looking for the commonalities. So Jesus leads me to Muzammil and to David. Is this proselytizing? It's not—it's the way I reach out. Because I am claimed by Christ I know that the Hebrew scripture is my scripture, too. Since it is, I can say, "Now what about Abraham?" Over the years I hadn't realized this, but my interest in Abraham was very real. I got to it through Jesus Christ, by working through his authority, which pulls the Hebrew scriptures into the Christian Church. Then I started working step by step through the prophets and Moses, and I came to Abraham and saw that I have interactions with Muslims and Jews because of him. I realized Abraham is in the Catholic liturgy: "Our Father in faith, Abraham," in the great prayer that transforms the Mass By working from Jesus to Abraham, I can see Abraham in Jesus' fullness. My first interest was not Abraham; I discovered him through Jesus. So even when I present Abraham in a public discourse, there are probably Christians present who say, "What's this about Abraham?" Whereas if I led them through Jesus to Abraham, they would begin to understand the dialogue.

2. SCRIPTURAL INTERPRETATION

SIDDIQI: I think we have to understand our differences, but I don't see that we should legitimize them. We don't say that differences are okay, at least from the Muslim point of view, because the general revelation of God demands a response; and the prophetic revelation as it came to Prophet Muhammad certainly demands a response from me and from everyone in the world. So there is a demand, but at the same time there is no forcing of this upon anyone. I can see your point, David, and George's, but we have to see why various positions were taken—why George talks about certain understandings of the words of the New Testament by the Church. I take those things very seriously and would like to see whether really there is a related message from the New Testament point of view and the words of Jesus himself. I question the record itself and would like to know if statements attributed to Jesus are really his or other people's. In the same way, in trying to understand the Muslim view, go to the Old Testament and say: these are the Jewish claims about the Torah, or about Moses; but I would like to know to what extent these are established by the text itself.

So the Muslim community seriously looks at the Torah, the Old Testament, because it sees itself as a continuation of the same tradition running from Abraham to Jesus, and then to Prophet Muhammad. And all of them bring the same message. On the one hand, in our dialogue, we have to see how the other two groups understand themselves and base our relationship with one another on that, not just on how we understand the others.

On the other hand, because we share the same history, we will have our own interpretation as well. That means the Muslim has the right to interpret the Old and New Testaments because they are part of his heritage. Just as the Christian interprets the Old Testament according to his understanding, the Muslim has the right to talk about Jesus. In fact, he has his own Christology which differs seriously from that of Christians.[24] Our interpretations of Abraham and Moses also differ in many places. This is an area we need to look at. In fact, Jews and Christians might find some illumination from Muslim interpretations of these figures, as I find illumination when studying Christian and Jewish literature.

GORDIS: I think, Muzammil, your formulation is extremely important and interesting. You pointed out the kinds of questions a Muslim will ask about Hebrew scripture or the New Testament, and that Jews and Christians read these books with different questions in mind. Also, there are differences in how the various writers formulated the Gospels, and in the Church Fathers' later interpretations of them.

The same phenomenon takes place in every group. Jews have a Christology, for example. It's not particularly important to them because Jesus is neither a prophetic nor a divine figure for Jews, but he is a historical figure. Jews also have an account of Muhammad as a great religious leader, which is different from that of Christians or Muslims. Christians, similarly, have a different account of post-Biblical Judaism from that of Jews. So all of our faiths have different historical accounts of the others' experiences.

But even within each of our own traditions there are different groups characterized by the kinds of questions they ask about their own traditions. For example, within Judaism there are traditionalists who will argue that the Bible was revealed literally to Moses on Mt. Sinai. Yet, the same kinds of questions that you say Muslims will ask about the Hebrew scripture or the Gospels, some liberal Jews will ask about the traditional Jewish assertions.

Now I'm wondering whether there are Muslims who will look within the Qur'an and the *Hadith* and ask whether, in fact, that literature is exactly what the traditional formulation says it is. I, for example, say about the Hebrew Bible that I accept the Documentary Hypothesis that the Torah or first five books of the Bible are a composite of at least four literary strands later edited into a continuous whole. That's what it says to me when I read it. I accept the notion of God's revelation to Moses on Mt. Sinai, and I can quote the classic Rabbinic tradition in Midrash *Rabbah* which asks, using a verse from the Book of Job (11:9): "It (the Torah) is wider and longer than all of the earth, and greater in breadth than the sea; could Moses have mastered and learned all of this in only 40 days?" The implied answer is that all God taught Moses was general principles, which suggests it was not a literal revelation but principles which were later filled out. This is more consistent with the notion of the expansion of the Bible towards a divinely revealed yet human document, rather than simply a product of literal divine revelation. But there are those within the Jewish tradition who will disagree and argue for literal revelation.

So it seems to me, and if I'm correct and correct me if I'm wrong, each of our traditions contain within it those who have not only alternative histories and theologies of the other faiths, but also of their own.

SIDDIQI: This is the case more so in Judaism and Christianity than in Islam, because Muslims do not have many interpretations of revelation. Mainstream Muslims believe the Qur'an is a literal revelation. The Divine word was spoken to the Prophet through the Angel Gabriel, in the same way revelation came to Moses and Jesus. So Muslims speak about the Gospel in the same way they speak about the Torah. Of course, they may say the present Gospel is not completely authentic. The Divine revelation was literal and the Gospel does contain part of it, but some of it is not there. And the Gospels contain other material not part of the revelation Jesus received. In a similar way, Muslims talk about the Torah which contains some of the revelation that came to Moses, as well as additional ideas. The Muslim view of revelation is very literal: God spoke to the prophets and this is the divine word that has been recorded. The assertion is that the Qur'an is the authentic record of the revelation Muhammad received, while the Old Testament and New Testament are not completely authentic records. So when Muslims read the various interpretations of scripture by Christians and Jews, these Muslims say: "This is what we mean. Why do they have different opinions on this or that? If it had been a literal record, Jews and Christians would not have different opinions because Muslims do not." Yes, Orthodox Jews made an assertion about the meaning of scripture, but more and more Jews have concluded that assertion was not right. We've been telling them that for the last 1400 years, haven't we?

GORDIS: But you have a much younger faith and haven't gotten to the point of maturity to be asking the same kinds of questions.

SIDDIQI: Well, we don't know what will happen in the next 1400 years, but what I'm talking about is now, the present situation.

GORDIS: Let me ask you one other question. You indicated that in Islam the revelation to the prophet Muhammad is not only the third of these great revelations, but the final one. You know that Christianity and Judaism don't accept that assertion, but there exists in Judaism a parallel phenomenon—that the prophecy of Malachi ended the period of prophecy. Afterwards, there was another kind of religious leadership, great leadership, but it moved away from prophecy to the authority of the Rabbis. This was an intellectual, and much more democratic, leadership; and the period of prophecy was over.

SIDDIQI: Is this an interpretation, or is this the prophet's own statement?

GORDIS: No, it's traditional. It couldn't be the prophet's own statement because Malachi was himself a prophet, but it's the traditional . . .

SIDDIQI: But is it dependent upon the final prophet?

GORDIS: No, but it is the normative Jewish tradition concerning prophecy. The fact that Malachi said it, wouldn't prove to an observer that prophecy ended with him. It could be just an assertion. My point is: obviously there is a difference of view as to when the period of prophecy ended, but both Islam and Judaism assert that prophecy goes to a certain point. In Islam it ends with the prophecy of Muhammad, in Judaism with the last of the Hebrew prophets, Malachi.

SIDDIQI: Muslims don't make this assertion because nobody has the right to. This is a prophetic statement—because the Prophet said it, we say it. Prophecy could have continued but it is said in the Qur'an that Prophet Muhammad is the final prophet. Because the statement comes from God and the Prophet himself, Muslims take it so strongly.

GORDIS: According to Islam, then, is prophecy the only source of truth?

SIDDIQI: In Islam there are two kinds of revelations. One is the definitive revelation of the word of God which comes to the chosen prophets. People differ in accepting or not accepting it. Those who do are the believers, the others the non-believers. The second kind of revelation is that available to all people. Some pious people have this continuous communication with God. But they do not have the authority to come out and say to people, "Listen, because God has spoken to me, you are commanded to do thus and so." So the revelation is for them personally. Some people may be influenced by their word, others not. This is called inspiration and is a continuous reality experienced by more and more people. But a targeted assertion by a person that he is the prophet of God and should be obeyed because of that—this happens to only a few individuals, and to no one after Prophet Muhammad.

3. THE CANON OR CONTENTS OF SCRIPTURE

GROSE: Now it's time for me to get into this. I think it's a question of canon. Canon means rule or measure. You have a cut-off point and say: this is it, the authoritative revelation is over. That's what establishes the canon.

SIDDIQI: But who determines that? My point is: do we have the right to say, "We have enough prophets, so let us stop this institution"?

GROSE: I see your point. But what I'm saying is each of the three scriptures has a canon and that its contents are an internal matter. The Qur'an says that's the way it is. It took the Christian leadership 300 or 400 years before they established a canon, and David said Jewish tradition established early on that Malachi is where the canon ends.

GORDIS: Only prophecy, and then a different type of leadership begins. It's not the end of religious truth or insight or development.

GROSE: Prophecy is equivalent to canon, it appears to me, in both Judaism and Islam.

GORDIS: No, because the Hebrew Bible includes other post-prophetic material.

GROSE: But in chronological order you come lastly to the prophets, and then there is the cut off.[25]

GORDIS: The wisdom literature follows the prophetic literature in the Hebrew Bible.

GROSE: Alright, I'd forgotten, but even the wisdom literature has an end point, and that is the final canon. So there is the phenomenon of canon in each of the three faiths. Now on the basis of canon I make this point: it's important for our dialogue and for American Christians to say, we will read the Hebrew scriptures—and I want them to call it that—to see what is of Christ in the Hebrew scriptures. They've been doing that a long time anyway. But Christians should also read the Hebrew scriptures to see what it's telling them on its own grounds. "What if Jesus hadn't come?" This would be Christians asking themselves the question. There are Christians who find the Trinity in the Hebrew scriptures. I don't find it there and think it's a great mistake and not fully honest to say the Trinity is there, as in the "we" of majesty.[26]

So, also, the Christian is to look into the Qur'an because many elements of the Bible are in the Qur'an. This is the same process that the Muslims use on both the Testaments, the two bodies of scripture. So this should free up the Christian, because that's my primary responsibility. My second responsibility is to help us free up one another. But primarily I want to free up my own community so they can enter into this kind of dialogue, read the Old Testament, and say, "I wonder what's there before Christ came?" I consider this a loyal act on the part of Christians. They should also be able to look at the

Qur'an and say, "What of the Bible do I find there?" and thus make the Qur'an "user friendly." Or to ask, "What is the Qur'an telling me that in its own terms speaks of Jesus Christ the way I understand him?" So we have these two ways of treating one another's canon: to see what it validates or enriches in our own tradition, and to see what scriptural material is unique and points out the contrasts with the other two.

I think Wilfred Cantwell Smith was the first scholar to help Christians understand that, for all the fundamentalism that emerges in Christianity, it is not a religion of a book. I offer this as a contrast to the Muslim assertion, for which I am grateful, because the Qur'an is inclusive in that God addresses Jews and Christians as "people of the book." It means Muslims are including these others as peoples of revelation. But to me Christians are not people of the book, but of the person, to whom the book bears testimony. I think this is standard throughout Christianity, notwithstanding the times when they almost let the book take over the person, as in fundamentalism. The givenness of Jesus in Christianity corresponds to the givenness of the Qur'an, and Christians need to understand that. There's nothing negotiable about the Qur'an—it's there. There's nothing negotiable about Jesus—He's there. You can then do interpretations in both cases, but the givenness is there. To me, the "givenness" in Judaism is peoplehood, a metaphysical spiritual reality. It's there. Leo Baeck developed this theme brilliantly in his book *The Essence of Judaism.*[27]

SIDDIQI: George, you brought up the question about the closing of the canon. And David mentioned the end of prophecy with the prophet Malachi. But, David, you also mentioned that truth does not come to an end with the end of prophecy. When you say that truth continues, while prophecy has come to an end, what is the position of the truth that comes after the prophet. Would it have the same kind of authority as the truth that was brought by the prophet? And I'll ask George the same question: if the canon has come to an end, what about the other books that were written after the canon? Do they have the same authority? From an Islamic point of view, when a Muslim says that Prophet Muhammad is the last prophet, and the Qur'an is the final revelation, he is not making a theological statement. There must be a statement from the prophet himself, from God himself. Because the Qur'an says this is the final prophet, he is taken as such by Muslims. That doesn't mean we will not have insights into this final revelation, but they will not have the same validity and will not be equal to the Qur'an. Many theologians have written after the Qur'an, but their works lack the status the Qur'an has.

So when Muslims make the assertion that Muhammad is the final prophet, it means two things. First, that they do not make this assertion on their own but because he made it. Because they believe in him, they accept his statement. Second, that they don't give the same status to other statements or books and to other people after him as they give to him and the Qur'an.

GROSE: Christians have two views on this question. For Protestants, the canon is closed. There are other theologians and thinkers, but the canon is closed. There is more of a continuum of immediate revelation in Roman Catholicism because the Pope, when he speaks *ex cathedra*—formally on a matter of faith or morals—does so with the authority of Christ. Those who hold the papal office have the keys of the kingdom, and the spiritual authority to pronounce new doctrine which may or may not, from a Protestant point of view, be found in the canon.

GORDIS: A word about what happens after prophecy. Prophecy is, in Judaism, a unique form of relationship between God and human beings, but not the only form. It has a high degree of continuing authority and is, therefore, central in Jewish tradition. But remember that, in the three-part division of the Hebrew Bible, it's the second of the three. Torah comes first, and is a formulation of the revelation of God to Moses, which is set apart from the classical Hebrew prophets. Prophecy is the second part. Then comes the Hagiographa or the sacred writings: the wisdom literature, including Psalms, Proverbs and Job; the books of Ezra-Nehemiah and Chronicles which are historical; and the five scrolls: Song of Songs, Ruth, Lamentations, Ecclesiastes and Esther. It is an eclectic grouping but also authoritative, and conveys truth. But even more important than the truth contained within the wisdom literature, is the tradition—based on a particular verse within the Book of Deuteronomy—which says, "It is not in heaven" (Deuteronomy 30:12). That is, authority over the interpretation of the tradition, over the development and growth of the religious life, "does not remain in heaven."

There is also the Talmudic story in which one authority, Rabbi Eliezer Ben Hyrcanus, attempts repeatedly to appeal to divine intervention in a debate in the Rabbinic academy. Each time, the rabbis refuse to accept his supernatural signs: a stream moving from its course, a tree being uprooted, etc. Finally, he appeals for direct divine intervention and says, "Let there be a *bat kol*, a still small voice from heaven." And the voice says, "Follow Rabbi Eliezer Ben Hyrcanus because the law is according to him." But the court rules, "Sorry, law is not made by voices from heaven because the Torah says, *'Lo bahshamayim hi*—it's not in heaven'" (Babylonian Talmud, *Baba Metzia* 59b). Law is given over to human beings. Because human beings are created in the Divine image with the power to reason and make decisions, religious authority goes over to them when the period of prophecy is over.

So there are differences in our traditions, as we've seen, and they take us back to the question of how we deal with differences. Here, perhaps, I stand somewhat apart from both of you. The divinity of Jesus is not a stumbling block for me. I simply don't accept it. I don't stumble because of it because I'm not on any path which it blocks. Nor is the fact that we engage in this theological enterprise and have differences a problem for me. Instead, it's enriching. It seems to me that, underlying the enterprise of dialogue, there must be some way that we can say to each other, "We accept the validity of your search for God and your formulation of the human experience in God's world, although we assert the truth of ours." If the nature of the enterprise is ultimately for me to convince you of the truth of my way, which necessarily implies the error of yours, then there is very little for us to talk to each other about. In that case, we're not dealing with a shared challenge but an attempt to invalidate the other. Certainly, theological evidence will say we are different. Somehow we have to say that the differences are also part of God's plan. And so, we need to accept the legitimacy of the others and their search, while at the same time not abandoning the truth claims that each of us makes. That seems to be a pre-condition for dialogue.

GROSE: All three of our faiths are world religions since they make an appeal to humanity at large. So we have to ask, "What is the validity of dialogue in the midst of this at-large appeal?" Because of my view that scripture doesn't stand on its own feet but testifies to the person Jesus, I can see the situational or time-bound aspect of what Paul was saying about Christ crucified as a stumbling block and folly (1 Corinthians 1:23). This was a "stumbling block" to first century Jews attracted to the Christian movement and "folly" to the Greeks and Romans. I can say this, but it doesn't destroy the authority of the scripture for me because the person Jesus is the ultimate authority for me.

SIDDIQI: I think Muslims do respect differences in the sense that Jews have their interpretation, Christians theirs, and other religions also. But the question is to what extent every interpretation is a legitimate one. The Muslim position is that there is a divine revelation that comes to Prophet Muhammad and makes a demand on people. It's not for only one people, not for only Arabs. In the Jewish situation, you speak, David, about the people of Israel; and you really don't have a world mission. Judaism never was and was not meant to be a mission for the whole world. It speaks about one people. The Jew can say, "Yes, something is valid for others, but not for us." Because the Prophet's revelation is for the whole world, one must respect differences. It is not possible in this world that all people will have the same opinion. But, at the same time, to say that two different positions are valid and legitimate is a position Muslims have difficulty with.

4. RESPECTING OUR DIFFERENCES

GORDIS: I'm not certain, Muzammil, that you're right about the degree of universalism within Judaism. Judaism contains within it, very prominently, both in the prophetic literature and in the liturgy, the notion of its universal concerns. "On that day when all the world will consecrate itself to God, the world shall be one."[28] So the universal thrust of Judaism is quite central, not peripheral. We might, at some point in our discussions, reflect on how the Muslim would view the non-acceptance of Muhammad as the last of the prophets by Christians and by Jews, and the how the Muslim would react to the pagan interpretation of the world. In other words, is there something about the fundamental monotheistic insight which might permit—you used the term "respect" but I'll use the stronger term—validity without conceding the truth of your own position?

SIDDIQI: We use the Qur'anic phrase "people of the book."

GORDIS: That's right. But I wonder if we haven't come closer to being able to attribute something between "respect" and "validity," or a special dimension of resonance between our three faiths, because of the monotheistic insight. Doesn't it distinguish us from other interpretations of reality from which we differ more fundamentally?

5. ABRAHAM, ISHMAEL AND ISAAC

GROSE: I think all three affirm that the same God has addressed each of them and acted in their midst. That's what is going to hold us together and goes beyond respect. This is another trinity!

As I said earlier, I am led into the Hebrew scriptures through Jesus Christ. I know the Hebrew scriptures stand without other support; but because I am led into them through Christ, I find there what points to Christ, as well as what Judaism has always said is there. I find that Jesus and Paul speak of the children of Abraham. Interestingly, Abraham is not an eponymous ancestor, one after whom descendants are named. There are no Abrahamites. This is a very telling matter in the text. There are all kinds of other tribal groupings, but no Abrahamites. Thus Abraham is positioned to belong to the three communities and all three claim him. From a Christian point of view, salvation history begins with Abraham. The earlier episodes in Genesis are signs of the destructiveness, self-destructiveness, of the human race; but through Abraham God enters to do his redeeming work. He is in covenant with Abraham and the dialogue in many ways is dependent upon that covenant. There is also a covenant between Allah or God and Abraham in the Qur'an that Abraham and Ishmael would build the Kaaba, the holiest shrine of Islam in Mecca. In the Hebrew Bible (Genesis 17:5) his name is changed when God declares he will be the father of many nations.

He has a first son, Ishmael. In the Jewish and Christian scriptures, Ishmael is not given the promise that he has been given all along in the Qur'an. One of my research tasks has been to see whether or not more significance could be given Ishmael in the Christian understanding of Genesis. I find grounds for that. He's Abraham's first child. He has a significant name, "God Hears" or "God Listens." When his mother Hagar flees from her mistress Sarah, she is told by the angel of God to go back and what the boy's name will be. So Ishmael is rescued while he is still in his mother's womb (Genesis 16:7-14). Then, when the Almighty says that a covenant people should be established with circumcision as the sign of it, Ishmael is there and Isaac is not yet born, according to the Genesis account (17:9-14). So he becomes *ben b'rith*, a son of the covenant by circumcision. This is telling. We know of Ishmael's banishment which has been taken so often to mean casting off his seed. But, after he and his mother are banished, they are again rescued—the second Divine rescue for Ishmael (Genesis 21:8-21). Then Abraham is buried by both Isaac and Ishmael (Genesis 25:9). So, whatever the banishment meant, Ishmael is back for the burial and is not out of the family.

Then there is the near sacrifice of Isaac (Genesis 22:1-19). In the history of Christian theological interpretation, it is simply called the sacrifice of Isaac. The Church made it a Christological text[29]—though Isaac was not actually sacrificed—as a foreshadowing of the sacrifice of Christ. In both cases there is reference to the only-born son. But while in Christian thought Jesus is the eternal, only begotten son made flesh, nevertheless it is not possible for Isaac to be the only born son because of Ishmael. So the onlyness of Isaac must mean something else. As some Jewish and Christian scholars have observed, he is the beloved covenant child. However, numerical oneness is not the predominant emphasis in the Genesis account. But Jerome's Latin translation of the Bible— which was followed in the European languages—deliberately made Isaac appear as the only son in existence. That, of course, makes Ishmael a non-person. Like the Hebrew text, the Septuagint clearly doesn't make him that. The Greek phrase is, "Take your beloved son, Isaac, whom you love" (Genesis 22:2). That's repetitive but is idiomatic in Greek. It means Isaac is beloved but, because of this idiomatic construction, that he is one beloved among other beloveds. This allows for Ishmael also to be beloved. He becomes then no longer a non-person, according to that episode, which is called, as we know, the binding of Isaac in Judaism and the sacrifice of Isaac in Christianity.

This illustrates the point I was making earlier. We want to see what Judaism says about the text, not what Christianity or Islam says about it, not what we may read into it for later historical, theological, or pietistic reasons.

In light of these considerations, I can, as a Christian, affirm the place of Islam in salvation history. I don't know all the implications of that, but I can't escape what I have discovered. It is difficult for me to affirm that Muhammad is a prophet in the same sense as Isaiah, Jeremiah, Jesus, and Moses are, simply because my canon got closed. Yet, I am left with the problem of having acknowledged the place of the Ishmael line in salvation history.[30] That leads to Muhammad and to a problem I have not yet resolved. But it points toward the inclusion of Muhammad as a prophet of God.

HUBBARD: What about the fact that Muhammad comes 600 years after Jesus?

GROSE: German theologian Jurgen Moltmann[31] has suggested we not get hung up completely on chronology. So, while Islam came after the other two canons were finished, this doesn't eliminate certain other historical possibilities. If we take a time warp view, we might even find that we could, from a Christian point of view, place Muhammad with Israel's prophets as a prophet of God. Here is Amos, here is Jeremiah, here is Muhammad. You see them then for what they are as prophets. Though this is possible, I'm not there yet; but I can see what I'm being drawn toward, because I am persuaded fully of the Ishmael line's place in salvation history.

I am further persuaded, as are many Christians, of what Paul declared in Romans 11. After describing the differences between Christianity and Judaism, he declares, "Does this mean that God has abandoned the Jewish people? By no means!" (Romans 11:1) Paul had already noted that the covenant with the Jewish people and the promises stand (Romans 9:4). So God hasn't gone back on his word." This is extremely important in our time and in light of anti-Semitism's history in Europe—that the Israelites, the Jews, are not an anomaly but a people with a covenant as valid now as it was at the beginning. And that doesn't diminish my own faith, my own Church, my own life in Christ.

I'd like to draw from the spirit of Phillips in his fine book *Your God Is Too Small* and say: I don't know the mind of the Almighty. I know certain things—who Jesus is to me, to the Christian community, to the world. But why can't the Almighty have more than one chosen people? Jesus, in what is the height of Christian worship, said, "This is my blood of the new covenant which is poured out for many" (Mark 14:24). Many early manuscripts of the New Testament read simply "covenant," not "new covenant." In other words, both continuity and discontinuity with Judaism. I know of only one instance of the English word "covenant" in the Qur'an. But from my perspective—and I can't say that all Christians think as I do—these three are covenant peoples, and there is no diminution in their covenant life with God. This doesn't in any way modify the distinctiveness that I know about Christianity, however.

***

The participants next had a technical exchange on the phrase "your only son, Isaac" (Genesis 22:2) in light of the discussion above of Ishmael's significance in the Genesis account. Dr. Grose felt that numerical oneness was not the issue in Genesis 22, but Dr. Gordis thought the translation "your only" (Hebrew: *yecheedcha*) was accurate nonetheless.

***

GROSE: What is Isaac then? What does "your only" mean in this context?

GORDIS: He is the central concern of Abraham in the account, and therefore the central concern in this story where God commands he be sacrificed.

GROSE: And the central of concern for the future?

GORDIS: Yes, for the future of the Jewish people.

SIDDIQI: From the Islamic standpoint, it really doesn't make much difference who was sacrificed. It could be Isaac, it could be Ishmael. The Qur'an doesn't say which one, although the Hadith speaks about Ishmael as the one who was offered for sacrifice. And the majority of Muslim commentaries on the Qur'an talk this way, though some mention Isaac also, because both of them are prophets according to Islam.

GORDIS: Your point is central here, Muzammil. The story is not really the story of Isaac or Ishmael, but Abraham. It begins with the phrase, "After these things God put Abraham—and Abraham's faith—to the test" (Genesis 22:1).

SIDDIQI: The Qur'an talks about Abraham's test, but also notes that father and son are submitting together. The Arabic word used for submission is *aslama*.[32]

GORDIS: "So the two of them went off together" (Genesis 22:6). Abraham and Isaac went together of one mind. So Isaac also was demonstrating his faith, but the overall framework of the story is of the test of Abraham's faith. By the way, it's a rather gruesome test of faith. What right does Abraham have to demonstrate his faith by killing his son?

SIDDIQI: But Ishmael will also be made a great nation (Genesis 16:10, 21:13). When and how is that purpose fulfilled? Is the coming of Muhammad in the line of Ishmael the fulfillment of that promise?

GORDIS: Let me try to answer your question in terms of what the Hebrew Bible says about Ishmael. The style of the Hebrew Bible's narrative portions is like an inverted pyramid. It begins with an account of the entire patriarchal family—the lineage, the genealogy. Then it puts them all aside and selects out the one it is interested in and continues that account. That model, applied to the Genesis story, tells us that Abraham had two children; but it concentrates on Isaac, Jacob and Jacob's 12 sons who are central from the Jewish perspective. However, the very poignant story of Hagar's banishment with her son Ishmael is narrated (Genesis 16). Abraham and Sarah both look bad in that story because, under pressure from Sarah, Abraham accedes to her demands that Hagar be sent away. It reports Abraham's sadness and, in an odd deus-ex-machina manner, how God says it's okay because Ishmael will also be the father of a great nation. I always ask myself, "What if God had not appeared at that moment and said, 'It's okay because Ishmael will be the father of a great nation'? What if Sarah and Abraham had done this to another son who was not going to be Ishmael? Would that make it right?" In fact, I think the story is included to make us sit up and say, "That's wrong." And yet, Ishmael, who was also Abraham's child, did become the father of a nation. This doesn't demean Ishmael and the nation that came from him, but it's not the center of attention of this account. So the Biblical narrative instructs morally not by presenting these characters as paragons of moral perfection. Abraham was saddened by what Sarah demanded; she was wrong in pressuring that way.

SIDDIQI: As David was mentioning, the account was written by people more interested in Isaac's line. They are not interested in Ishmael anyway, so they dump him out. So it cannot be called a very objective account of the story but is written from the perspective of the Isaac line. If you take the position that it is all Word of God, certain questions arise. But if you take it as an account written by human beings under the inspiration of God, then one can say that these writers had problems with Ishmael, and so they ignored him.

GORDIS: Or they had a special interest that focused only on Isaac.

SIDDIQI: Just focused on Isaac, and kept talking about him.

GROSE: From my perspective the human element is in all scripture. Now, if we just look at the uniqueness of Isaac, we're not going to think much about Ishmael. But we do find these references to Ishmael which Genesis will not give up on. What I see, in pulling them together, is that Ishmael—in some mysterious and not fully demonstrable way—is also a covenant child in the Abrahamic sense.

SIDDIQI: David, you mentioned earlier that, from the Jewish point, there is nothing called "salvation history."

GORDIS: No, I'm saying that term is not one with which Jews are comfortable.

SIDDIQI: This is connected to the problem of divine revelation. Some people talk about it in terms of a literal revelation, but others in terms of God's acts in history.

GORDIS: True, but the term for the Jewish understanding of this is not salvation history. The term revelation has two distinct meanings: as an event and as a process. Revelation as an event talks about specific moments in which there was a self-opening of God to human beings and a specific literal product of that event—the Torah—which has had a momentous impact on the world. Others, who may agree or disagree with the notion of revelation as an event, would argue that revelation includes the notion of a process. They say that the nature of the world—the nature of human experience and human history—is such that human beings act in a world of God. God's will makes itself known through human experience and through history. So it's history, not salvation history. Salvation itself is talked about separately as the goal of history. Explanations of how salvation is achieved range from some apocalyptic event overturning reality to the idea of an ultimate self-fulfillment—human beings attaining the maximum they are capable of. God will then be defined as that characteristic of the world making the process of self-fulfillment possible.

GROSE: I think it's well that you question the term salvation history. German distinguishes between *historie*, chronological events that historians write about, and *geschichte*, events loaded with significance. In a Christian setting, *geschichte* means the special ways God dealt with the human race, something more in keeping with the first position you were describing, David.

GORDIS: Still, when I hear "salvation history," it represents a kind of Christological idiom. It's too other worldly, whereas the process of history in a Jewish way means improving or redeeming the world through human activity. "Salvation history" is not comfortable vocabulary for me as the kind of Jew that I am. But I don't think even fundamentalist Jews would be comfortable with the term.

SIDDIQI: Christians talk about God in history from the point of view of salvation history. From the Islamic perspective, and I also think from the Jewish perspective, there is no such thing as God in history.

GORDIS: No, "God in history" is in fact a more comfortable notion.

SIDDIQI: God is directing history, of course, and everything is under his rule; but God certainly doesn't appear in history. That's because we don't talk about God in man, God in the world.

GORDIS: I'm still not sure, Muzammil, that I would agree with you.

For example, the central story or myth—in the positive sense of the term—of Christianity is the life and death of Jesus. Similarly, the central myth of Judaism is precisely God in history in the events of the Exodus.

SIDDIQI: That's God acting, not God in history.

GORDIS: What's the difference?

SIDDIQI: God's redeeming acts, the tablets given at Mt. Sinai and the blessings are there, but not God himself as a person.

GORDIS: Oh, not as a person. God does not become man. In that sense, I understand. However, the theme reiterated in Jewish liturgy is that many acts are performed in order to remind us of the two fundamental appearances of God in history. One is creation, and *zecher lamaasei bereshit* is a recollection of the creation; while *zecher liytziot mizraim* is a reminder of the Exodus from Egypt. The Exodus means the beginning of freedom for the Israelites from physical bondage; but it extends to the giving of the Torah, which means freedom from spiritual bondage—the affirmation of the spiritual quality of the Jewish people. So that's the closest we come in Judaism to talking about God as acting in history, although you are quite right: God does not become man and appear either in Islam or Judaism.

GROSE: The word "salvation" has such strong Christian associations that I have often replaced it with "rescue." In all three of our communities, God rescues—at the Red Sea crossing; at the cross; at the battle of Badr in 624, the first time the Muslim community encountered the pagans and came out victorious. There were only 300 of Muhammad's followers fighting against 900 polytheists. God won the battle. And, as Muzammil has reminded us, indeed the Qur'an itself is *furqan* (Surah 25:1), the criterion of truth which rescues. So I like the rescue theme.

HUBBARD: Are there any loose ends we need to tie up at this point?

SIDDIQI: George, you made a very good point earlier about taking Muhammad as a prophet of God like the earlier prophets, even though he comes later chronologically. But if Muhammad is recognized by Christians as a true prophet of God, then what God says through him in the Qur'an about Jesus contradicts Christian claims about Jesus. How are you going to deal with this?

GROSE: I don't know because I'm not actually ready to say that Muhammad is a prophet of God, though I can see that I am moving in that direction. However, it's impossible for me to accept what the Qur'an says about Jesus' not being crucified (Surah 4:157) because his crucifixion is part of the givenness of Jesus for me. I'm left with two choices: one, to continue to say Muhammad is a prophetic figure but not a prophet in the sense of the biblical prophets; or, two, just as Muslims say there are possible errors or editorial changes in the two other covenant works, the Hebrew and Christian scriptures, so, too, the Qur'an is subject to error. Thus I would say, in this instance, that the Qur'an is in error but not the prophet Muhammad.

SIDDIQI: George, I am glad to hear that you are moving toward the direction of recognizing Prophet Muhammad as God's prophet. However, you are making a dogmatic assertion by saying that the Qur'an is in error simply because it differs from the New Testament. Historically, it is an established fact that the Qur'an is the same today as Prophet Mohammed left it. However, one cannot say the same thing about the New Testament. So one has to see which text is more reliable: the Qur'an, in giving the message taught by Muhammad; or the New Testament, in giving the message taught by Jesus. I must say that Muslims are here on a more sound ground.

6. THREE FAITHS, ONE GOD

HUBBARD: Let me return to something that David alluded to earlier. The Medieval Jewish philosopher Maimonides said something to the effect that Christians and Muslims are vehicles of God's providence to bring the world ethical monotheism. Thus these two religions, which draw from Judaism in some way, become conduits to make the light of monotheism available to the world at large. This relates closely to the question David brought up earlier: is the world actually better because of our differences? In other words, David seems to think that the fact there isn't just Judaism or Christianity or Islam is in some sense by divine design, or the way things ought to be. Would you comment on this, David.

GORDIS: Maimonides did say that the monotheistic idea had its roots in Judaism and then spread to Christianity and Islam. There is also an apocalyptic aspect here because ethical monotheism prepares the world for the final or Messianic era. The world will not necessarily become Jewish then, but will become committed to the worship of God—each group in its own way. So Jews, Christians, and Muslims all are partners in preparing the world for the ultimate redemption, the Messianic era, by teaching and spreading the monotheistic idea. This, in turn, relates to the notion that the world is a diverse place and that the lesson of monotheism has to be articulated in ways acceptable to a very diverse population. People who are different are going to absorb that lesson in a variety of ways. For Christians, Christianity is the way ethical monotheism becomes absorbed, taught, and spread. For Muslims, Islam is the way; for Jews, Judaism.

7. CONVERT MAKING

HUBBARD: How then does that relate—at least for you, George—to the idea that Christianity is a missionary religion which preaches that one should make disciples of all nations (Matthew 28:19) or to the text from John's Gospel, "I am the way, the truth, and the life, and nobody comes to the Father, except by way of me" (John 14:6). Is what David just articulated compatible with Christianity in terms of this missionary thrust, or with the idea that Jesus is the only way to salvation?

GROSE: Christianity is a missionary religion, there's no doubt about it. And I'm a missionary—but a somewhat new kind of missionary because I'm committed to dialogue. The history of the Church's missionary activity hasn't emphasized dialogue until very recently. I do preach Christianity in churches, and resemble other preachers in that way. But apparently in this dialogue work I'm different, and there are only a few Christians like me. I think this is the *kairos*, the special time, when I am called to do the work of Jewish-Christian-Muslim dialogue. Maybe another generation wasn't called to do this in the Church, but I am. I hope there are others around me who will more and more see this as the Church's mission. Part of my stance is that we don't have to worry about the truth. I think we all know that we're not here to defend the truth because it doesn't have to be defended. However, such defending is certainly something that Christianity has been caught up in for a long time.

Now let's turn to the question of Jesus' statement in John 14:6, "I am the way, the truth, and the life. No one comes to the Father but by me." I've seen Christian theologians finesse this saying. People ask them about it in a public setting; and either they won't even talk about it, or they do so and insist Christianity is the only way to salvation.

In my opinion—after working on the matter recently—the words "but by me," or "except by me," can mean several things. The usual way the phrase is taken is that Christ is the instrument of salvation, and it is only through him directly that one is saved. But I've found another way expressive of what I myself believe, though not necessarily what the Church at large believes. The words may be just as authoritatively rendered "no one comes to the Father except by the *benefits* (of Christ).[33] In other words, Jesus died for the sins of the whole world, but there is no place for this belief in Judaism and Islam. However, because I believe it, I can say that Jesus Christ—in all his fullness to me—has blessed both the Jews and the Muslims. In a way it doesn't matter whether they know it or not.

SIDDIQI: And does it matter whether they accept him or not?

GROSE: No, but the blessing, the salvation, still applies because it flows through Abraham. So I am introducing a new type of Christian theology, but it's not one that everybody holds. Muzammil, you just raised indirectly the question of proselytizing. I know that Jesus died for me, and I also believe he died for the Jews and the Muslims. They don't know that; but because I believe he died for them as well as me, they are precious to me. That's not the only reason they are precious, but it is a paramount one. So I find in Christ how precious the Jews and Muslims are.

GORDIS: But when Muzammil asked you whether it matters if we accept the Christian message or not, you said it doesn't. If it doesn't matter, why the proselytizing? Why the missionary activity?

GROSE: I can explain my position on that by relating an incident that happened during a Jewish-Christian-Muslim dialogue some years back at San Diego State University. A number of fundamentalist Christians in the audience were directing questions at me, some of them just plain unsuitable, such as why I was associating with Jews and Muslims. But another was, "What are you doing to convert your colleagues? Tell us, we want to know." So I said, "I think Christians should be more biblical, not less," and spoke about the end of the Gospel of Matthew (28:18-20) and the beginning of the Acts of the Apostles (1:8). Matthew speaks of making disciples of all nations, and Acts speaks of how his followers should be witnesses, hailing from Jerusalem and going out to the ends of the earth. I said it's quite clear to me that we are called to be witnesses, and that the phrase "make disciples" has been taken so often in the imperial sense that we will take upon ourselves the authority even to compel others to become Christians. In researching my doctoral thesis, however, I found that making disciples comes from a Hebrew phrase in *The Sayings of the Fathers*.[34] This phrase, *vehe`midu talmidim harbay*, "raise up many disciples," (*Sayings* 1:1) describes how a rabbi gathers his disciples. It doesn't mean he coerces them; but taken out of its Hebrew context into Greek, Latin and English, it has a quirky side to it. The first way of taking it in English is that you *make* people become disciples. Consequently, I prefer, "You shall be my witnesses" (Acts 1:8).

So I responded to these fundamentalist questioners: "I can't get away from being a witness to Christ. That's what it means to be a Christian. But I do not convert anybody—conversion is the work of the Holy Spirit. That's what I meant when I said we ought to be more Biblical. It is spiritually dangerous for anyone to arrogate to himself or herself what is the work of the Holy Spirit. So each of us Christians is a witness, none of us any more or less than the other. As far as conversions from one faith community to another are concerned—and they do occur—I can't explain them, and I don't know who can. You can talk about circumstances, personal friendships, whatever. So it is the work of the Holy Spirit, and I'm not going to worry about that. I've got my task as a witness."

These remarks seemed to help that night and liberated the scene. People were more relaxed and open and direct in the things they talked about.

HUBBARD: Let me ask you, Muzammil, a final question, which is parallel to the one George just answered. If a very traditional Muslim had come up to you at that same San Diego State gathering and said, "What are you doing talking to these people? Shouldn't you be making them Muslims?" What would your response have been?

SIDDIQI: Making Muslims is not the job of the Muslim. The Qur'an uses the terminology *kunu shuhada 'lillah* (Surahs 4:135, 22:78), "so that you become witnesses of God to mankind." But you are also a witness in the other sense of giving testimony to God by declaration, a verbal testimony. That is what a Muslim does when he says the Muslim creed, the *Shahadah*—"I bear witness that there is no God but Allah." It is very interesting that a Muslim doesn't say, "I *believe* that there is no God but Allah." Of course, they do believe; but very often the act of faith means to declare, to bear witness. That's the first part of Islam, to make the declaration or *Shahadah*. So you make a testimony that there is no God but Allah, and Muhammad is his prophet. They should become part of your life, and your life should bear witness to this. Now one has to bear this witness in all compassion—in all goodness—to other people. This is why the Qur'an says there is no compulsion in matters of religion (Surah 2:256).

With reference to the Jewish and Christian communities, the Qur'an further says, "Do not argue with them except in the most beautiful manner" (Surah 29:46). Dialogue and discuss matters with them "in the most beautiful manner." There is a special relationship that Muslims should have with Christians and Jews because they are recognized as the "people of the book." That doesn't mean, of course, you exclude other people, such as Hindus and Buddhists. Muslims have relations with them also. The question is often raised as to whether Muslims think that non-Muslims are going to hell. The Islamic position is that it is really none of our business who is going to hell and who to heaven. That's God's job—He is the one who is going to determine it. The point here is that we have God's message to Prophet Muhammad, which is historically authentic, the true message of God. This message has to be presented in the best possible manner to the world, and it is up to God to see why a person is accepting or not accepting that message. Perhaps he's not convinced of it, even though I've tried my best to present it. Or maybe there are other reasons that only God knows. So one should not make a judgement about someone's fate. An Egyptian author, Hasan al-Hudaibi, put it very nicely in his book *Du'at la Qudat* ("Conveyers Not Judges") where he said we are the people who call others, not the people who make judgement upon them. God makes judgement. We are not judges, just people who enlighten.

HUBBARD: I could say in closing the session, apropos of the Qur'an, that today's dialogue has been stated "in a most beautiful manner."

CHAPTER THREE

THE NATURE AND ROLE OF REVELATION IN EACH TRADITION

1. REVELATION

HUBBARD: As we take up the question of revelation, I'd like each of you to comment on what it means to have a sacred scripture which becomes the vessel of a religious tradition's history and experience and is the product of divine inspiration. David, would you begin.

GORDIS: At the root of Jewish belief is the principle that Moses received the Torah from God on Mount Sinai in that most quintessential moment of the theophany. But, beginning with the very earliest sources, the question of what that means within the text of the Torah and how it is articulated in the tradition becomes a live one. For example, does one believe God literally gave the Torah word for word to Moses? Yes, in some ways. On the other hand, does this mean that certain broad principles were given, rather than the literal text of the Torah? Yes, and the tradition speaks in both those ways. Let me mention two examples from the midrashic literature One source says: "Everything that an advanced student of the Torah and of the tradition is ever destined to say and to comment on, was already given to Moses on Sinai" (Midrash *Tanhuma* Jethro 11). In other words, not only the text of the Torah but all the discussions in the Talmud of both legal and extra-legal material are all included in that first revelation. So, in a sense, it's being played out, but it was all given, all there.

But another source in the Midrash (*Shemot Rabbah* 41,6) asks the question from an almost diametrically opposite point of view. It uses a verse from the Book of Job (11:9) which proclaims that "If God's wisdom is lengthier than the earth and broader than the sea"—interpreting wisdom as the Torah—how could Moses have learned it in only forty days? The implied answer is no, that would be impossible; God only taught Moses general principles. Now, of course, the tension one feels between the sense of the general act of revelation on Sinai and the more literalist act of revelation—each of which has a basis in the tradition—becomes compounded when one looks at the history of the study of scripture. Here one finds the approach of the traditionalists who argue that the history is irrelevant.

But one also has to take into consideration the work of modern biblical scholarship and the Documentary Hypothesis of Wellhausen which sees the Torah as the product of a lengthy human process rather than as a single document given at one time.[35] So, at least for this introductory comment, let me encapsulate it this way: undoubtedly, no matter what one's theory is about the actual words of the Torah text, all traditional Jews affirm the act of theophany, of divine revelation to Moses and, through Moses, to the Jewish people at Sinai. Part of the centrality of that story is that 600,000 people were witnesses to it at the base of the mountain and attest to its historical accuracy.

The Torah then became the central, dominant document that defined the subsequent development of the Jewish people. It became the core of rabbinic literature, even after the text of the Mishnah became gradually separated from the text of the Torah and moved from commentary to independent legal and non-legal text. The Torah became central because it's considered to be divine, one way or another. The range of views within the Jewish community embraces those who emphasize the literal notion of revelation, and those who see revelation more as a process or continuing relationship with God in rediscovering its meaning in each generation.

GROSE: Thank you, Dr. Gordis. I was intrigued by your description of the later prophetic and Talmudic developments, all being actually inherent in what was given to Moses. . .

GORDIS: One perspective...

GROSE: ... one perspective. Your description of Talmudic development has an analog in Catholic dogma. The Pope, who is the vicar of Christ on earth, when he speaks *ex cathedra,* in his official capacity, establishes dogma. For example, the Assumption of Mary—that Mary did not die but was bodily assumed into heaven—was declared *ex cathedra* from the See of Peter. As such, in Catholic understanding, it was not a new doctrine but was always inherent in the Gospel and the Apostolic Tradition of which the Pope is arbiter.

Another intriguing analog is that of the sovereignty of God in Calvinist Protestantism and Islam. Whether there is any historical connection between the two isn't known. However, the chief Protestant analog to the development of Talmud is that all truth is inherent in the Bible. And the Holy Spirit guides authentic interpretation of it. As Pastor Robinson of the English Pilgrims to America said, "There is yet more truth to break from God's Holy Word."

There is a three-fold way of describing the word of God in the Presbyterian Church, which is similar to other Protestant churches: Jesus Christ is the living word of God; the Scriptures are the word of God written; Baptism and the Lord's Supper are the visible Word.

HUBBARD: What does it mean to say that "Jesus is the living word of God?"

GROSE: It's more correct to say simply "word of God." This is drawn from the prologue to John's Gospel: "In the beginning was the Word, and the Word was with God, and the Word was God....And the Word was made flesh and dwelt among us" (John 1:1, 14).

HUBBARD: But how do you, as a Christian, understand that phraseology? How is a person or a figure a word?

GROSE: Behind the Prologue of John is Genesis. God spoke and it came to be. He said, "'Let there be light;' and there was light" (Genesis 1:3). My understanding is that in Hebrew "word" or "deed" is expressed by the same term. The Temple was Solomon's word. That is, it was his deed; he built it. So throughout. In the Greek heritage "word" or *logos* has a different meaning as the rational principle of the universe, the eternal principle of order amidst flux—so the Greek philosopher Heraclitus. To the Stoics, the *Logos* was the mind of God, penetrating and guiding all things. To Christians this word or *Logos*, as understood through both the Hebrew Bible and Greek philosophy, came together in Jesus Christ, the Word incarnate.

GORDIS: And John says the Christians understand the word of God? Jesus is the word of God?

GROSE: Jesus is the word of God. Christians base it strongly on John's Prologue (John 1). You see there the sources of the terminology and the way it's used.

SIDDIQI: But, generally, we don't call a human being a word. But you say Jesus is the word. So in what sense are you using it?

GROSE: Very well. Isn't it Isaiah, where God sends forth his word to accomplish that which he purposes and it does not return to him void (Isaiah 55:10-11)?

GORDIS: But again, you're giving me a source. You're not telling me what it means.

GROSE: No, I'm telling you what it means to me. Because Jesus came according to God's purpose, and accomplished what he intended—as expressed in the Isaiah reference.

GORDIS: And what does that express to you when it says that God sent forth the word?

GROSE: To me, it's very important that the Old Testament, the Hebrew Bible, by the expression *davar*, means an action or a deed. Something was done, and that is the Word.

SIDDIQI: Is this a metaphor?

GROSE: Yes.

SIDDIQI: Are you saying that Jesus came by the word of God?

GROSE: Yes, in the flesh—incarnate. This is the Christian doctrine of the Incarnation. He was God's action; or the sending of him was God's action. And since, in Christian understanding, he is the Word of God made flesh, then it is continuing action. That is the Hebrew and Greek understanding coming through on the Christians, and John's prologue says "Word of God."

HUBBARD: Let me be sure I understand you. When you say Jesus is God's word, I think you mean he is the embodiment of God's desire, purpose and action—all coming together in Jesus.

GROSE: Yes. When we say Jesus is the word of God, then we see that he is the embodiment of God's mind, intent and purpose. Moreover, he is the actualization of that purpose. And Jesus is this in human flesh. With John's Gospel, again, as a point of reference, "In the beginning was the Word..." (1:1). With Genesis as a point of reference, "And God said, 'Let there be light;' and there was light" (1:3). And this also is in the declaration of John's prologue for, even there, the Son of God was present, because it was through him that God created the world. That's an astronomically high Christology: the Son of God was even involved in creation. That's the way John's Gospel works, and there's something similar in Paul's letters to the Ephesians (1:3-6) and Colossians (1:15-20).

HUBBARD: It's interesting that *Genesis Rabbah* in the Midrash states that God created the world through the Torah.

GROSE: Another analogy. A very telling one.

HUBBARD: Philo[36] takes it a step further when he talks about God creating through his word.

SIDDIQI: But I think Philo uses it more like a blueprint. This does not seem to be a Hebrew meaning. Is it?

GROSE: All right, this is the Greek influence coming in.

SIDDIQI: In the Qur'an Jesus is also called "a word from God," indicating his miraculous birth. His mother received a word from God that she would bear a child. She indicated that she was not married, had not known a man. The angel of God told her that it was God's decision and it must come to pass (Surah 19:20-21). So Jesus is called "a word from God" in a sense that he was born in a special way by a special command of God. That is our understanding of the "word." Tell me what John is saying. Is he using this metaphor in a Hebrew sense, in a Greek sense, or what?

GROSE: John, whose Gospel dates from about 90 A.D., is appealing to a two-fold audience: to the Judaic mentality and the Greco-Roman. The Gospel is already out in the Gentile world and John is addressing both Jewish and Gentile Christianity. He picks up the Semitic aspect, the vitality of God's activity, fulfilling his purpose or *davar*. God's word goes forth to accomplish that which he purposes and does not return to him void.[37] Now I would call that a Christological text out of the Old Testament, applying right to Jesus. And you guys can't stop me; it may not be permissible from a certain point of view, but I'll do it anyway; there it is. I've not read that any interpreter calls it a Christological text, but probably someone has—these texts have all been pored over for hundreds of years.

GORDIS: No possible distortion has been avoided.

GROSE: That's the nicest thing you could possibly say. Anyway, out of the vitality of the scriptural period of Judaism comes Jesus who is God's predestined purpose. He's going about teaching and healing and doing his prophetic thing. On the other hand, to the Greeks, "word" or *logos* is something else: final, ultimate truth. But that's not a Semitic way of thinking, whether Arabic or Jewish, because one doesn't ask about ultimate truth. But Greeks did; and they identified it with the *logos* of God, as did Philo.

So *logos* has a double reference, Semitic and Greco-Roman. When John uses *logos* he knows that a lot of Jewish people, although they speak Greek—the language of the Mediterranean world—are really Semites in their heritage. Consequently, John is addressing the Semitic mentality and the Greek mentality in the same Prologue (John 1). He has enriched my life because of this double perspective.

What I've just described enriches what I already personally knew. I didn't became a Christian because I first found these philological connections. I think that's what you're probing from me. I believe Jesus is alive, having conquered sin and death. Yet, according to the Qur'an (Surahs 3:55; 4:157, 158), Jesus was not killed and raised. Rather, like Enoch (Gen. 5:24) and Elijah (2 Kings 2:11), God took him to heaven and he did not pass through death.

SIDDIQI: I believe Jesus is alive, but not in the same way as we are alive now. All other prophets are alive, too, but the life that we are talking about is a different type of life. It is not like our physical life.

GROSE: All right.

SIDDIQI: And the martyrs are alive, too. The Qur'an says, "Do not call those who are killed in the faith of God, dead. They are alive" (2:154).

GROSE: Yes. But the martyrs did die.

SIDDIQI: Yes.

GROSE: They went through death.

SIDDIQI: And prophets, too, went through death, but they are alive.

GROSE: All right. He must be more than alive, because I used to be able to say, in Christian circles, "Jesus is alive." That was part of my experience, something I know. But that's not enough—and that's what all of you have helped me see—that I could just as well be a Muslim and say the same thing. So I must also include Jesus's power and identity: he is the incarnate, crucified and risen Lord. In this connection, I know someone to whom Jesus has appeared.

SIDDIQI: How did he appear? Did he appear in a dream, in a vision, or in a real physical sense?

GROSE: The person to whom he appeared said that Jesus came to him in light which filled his bedroom, though it was nighttime. He then became a Christian.

SIDDIQI: Does the appearance mean that Jesus was alive more than anyone else who also may appear in a vision or dream?

GROSE: Yes, that was what I meant by that.

SIDDIQI: There have been a lot of appearances of religious figures, all over the world, on numerous occasions. People state, "I have seen my rabbi, I have seen my guru, I have seen my sheikh," something like that.

GROSE: Well, clearly, these appearances were in a Christian setting.

SIDDIQI: You were using the example of Jesus' being alive because people saw him. You, yourself, are a witness for that and know those who saw him. So does it make a special case?

GROSE: It confirms to me what I already knew from the scriptural account. You come to the place where, finally, it's a question of faith.

But I also noted that to say, "Jesus is alive," used to be quite sufficient for me—if a Christian said it. But I've been able to see lately, in my life together with Jews and Muslims, that it's a true statement; but it's not sufficient for my acceptance of Christianity. Muslims also believe Jesus is alive, so it's clearly not sufficient. But it's a powerful persuader, and I have several others. To me, these accounts of visions confirm scriptural accounts and the resurrection. You asked me personal things. I'm telling you very personal things, and it's kept me going on a lot of dark days. I know this. It is not just something I've read in a book, even the Bible. So I think as far as spiritual experiences go, I would accept that the other religions have them. But these appearances occurred in Christian worship or brought a person to Christ as Lord and Savior.

I later had realized that the risen Lord still has the stigmata, the nail marks in his hands and feet from the crucifixion (John 20:24-29), that he bears the marks of his wounds even now. This is part of his identification, to tell us, for example, one way to identify him, to show that it was himself and not some vague spirit. This makes an appearance very Christian because Jesus bears the marks, even now. This is confirmed by the Book of Revelation, in which the author saw in a vision the throne of God, and beside it a lamb, "standing as though it had been slain" (Rev. 5:6). How can a lamb stand if it has been slain? This has been understood as an allusion to the resurrection of Jesus: he was slain as the lamb of God but is now alive. All of this comes together now for me—I'm giving personal testimony. This scriptural enrichment brings me a lot of joy, and I find it also connecting outward to my colleagues.

HUBBARD: Thank you. Muzammil, will you please comment on the question of revelation.

SIDDIQI: In Islam, there are at least two kinds of revelation. One is a revelation in the very general sense of the word which means inspiration—to do good, or inspiration in nature, even God's inspiration, the honey bee as in the Qur'an Surah 66:68. God inspires the bee; he goes to collect juice from the flowers and makes honey out of them.

It's the inspiration that directs life. The world moves by this divine inspiration.

In Islam, there is also another specific revelation that comes to the prophets of God. It is not like a poet's inspiration, or an artist's or saint's or mystic's. It is the inspiration for which God chose the prophet. He is called *nabi*, the one who is spoken to, who is informed; and he is to give a very important message to those who are to receive the messenger. The divine word, in the very real sense of the term, comes upon the chosen prophets. God selects them and then, in a sense, forces his word upon them. I like the expression from the Old Testament, "I have put my words into your mouth," or something like that.

HUBBARD: It's Jeremiah Chapter One (1:9).

SIDDIQI: Jeremiah, yes. That's more or less the Islamic concept of revelation. It is called *wahee*, a whispering, a kind of communication between God and man which happens through the Angel Gabriel, the carrier of revelation. God speaks to Gabriel who brings this message to the prophet. Some scholars have speculated on why there is need for an angel, since God can speak directly to a prophet. It is to keep the objective nature of the revelation, so that it doesn't become like a subjective feeling. Instead, there is an outside agent, an angel, through whom God sends this message to the prophet. So it's not like someone saying, "I'm inspired, and God has spoken this to me." But an angel comes and gives the message to the prophet, and sometimes people even witness it. He is sitting in the company of people who see that something special is happening to him. He utters words that are very different from what he normally speaks. So the revelation is always kept separate from even the words of the prophet. Even though this prophet's words carry a lot of weight and authority, they are not the Qur'an. The Qur'an in a very specific sense is a revelation of *the* word of God. This word of God is not an open-ended thing so that anybody can say at any time that something is also included in the word of God.

I was getting a sense that all the rabbis that spoke in later generations

were also included in the revelation at Mount Sinai. Prophets' words
are not included in the Qur'an, although they are in the explanation of
the Qur'an, no doubt about that; but they are kept separate. That's why
in Islam there is never a question about what is Qur'an and what is not
Qur'an. Qur'an and *Hadith* are kept separate. And the words of the
later scholars and jurists were never incorporated into the Qur'an.
They are called commentaries or explanations, and some are better than
others. You can always tell them from the Qur'an itself and can
question them. But the Qur'an will remain specific because God has
spoken these words which are not the prophet's, but which the prophet
has heard. As the Qur'an says, it is upon his tongue and upon his heart
that the revelation came.

Later, in the first and second centuries of the Islamic era, a question
was raised about the Qur'an whether it was created or non-created.
This was, perhaps, due to the influence of Greek thought as the Greek
books were being translated and read by Muslims. The rationalists, the
Mu'tazalites said that since the Qur'an spoke about things that
happened in the time of Prophet Muhammad and at other times in
history, then how could we say that this was the eternal word of God?
In other words, they were saying that the events that happened in
history, how could they be spoken eternally? So they came to the
conclusion that the Qur'an was created in time. Just as God created the
world, so He created the Qur'an, they said. According to them Qur'an
was not the spoken word of God, but the created word. The orthodox
position is that the Qur'an is the spoken word of God and it is eternal,
as God's speech is eternal. They said, "The paper on which the Qur'an
is written is created, the ink is created, the events that it speaks of are
created, our reading of it is created, our looking at it is created, but
God's own spoken words are not created. Those are eternal words.
When you read the Qur'an you come in touch with the eternal divine
words. God speaks to you directly in a special way.

Muslims do not worship the Qur'an. There is no bibliolatry in Islam.
Muslims do not believe that because the Qur'an is the word of God so
it is God. The copies of Qur'an are handled with great reverence and
respect, but it is never worshipped. Muslims do not even hold the
Qur'an in their hands when they pray. One memorizes the Qur'an and

in prayers reads it from memory. The book is never brought before
the people in a procession, so that it may not appear like an idol, an
icon or a relic. Reading of the Qur'an is an act of worship, so
Muslims read the Qur'an, listen to it, study it. One gets a special
feeling when the Qur'an is recited.

It is also to be emphasized that Muslims take all precautions not to
mix or add anything with the words of God and also not to take away
anything from them. To change the word of God is called *tahrif*. It is
corruption and is a grave sin. The Qur'an says that is what Jews and
Christians did to the divine word (Surahs 4:46, 5:13). They did not
keep the divine word in its purity and authenticity.

2. THE EFFECTS OF DIALOGUE

GORDIS: Might we pause and reflect on the nature of our
conversation up to now. We have been sharing our knowledge on
various points. But how, ultimately, will we be affected by this
experience? What is your spiritual reality? What does it have to do
with mine? I want to be able to say that maybe we have different
points of view, but I'm an enlarged person spiritually—I operate in an
enhanced way—because of my exposure to your spirituality. And not
just on a cognitive level. That, I think, is one of the desirable products
of dialogue. It has something to do with truth, and what we mean by
parallel search; but, to me, it's more important than a sharing of
information and getting to know each other. It's something which may
not be as linear or as verbal as that but which we need to explore.

SIDDIQI: The problem is that all our three traditions share a great
deal. But, at the same time, within our three traditions there is some
part which we do not share. There are actually parts in your tradition
which I reject and parts in my tradition which you reject.

GORDIS: Absolutely.

SIDDIQI: And that is part of our faith, our understanding of our
tradition and ourselves.

GORDIS: Yes.

SIDDIQI: Speaking as a Muslim, I accept Jesus very much as a prophet of God, as a spiritual person, but I do not accept his being called the Son of God. I just cannot accept it. That is alien to my understanding of God and His nature.

GORDIS: You're putting your finger exactly on it. That's what I'm asking: In view of our differences and particularities, what does Muhammad as a spiritual human being have to do with my spirituality? I feel that it can be enhanced, despite the fact that you come from a different tradition and we have disagreements. I feel that when George talks about his personal religious experience, it's not mine; but I am moved by it. I am spiritually expanded by it, despite the fact that I don't accept the reality of his perception of it as the person who went through it.

GROSE: I think that's beautiful. Isn't there a Talmudic saying that if someone saves another's life, it's as if he has saved the whole world?

GORDIS: Right.

GROSE: Every time I celebrate the Lord's Supper, perform a baptism, read the scripture, it's an element of what's going on in the whole world. Here we were in a building with a congregation, all of whom I knew by name, and what was happening there was happening to the whole world. And I think the same could be said of other churches. If that is the case, then every time the sun goes down on Friday, the Sabbath becomes the Sabbath for the whole world, not just in a certain synagogue. Every Friday when the Muslim call to prayer is given, the whole world is called, not just those in that particular mosque. You can see what I'm developing here. So the power of each of these moments is released and actualized every time worshippers get together to do what God commands. That power affects the whole world.

So whatever is done in keeping with the word of God, as Isaiah said, goes out and accomplishes His purpose. And it's all there in the act of worship, whether it's at the Muslim mosque in Garden Grove, or here at the University of Judaism, or in any church—it's really going on for the sake of the whole world. The whole world is in on that particular action.

HUBBARD: Your idea, George, reminds me of the Jewish Cabalistic or mystical notion that all human activity has cosmic consequences, that what a person does in one place can influence what happens elsewhere.[38]

GORDIS: I'm not suggesting that any one of us is going to give up our particular allegiance. We come from the authority of those positions to talk to each other. But I am suggesting we ought to be changed by this experience, opened up to hear each other in a way that we might not have been able to before.

GROSE: I must say, I've had many years of suffering over this, and moments of tremendous joy, too, some of it tremendously vivid.

SIDDIQI: I like what both of you are saying. I agree with you that we must have openness, we must expand ourselves by knowing and appreciating each other. A religion is like a country that you know exists somewhere. But then you go there and spend a few days. After that, when you hear about it or read something about it in the newspaper, somehow it affects you. You feel, I was there, I met its people, I sat with them, I ate with them. I think it is the same thing with the dialogue: once you sit with the people of other faiths and listen to them, you know their feelings. It is not like you are reading about them in a book. They are no more distant people, they become part of your own imaginative self. This kind of relationship, certainly, gives a deeper feeling, removes distance, prejudice, hate and estrangement. I think this experience is very important. Otherwise, we will just keep referring to other faiths without any human feelings for their adherents. We do have our differences which we should dialogue and carry on discussions about, but we must not lose sight of others' spirituality and must give them proper respect as fellow human beings.

GORDIS: Could I just overstate something, and then maybe discard it? There's a certain risk in our dialogue. The risk is—let's confess it—we're fairly knowledgeable about our own traditions. So there is an inclination, when we listen to each other, for me to say, "Okay, I'm going to compare this with Judaism." Instead of listening to you, I am listening only in terms of being clear about what I'm saying, rather than being open to what you're saying. After we do the listening and comparing, have we gotten to the point where—without giving up our particularities—we are also listening to the other as a human being, a spiritual being whom we admire and care for? Does what we say resonate, so that there is more than just understanding? Even though I'm not going to become a Muslim, Muzammil, and you're not going to become a Jew, and neither of us is going to become a Christian—unless George is successful. He's working at it!

GROSE: You're going to make an evangelist out of me yet if you keep talking about it!

GORDIS: You are an evangelist. Didn't you tell us that the first day?

GROSE: Yes—an inevitable comment!

GORDIS: But my point is a serious one. We must not only sit and compare: "Okay, you said this—well, I found it in the Midrash." And you say, "No, it doesn't parallel, one comes from the other." In the constant listening to the other position—in the openness—there's a certain closure. We only want to internalize the other in terms of what we know to be true, and the dialogue takes on a respectful but almost dismissive character. We're not, for example, listening to Christianity, we're saying, "Okay, what is this guy, this Christian, who obviously is wrong, getting at?" I'm overstating it, but I think the point is there. I'm just talking about myself. When I hear Muzammil say revelation is even more inclusive than I believe, I have to overcome the tendency simply to think "Is he right? In certain ways he is, in other ways he's wrong. What other verses or sentences could be quoted?" When I do this, I'm not really hearing you except in comparative terms. The experience of dialogue is more than a course in comparative religion. It's a much more human and holistic experience. We kid about it, but I don't feel threatened at all. I don't think we're having a contest about which religion is better, which is right. I think we're beyond that.

SIDDIQI: I see what you're looking for. The point is, how to do it?

GORDIS: Exactly. All I'm suggesting is, could we spend an hour sitting and talking with each other about this, maybe not now, but after giving it some thought beforehand? It involves the meaning beyond what we've explored so far in our coming together.

SIDDIQI: Our traditions are basically prophetic, not mystical, even though we do have mystical elements in all our religious traditions. Prophets talk clearly. They define, demarcate, distinguish between what is right and wrong, what is true and what is false. Mystics are different. They see unity even in apparènt contradictions. They are inclusivist, not exclusivist. It is, I think, difficult to be prophetic and mystical at the same time. On the human level, we have to be together and be open to each other and respect each other. But it is the intellectual level where I do not see how we can reconcile our differences. As I said earlier, within our traditions we do have elements that do not agree with each other.

GORDIS: Look at the problem that I have. Your scripture and the father of your faith, Muzammil, is not the father of faith or the author of scripture to me. As a Jew, I am in worse shape. I have more difficulty with it. The problem is, in view of the fact that we tend to be involved in traditions which are particularistic, both of us will say, "This business of the embodiment of God in a human being doesn't make sense. We don't accept it." It diminishes the notion of monotheism to the Jew or the Muslim. That's why we look in different ways. It is a problem. I don't have the answer, but I am saying we'd be settling for something much more pedestrian if we didn't make the effort to find the answer. The question I'm looking for an answer to is: Let's assume we're not going to persuade each other of the rightness of our respective positions, that we're going to be different, and that our traditions are distinct. Can we, then—in a world which desperately needs a religious vision which can transcend the difference while not breaking it—be instruments of creating something to make the world better, a world that depends on human beings to be able to relate to each other in their difference? If we can't do it here, and really respond beyond being informed by one another, there's no hope it's going to be done anywhere else.

GROSE: Being informed, but being informed by the word of God. That's something to be stated. We are giving each other information, but it's not just that, because there are a lot of people who, for example, are teaching world religions, Buddhism, Hinduism and all the others. I have taught world religions. I especially enjoy teaching Judaism, Christianity and Islam. That's part of my commitment. In a way, I am a promoter of Judaism, Christianity and Islam as a Christian. It's a strange situation, I know. I am not a promoter of Hinduism, Buddhism, and the others. I am for whatever will enhance the vision of God in Judaism, Christianity and Islam. I struggle to be objective whenever I am challenged to do any teaching of eastern religions, especially because the humanity of these believers grips me, and I know I must speak with them.

SIDDIQI: I have a human concern which is not limited to the family of Abraham only. Half of the people in this world are not Muslims, Christians or Jews.

GROSE: They're Buddhists. They're others.

SIDDIQI: And Hindus, Jains, Confucians, Taoists, Shintoists, Sikhs, etc.

GROSE: So I have a limitation because of my serious commitment to the dialogue of the three monotheistic faiths. But that has given me an advantage: my focus on the three. I would like to say a couple of things about how this has enriched my life. I remember when the late Rabbi Dr. Henry Front[39] was dying. I went to see him at Cedars Sinai Hospital in Los Angeles. I just had the feeling that things weren't going too well. There was Henry, lying in his bed. His wife, Regina, was there, holding his hand. She said, "Henry's got a terrific headache and he's in terrible pain." I said, "I'd like to pray with you." So I prayed for his headache in the name of the God of Israel, of Ishmael, and of God the Father and the Lord Jesus Christ. That had a profound effect on me, and Henri's headache abated.

It was only a couple of days ago that I was talking to Dr. Abdelmagead El-Biali, a businessman in Whittier. In a testimony to me of Islamic spirituality, he said, "*Inshallah* (Allah willing), Dr. George, we do the best we can." Many devout Muslims talk about God freely. Lots of Christians don't, and I think it's a shortcoming of Christianity. It's in them, but they can't seem to get it out. But I really think it's a stifling of their life with God, that they can't speak freely about Him.

GORDIS: Traditional Jews do exactly the same thing as Dr. El-Biali. They say, "I'll see you next week, *im yirtzeh Hashem*, God willing."

GROSE: So I have the sense there are Muslims who walk with God, just as I have the sense there are Jews who do.

GORDIS: A Jew asks, "How are you," and the person answers, "Thank God." So what are they giving you? You're supposed to praise God for both good and evil. And the answer is irrelevant, right? And if they are saying only thank God because things are fine, then they are being sacrilegious.

3. THE CANON OF SCRIPTURE

HUBBARD: Muzammil was talking earlier about the possible corruption of the word of God in Jewish and Christian scripture. Would each of you comment on this and on the related question of how these scriptures are authenticated—how we know they are God's word.

SIDDIQI: I look at the Jewish and Christian scriptures with respect, of course. The Qur'an talks about God's revelation to Moses in the form of Torah and to Jesus in the form of *injil*, Gospel. But I want to emphasize that Islam speaks more of verbal revelation. In the light of this, it appears that there were verbal changes in both Torah and the Gospels. You have spoken of historical developments. This means, then, that according to the Islamic concept of revelation your scriptures do not meet the criteria of authentic verbal revelation. But I want to hear David and George on this.

GORDIS: The issue is canonization. At a point known in the Jewish religion as *mikan vaeylach*, "from now on," prophecy ended; and what comes after that decision was made is not canonical. Those who framed it that way understood that there were other works, other figures circulating, who made claims to prophecy or to canonical standing. Remember that the Hebrew Bible is divided into three sections of descending order of sacred claim. All of it is biblical and canonical, but the Torah, the five books of Moses, have claim to the highest authority. They are what was revealed to Moses on Sinai, according to the tradition.

On the next level are the prophets, *Nevi'im* in Hebrew, who are subdivided into two types: the classical prophets, Isaiah, Jeremiah, Ezekiel and the twelve minor prophets;[40] and the former prophets, which are more historical works: the books of Joshua, Judges, First and Second Samuel, and First and Second Kings. All of these are viewed as works of enormous authority, but they are not as authoritative as the Torah.

The third section of the Hebrew Bible, the sacred writings or hagiographa, *Kethubim* in Hebrew, are a much more heterogeneous collection. In particular, there was sometimes debate as to whether a work should be included or not. The most well-known debate was over the Song of Songs because of its very graphic sexual imagery. It was finally included because it was understood as an allegory of God's relationship to the people of Israel. Similarly, no one would say that the book of Esther, which belongs to the genre of king and courtier literature, is on the same level as the book of Isaiah in terms of its majesty and historic import. Nevertheless, these three sections of the Hebrew Bible are all canonical.

There is no internal seal which tells you that this is biblical and this is not. Other works in the Jewish Apocrypha and Pseudepigrapha[41] could have been included in the canon but were not. That was an evolved judgment that the community came to early on but in stages. Are there corruptions? That depends on what you mean. We have at a very early stage after the Hebrew Bible was canonized the tradition of the Masoretes, careful students of the Bible whose function was to preserve its text and make certain no changes occurred.

SIDDIQI: What century?

GORDIS: Some of the work of the Masoretes is felt to go back to the second century.

GROSE: Common Era?

GORDIS: Yes. What did they do? They created an entire apparatus of notations on the text of the Hebrew Bible which calls attention to special features. There were times when they had alternate readings and would designate one as the *kateev*, the "written text," and other as *keray*, "the way it should be read". So they were able to keep both readings. The meaning of the text was preserved in one version and the orthography, the actual Hebrew letters, in the other.

One important feature, related more closely to the question of corruption, is how Jews read the Bible—particularly the Torah. They did so with the assumption that there is no accidental characteristic of the text. This relates to the fact of absolute, literal revelation. If, in two places of the Torah, the same verb or noun is used, and the authorities felt a different word could have been used, that's felt to be suggestive. For example, the law of sacrifice says the daily sacrifice is to be performed "in its appointed time" *bemoado*. And then, with reference to the sacrifice for the festival of Passover, it also says, "in its appointed time." The question arises: what happens if Passover comes on Saturday night? They have to prepare the paschal sacrifice in the afternoon on Saturday, but you're not allowed to prepare a sacrifice, which is work, on the Sabbath. So does the preparation of the paschal sacrifice set aside the Sabbath prohibition or not? One way they solved the problem was by saying, Look, the Torah says *bemoado*, "in its appointed time" with regards to the daily sacrifice and uses the same term *bemoado* when it talks about the paschal sacrifice. So just as the daily sacrifice is to be done at its appointed time, no matter what day it is, so also the paschal sacrifice is to be performed even if it comes on the Sabbath (Babylonian Talmud, *Pesahim* 66a).

That's a technical application of the rule, but it shows how every detail of the Torah, every vocalization, every use of a term, is so rich that there are levels of meaning and interpretation available. Therefore, any notion of a corruption or an error would be very serious, indeed. That's why there's meticulous attention to detail in the preservation of biblical text.

SIDDIQI: I have two questions, David. One, how do you deal with modern biblical criticism, especially the Documentary Hypothesis of the composition of the Torah, which you mentioned at the beginning of this chapter? The second is: when canonization of the biblical books has taken place, are some books more authoritative than others? If, for example, there is a contradiction between the Torah and the Book of Proverbs, which would have the preference? Or do they all have the same authority?

GORDIS: Officially, in theory, all of the Bible is authoritative. In practice, there's no question that the Torah, the five books of Moses, is the central product of revelation and therefore more authoritative than the rest. But they are all canonical, and all the books of the Hebrew Bible, going right down to the Books of Chronicles, can be used in the Midrash as evidence. But that hierarchy de facto exists.

Now, the other question is one we all need to deal with in some way. In the Jewish community, as in other communities, there are those we might call traditionalists, or literalists, who would reject the whole notion of a Documentary Hypothesis. Then there are those who embrace the theory and conclude that there's no sacred character to the Bible, that it's just another book with errors. Finally, there are those who accept the Documentary Hypothesis but whose religious faith isn't impeded thereby. I belong to the last group. My belief is that God did not create us in such a way as to mislead us—we are supposed to use our minds to enhance our understanding even of our religious tradition. And if we conclude that the Documentary Hypothesis makes sense, then that does not in any sense impede our faith. The revelation of scripture was to a community, and it's a process that continues in time. So it doesn't matter that individual sources were brought together in the Torah. What's important is that they came together and functioned as scripture; and, therefore, all the concentration on scripture and the inferences from it are perfectly proper.

The authority of scripture and tradition comes not from revelation as a one-time event, but as a process. That process, I find, involves a relationship between God and the Jewish people in time. Therefore, while a theophany took place on Sinai—and I did mention earlier that the Talmud says the Torah was literally given to Moses—it was only general tradition that was given to Moses. The tradition itself says that authority is embodied in the people who through time are in a constant relationship to God, and this is called revelation. So the way scripture came together over time in no sense compromises my religious faith.

SIDDIQI: But doesn't your position contradict a centuries-old literalist view that says the Torah was all given verbally, that every word of it is God's? As an outsider—and I use a strong word—it seems like you are making virtue out of necessity.

GORDIS: There are certainly Jews who reacted that way and who, in fact, accept the tradition that the entire scripture was revealed literally to Moses on Sinai. If they should happen to read Wellhausen or another modern biblical critic, and suddenly be confronted by the idea that the Torah was not given all at once but developed over several centuries, of course, this would challenge them. They would either have to refute this theory or accept it and adjust their original understanding. My point is that while there are many who believe the literalist tradition, a sensitive reading of what Jewish tradition says about the Bible does not suggest the exclusive notion of literalism. It exists side by side in the very earliest tradition with a sense of the Torah's coming together over time and with a human component.

4. THE HUMAN ELEMENT IN SCRIPTURE

HUBBARD: We've been discussing the human element in the composition of scripture, whether it's the Documentary Hypothesis of the composition of the Torah or the Two-source Theory of the composition of the Gospels of Matthew and Luke.[42] George, how is it possible from a Christian perspective to have the inspired word of God along with a human element that is subject to various modes of biblical criticism or literary investigation?

GROSE: I'll start with the Old Testament because, for the early Church, the only scripture they had was the Septuagint, the Greek translation of the Hebrew scriptures. The New Testament writings constantly quote scripture with the phrase "as it is written," or the like. And scripture was the Hebrew Bible in its Greek or Septuagint form used at the time by the many Greek-speaking Jews. So the Church didn't use the Hebrew text directly but the Septuagint. Yet the Church accepted the whole canonization process of Judaism without question and it became their Old Testament.

GORDIS: They didn't assert that Moses received the Bible in Greek, did they?

GROSE: No, they accepted the Septuagint as the word of God.

GORDIS: But again, it was not divinely inspired, not the same thing. It was a translation, right? So they were translators.

GROSE: Yes, they were translators; but there's a position in Judaism to the effect that the Septuagint is divinely inspired.

GORDIS: Yes. There's a legend that says that all 70 translators sat in different rooms and, miraculously, they all came out with the same translation.[43]

GROSE: Yes.

GORDIS: But they were translators.

GROSE: Very well. But the Church...

SIDDIQI: Seventy translators?

GORDIS: Seventy translators was part of it, but the main point is absolute convergence. Though they worked separately, all came out with the same text.

GROSE: Which is, in a way, to say it is divinely inspired. The Church accepted the Septuagint as divinely inspired. Indeed, as I said, it is widely quoted in the New Testament. The Christians moved quickly out of the Jewish community into the Gentile world. And they took the whole cloth, the canon of the Jewish people; but most knew very little about how it came to be. This was the scripture of the Jews which prophesied to them the coming of the Christ. They just took it. It was scripture—the only one they had at first.

But what about the New Testament? We know that Paul's letters were the first writings that circulated. They had his immense authority as an apostle, but it wasn't a question yet of canonicity. Then certain gospels came into existence. So it's really a two-phase answer about the character of scripture: there was Hebrew scripture in its Septuagint version, which Christianity was very literalist about accepting and had unquestioned authority; and there were the letters of Paul and the gospels which gradually gained authority.

Tatian, one of the Church Fathers, produced a melding of the four gospels, the *Diatessaron* which means "through four." It was used extensively in Syria, but never really took off in the Church at large which held to the four-fold gospel. This decision by the Church at large really established the nature of scriptural authority in Christianity. The phrase was, "These are the books that may be read in church;" and it established canonicity, even though church leaders didn't use the word "canon" until later. Other books could be read for spiritual edification [44] and still others were rejected. [45] Gradually these bishops' lists of approved writings coalesce in about the third or fourth century in the West, and the fifth century in the East. There never was an ecumenical Church council to declare that what we now have is New Testament scripture. It was only the Council of Trent (1545-63), the Counter-Reformation council, that listed the books of the Bible for the Catholic Church. So out of the organic life of the Church came the New Testament.

The Catholic Church and the Protestants have different positions on this. Catholics say it is on the authority of the Holy Spirit, working through the Church, that the list of writings which now comprise the New Testament was established. Protestants tend to declare that the Holy Spirit, working with the individual authors of the writings, established what was canonical. I myself am more Catholic and think it is the work of the Church; but that doesn't bother me as a Protestant because it is the work of the Holy Spirit either way. The human element didn't really come up as an issue with regards to the Septuagint because the Church just accepted it. The faith of the Church is that the four gospels witness to the same person, Jesus, about the same things he said and about what happened to and through him. Yet, the very four-fold gospel challenges any fundamentalism—any taking of the scriptures as literally true in every respect. If the Church had adopted the *Diatessaron*, then we might consider verbal inerrancy; but the four-fold Gospel undercuts anything like what is called nineteenth- and twentieth-century fundamentalism. There are several authorities in Catholicism, but the Pope, the Vicar of Christ, interprets the other two—scripture and tradition. Protestants have no Pope, and the only tradition they would consciously accept is one associated with earliest Christianity. That means that they're focused right in on the scripture, which might lead to fundamentalism. But this doesn't happen because the four-fold Gospel won't permit it.

If Protestants don't take the Bible literally, how do they interpret it? Here we need to focus on Calvin. He was more textual, in a certain sense, than Luther who was quite close to the Catholic tradition, even though he was the first major figure to break with it. Luther had the principle of salvation by faith as the hermeneutical or interpretative key to the whole business. Calvin is closer to the rabbinic tradition of examining carefully every semicolon, every word, how one word relates to the next. But Calvin was not, in the modern sense, a fundamentalist—that was some later Calvinism and offshoots of it—because he was trained in classical humanism and used the canons of rational, logical thought in interpreting scripture. He used the classical authors for illustration. He also used the Church Fathers, which is very interesting because Protestants don't think this is part of their tradition. But he was constantly quoting the Catholic Fathers, agreeing with them sometimes, not agreeing with them sometimes....

HUBBARD: Do you mean Augustine, Chrysostom, Jerome and the others?

GROSE: Yes, both the Greek and the Latin Fathers,[46] as well as the classical humanists. So Calvin had a very rich intellectual tradition, took the text seriously and didn't skip anything. He was a very systematic thinker. How, then, does one cope with apparent or real contradictions which exist in the New Testament? Calvin's first principle of interpretation is: Let the scripture interpret the scripture. If something's not clear or appears to be contradictory, you look around to find another passage that sheds light on the problem. I think the Qur'an works the same way: if a passage is not clear, there is a related one which will provide clarification. In this way, we have a similar approach in the three faiths to handling such texts. Present-day thinking in the Calvinist churches, specifically the Presbyterian, is that the Word of God is known in three ways: Jesus, the living word of God; the scripture, the written word of God; and the visual word of God—bread, wine, water. In this way, scripture and sacrament are derivative from Jesus, the Word of God, which we discussed earlier. So the scripture is not above Jesus. That's one problem with fundamentalism—taking away from Jesus by holding the Bible above him. But scripture belongs to him, not the other way around. In practice, I use all forms of biblical criticism in my own study and reflection on the Hebrew Bible and the New Testament. The Four-Source theory or Documentary Hypothesis of the Torah's origins is very useful to me, as is a knowledge of "Q". and the other sources in understanding the gospels.

GORDIS: As I understand it, the question is: at the point one says that there is a human component in scripture, how does one make the distinction between what is human and what is divine? And you were also interested, Ben, in how I view the Documentary Hypothesis.

SIDDIQI: There are several points: Is part of the Bible God's word, part of it human words? Are the words human but the ideas divine? Are all the ideas divine or just some of them? If this is like inspiration, then is it possible that people also had their own ideas mingled with divine ideas. It seems to me you are saying all these things when you talk about Old and New Testaments.

GORDIS: Right. So the question is how you distinguish the divine from the human. People will differ on this even within a tradition such as Judaism. Let me tell you how I deal with it and state at the outset that others will do so somewhat differently. The fact that a question creates problems is not a reason for me to pretend the question doesn't exist. For example, let's assume that accepting the Documentary Hypothesis raises a whole nest of questions about the Torah: How did it come together? When? etc. That in itself is not a reason to reject the Hypothesis. It may be convenient to do so, but one does so at the expense of truth by engaging in self-delusion. One could pretend that the issues don't exist because they're difficult to deal with. But I don't view that as the highest expression of my religious or intellectual self. If the problem of distinct sources within the Torah exists, I feel God challenges me to use my mind to understand and deal with it.

There's something that I want to say about language. There is a Hebrew expression, *diber Torah bilshoa b'nei adam,* "The Torah speaks in human language." This idea is embedded in two views of how you interpret the Torah and two schools of interpreters: Rabbi Akiba's and Rabbi Ishmael's—who is named for Ishmael in the Bible. Akiba was essentially a mystic and went, in a way, to an extreme in interpreting each specific characteristic of the Torah. Every minor detail in the text would be available as significant—hinting at something, suggesting something, implying something. Ishmael, on the other hand—although he also had an approach to interpreting the text so as to derive levels of meaning beyond the purely literal—held the general principle that the Torah spoke a human language. Therefore, he felt one shouldn't go overboard in finding these characteristics because the Torah is formed in human language. So one can't say that every characteristic of that language is divine in a direct sense.

I want to generalize from that principle of Rabbi Ishmael to a basic truth about language: it is a human phenomenon. To the extent that there is a divine language, it is a device for human beings to understand God. God doesn't speak in Greek rather than Hebrew, or Hebrew rather than Aramaic, or Aramaic rather than English. God, in my view, is not specific to a language—the Septuagint is not more or less God's word than the Hebrew Bible. The prophets do claim that they speak God's word when they say, *vayehi dvar Adonay elay lemor*, "God's word came to me saying..."; or, *Koh amar Adonay,* "Thus the Lord spoke", at the beginning of a piece of prophecy; or *dvar Adonay,* "God's word," at the end. Even though they're speaking God's word, they're actually conveying their sense of God's message.

Thus, even the most literal divine communication is still a translation into something human because language is human. So the distinction between what is God's word and what is a human's word is a continuous problem. This is related to the issue of religious arrogance where we try to elevate that which is human into the divine or to reach an understanding of the divine which is beyond human experience. In this connection, Moses Maimonides[47] spoke about God in terms of negative attributes: because the divine is beyond human experience, one can only say what God is not. God does contact us through revelation, but the written product of that revelation is a human phenomenon since its translation into language is human.

SIDDIQI: What you are saying is quite interesting. You are trying to understand the divine element in the human language. But the question I have is: how do you separate the two, according to what criteria? How do you know that this part is divine, permanent, eternal and authoritative; and this other element is human and can be dispensed with? There is another question that is related to this: if your scripture is such a mix of divine and human, then why do you call it a "canon"? What was the need for canonization?

GORDIS: That's the point. The judgment over what is authoritative, what is canonical, is given over to the community through revelation as a process. Much as George described it, there is no command of God that these books are in and these others out. It happens through a process of communal judgment, the product of a partnership of the divine and human. Thus, certain ideas, texts, values, commitments and commandments are considered authoritative. And it isn't a process which happens once and for all time. For example, the Book of Leviticus (13:1-8) gives me perfectly simple instructions if I find I have an eruption on my skin which could indicate leprosy. I'm supposed to go to the priest who will look at the particular symptoms I have and decide whether I should be excluded from the camp for seven days and then reexamined and so forth. This is part of the Torah and was looked upon as authoritative by the community. But today even the most literal fundamentalist, when he has a dermatological condition, doesn't go to the priest but to the dermatologist. I'm using that as a kind of *reductio ad absurdum* illustration of how the communal consensus changes. Another example is Deuteronomy 23:19-20 which commands the Jewish community not to take interest from another Jew, though it was permitted to take interest from a non-Jew. That was viewed as authoritative, and one can understand the context in which it arose. But the community as a whole rejects that as authoritative now as part of the dynamic of revelation which is part of a divine partnership in an evolving process.

HUBBARD: The Jewish community no longer stones those caught in the act of adultery as commanded in Deuteronomy (22:23-4) and did not do so even in rabbinic times. Lesser punishments were substituted. Similarly, the early Church never cut off peoples' hands despite Jesus' words that if your hand scandalizes you, you should cut it off; if your eye scandalizes you, you should pluck it out (Matthew 5:29-30). I suppose one could say Jesus was speaking hyperbolically or metaphorically. Even a fundamentalist will grant that you don't cut off hands or pluck out eyes if they lead you into sin. If I could go a step further. It strikes me, Muzammil, that if you don't worship the Qur'an, then in some sense it is human and open to criticism and analysis. Is that fair, or am I reading too much into your statement that it's human and not divine?

SIDDIQI: No. Worshipping the Qur'an is worshipping the book and, in Islam, nothing can be worshipped except God. So no visible image or portrait of God is made. But the Qur'an is the direction, the guidance, and has to be taken very seriously. Muslims do not regard the Qur'an as human and divine both. The Qur'an is totally the divine word and it is preserved as such without any change. God spoke to the Prophet through His angel Gabriel. But God used the Arabic language for this revelation. Arabic is a human language and, in order to understand the words of God in the Qur'an and grasp the divine purpose, we have to know the Arabic language—its grammar, idiom, vocabulary and structure.

The Qur'an also requires understanding of its textual and historical context: when was it revealed, where—in Mecca or Medina—before the *Hijrah*,[48] Muhammad and his followers' migration from Mecca to Medina, or after; and under what circumstances? This is called *sha'n nuzul* in Arabic. These are the circumstances of revelation. Some passages have literal meaning and some are metaphorical. There are many ways of interpreting the Qur'an. Scholars note that there are some words in the Qur'an that cannot be taken in their most obvious meanings. For example, there are sometimes verbal imperatives used, but every imperative does not mean that it is a command and it must be done. In Surah 5:2 God says, "When you are clear of the sacred precincts and pilgrim garb, then you hunt." Although the word "hunt" is in the imperative here, it only means "you may hunt." No one has said that it is the command of God to go hunting after pilgrimage.[49]

HUBBARD: Is that a form of literary criticism?

SIDDIQI: This is more an exegetical[50] kind of work. We have some highly developed principles of exegesis prepared by the *mufassirun* or exegetes and these are known as *Usua al-Tafsir*. This is an ongoing work. Also in the study of the Qur'an, one has to know the abrogating and abrogated verses, *nasikh wa mansukh* and the general and particular verses, *'umum wa khusus*, etc. The Hadith—whatever the Prophet Muhammad said and did, and things that happened in his lifetime which he approved of—also is employed in the interpretation of the Qur'an. The Hadith sometimes elaborates the concise passages of the Qur'an. For example, in the Qur'an God commands the believers to pray; but it is the Hadith that explains that it has to be five times a day and should be done in one way if you want to pray individually, or in another if you want to pray in congregation.

HUBBARD: So the *Hadith* is in some ways similar to the Torah.

GORDIS: Let me ask you about that. There are obviously many phrases, sayings and stories in the Qur'an which occur earlier in the Hebrew Bible, rabbinical literature, etc. Do you consider those occurrences prior revelations which influence what is said in the Qur'an?

SIDDIQI: The Qur'an is not the first time God has revealed His message. The Gospels and other revelations are recognized as well. But, if there are parallels, it is not because the prophet was sitting and collecting these sayings from different sources. The prophet was only a recipient of the revelation, not a maker of it.

GORDIS: I understand. So it's not even a degree of influence?

SIDDIQI: It is not an influence but more like parallels which are very helpful in understanding the Qur'an. For example, we often find a text in the Qur'an and that has a parallel in the Hebrew Bible or the New Testament.

GORDIS: Or in rabbinic literature.

SIDDIQI: It is quite possible that there are some rabbinic teachings that represent part of the divine revelation. Wherever there are similarities between the Qur'an and other previous scriptures, they are acknowledged wholeheartedly without any embarrassment. To a Muslim, they indicate that the Hebrew Bible and the New Testament are authentic in this particular case.

Prophet Muhammad is the one who received the message. God spoke to him as He spoke to Abraham, Moses, Jesus and others. Although the examples are not too numerous, if there is a statement or phrase which looks exactly the same in the Qur'an as in the Hebrew Bible or the Gospels, then we may say here God is repeating His words. He is, we might say, quoting Himself from words He revealed previously. Let me mention a few passages where the Qur'an says clearly that such words were given to the Israelites, to King David, to Jesus, etc.: Surahs 5:45, 21:105, 48:29.

GORDIS: Let me give a contrasting view, not of the Qur'an but of something in the Hebrew Bible. It is full of sacrifices, starting with Noah and running straight through. Did God command Noah to tell the children of Israel to perform these animal sacrifices? Is this independent of the fact that you had the practice of animal sacrifice elsewhere in the Ancient Near East? I don't believe so. Of course, I've talked about a divine-human partnership in the Bible. Therefore, my sense is that sacrifice in the Hebrew Bible is radically different from sacrifice elsewhere in the Near East. Such sacrifice was in the context of pagan culture where human beings nurtured the gods and the gods provided fertility, success, etc. Sacrifice in a monotheistic religion is completely different, but my sense is that the Israelites and the Hebrew scriptures received and were influenced by the institution of sacrifice in the ancient world. They transformed it, and this transformation was part of the great revelation of monotheism as embodied in the Hebrew Bible. But the practice is not uninfluenced or independent—it's not simply coincidental that sacrifice existed before it is enjoined in the Hebrew Bible. Do you see the difference of approach?

SIDDIQI: When I hear your interpretation, immediately I think that David Gordis is recognizing *Tahnif* which is the human element in the Bible and a corruption from the Islamic point of view.

GORDIS: Are there Muslims who would take an approach similar to mine?

SIDDIQI: In studying the Qur'an?

GORDIS: Yes.

SIDDIQI: There might be some, but they would not be recognized as Muslim approaches.

GORDIS: There isn't any proof.

SIDDIQI: It's not like there's a school of thought or interpretation of this type.

GORDIS: There certainly are Christians who would recognize the human element.

SIDDIQI: There might be some so-called Muslim here or somewhere who would say that there is a human element in the Qur'an; but there is, to my knowledge, no sect, group or seminary that espouses this type of approach. Those who do so are outright rejected as wrong.

GORDIS: Heretics?

SIDDIQI: Yes, heretics or whatever you may call them.

GORDIS: So I wouldn't make a good Muslim?!

SIDDIQI: I'm doubtful. But we do have some people who without questioning...

GORDIS: Listen, you'd better be careful, Muzammil, because I wouldn't make a good Muslim. I'd have to go back to George and see if I could become a good Christian!

SIDDIQI: I leave this to your own decision. But, as I started to say, there are some Muslims who—without questioning the divine origin of the Qur'an—have explained away some of its passages through ingenious interpretations. We had a famous Muslim scholar of last century, Sayyed Ahmad Khan of India,[51] who denied Jesus's virgin birth and, in his interpretation of the Qur'an, did away with this miracle.

GROSE: So somebody who's a Muslim said this.

SIDDIQI: Yes. The point is that we do have people who have made all kinds of interpretations but they and their interpretations are not accepted by Muslims in general. Likewise, there were some who also denied that God parted the Sea for Moses and his followers when they were leaving Egypt (Exodus 14:21-22). They say what really happened was that it was the time of low tide, and Moses thought God had done that especially for him.

GROSE: When a Muslim scholar says something like that, he doesn't participate in the mainstream—is that what you're saying?

SIDDIQI: Yes.

GROSE: David was talking about the human element in scripture and how can we take one another for what we are and be enriched by it. It reminds me that God's word came to the Hebrews in Hebrew and to the Christians through Greek.

SIDDIQI: The Hebrew people do say—and Muslims recognize—that the divine word came in Hebrew. But they don't say it came in Greek.

GROSE: They don't? Why not?

SIDDIQI: They don't know whether Jesus spoke Greek.

GORDIS: Incidentally, the Septuagint is not simply a translation. During the period from the end of the Old Testament or Hebrew Bible until the first Midrashic or rabbinic literature—about 200 B.C.E. to 200 C.E.—we have scant texts of Jewish biblical commentary. But the Septuagint contains interpretations of the Hebrew text which are part of the rabbinic interpretation of scripture. In other words, the interpretation is put into the translation.

GROSE: Look, I've got something to say that bears on both your positions. If one takes, as I have taken, an incarnational view of truth, and that language is a human activity, then the fact that the Qur'an is in Arabic, the Torah in Hebrew and the New Testament in Greek doesn't lessen their authority. If in Jesus there is full authority and it is in a human or incarnational context, then why can't there be a similar incarnation in the Qur'an as the divine word in a human language, Arabic? Or an incarnation of the divine word found in another human language, Hebrew? This should not be seen as a lessening of the authority of the scripture. The Qur'an is in Arabic, but that doesn't mean God speaks Arabic; because God has also given his word in Hebrew. There may be some Muslims who think God speaks Arabic, just as there are some Christians who think God speaks Greek. But there is nothing wrong with my point of view that the Qur'an is both divine and human—and that doesn't lessen its authority one whit.

SIDDIQI: It is human in the sense that God has chosen a human language to speak. But it is not human in the sense that humans formulated this word and then attributed it to God or called it a divine word. This is a basic difference between us. However, in order to understand the Qur'an, we have to study the Arabic culture and poetry of pre-Islamic times. A lot of the Qur'anic expressions are found there.

GROSE: What David is describing as the human component really isn't any different from what you're talking about.

5. TRUTH IN THE WORLD'S RELIGIONS

GORDIS: It's interesting how we've come to more of a consensus, so this may be a good place to bring this discussion to a close. We do have differences, but the question about language and the human-divine intersection relates to the larger picture. We have things which divide us—cultural, traditional, particularistic—but there are truths which we share. These become apparent as we articulate them and see their social settings in the human experience. I'm not aiming for us to get to the point of saying that the Hebrew Bible is authoritative for you or that the Qur'an is authoritative for me. It's not going to be authoritative for me the way it is for Muzammil. And the New Testament is not going to be authoritative for me the way it is for George. But I want

to be open to the New Testament and to the Qur'an to discover truths
in them. I want to hear God's word and God's voice in them because
God's voice is truth.   In Jewish tradition, *Hotama shel Hakadosh,
baruch Hu, emet,* "The seal of the Holy One, blessed be He, is truth."
Truth is not exclusive and is present in what you say to me and what
I understand about your beliefs. I want to have access so as to be
enriched by that truth—the truth found in Arabic, Greek, Hebrew,
Aramaic, etc.

The exercise we're engaged in will help me dispel the sense that I
relate to the other in an almost condescending way. Right? I think
each of our religious communities is, by and large, accustomed to
relating to the other in a condescending way with an emphasis on the
particular and the lack of openness. But now we're saying, okay, we're
different; but that shouldn't stop me from learning those things that can
help me to find truth. And it does come in every language and doesn't
end with one revelation. I would also add that it doesn't end with
Judaism, Christianity and Islam, either. For me, unlike the position
that you were taking, George—and here we have a different
perception—I'm excited about finding this kind of truth in Hinduism
and Buddhism. Because here there's also a search for the truth. I
mean, Buddhists were created by God, too. They're part of God's
world.

GROSE: I guess I'm moving out from a position that's very Catholic
regarding the Holy Spirit and the Church.

GORDIS: Catholic with a capital C?

GROSE: Yes. The Holy Spirit, for a long time in Christianity, was
understood as operative in the Church: the priest says certain words or
a certain prayer, and the action takes place on the altar. Protestants,
not that they are superior to Catholics, historically began to entertain
the thought that the Holy Spirit was free from human control, even the
control of the Church. Now, one of the issues in Christianity in the
past thirty to forty years is the doctrine of the Holy Spirit. The World
Council of Churches worked on this at its sixth assembly in Vancouver

in 1983. The Holy Spirit is not the humanistic notion that there's vitality in human beings. Rather, it's God's inbreaking vitality, God's Spirit. If our communities—Jewish, Christian, Muslim—take their place together in a family, they'll hold up the oneness of God over all forms of idolatry. So it is almost certain that God's Holy Spirit is working in these communities.

This is not a customary Christian position, but why can't the Holy Spirit work in communities other than the Christian? I think of Harvard theologian Harvey Cox's phrase, "the others who are nearest." In dealing with, considering and being in the presence of the others who are nearest, would it not seem perfectly real that God in His infinite wisdom is sending His Holy Spirit to these others who are near us? Among those who are nearest, God has revealed Himself in His oneness over against all forms of idolatry; and the distinction between the Creator and the created is known. If that's the case, then what you spoke of, David, as the real search is: let's see what the truth may be in "the others." What is God telling me through David, as well as Muzammil? I've long thought that I'm being told something by Judaism as well as Islam, by those traditions that are nearest. To me, that can be explained and justified in Christianity in the doctrinal considerations about the Holy Spirit. This is a theological enterprise, a fresh doctrine of the Holy Spirit for Christianity which finds truth through Judaism and Islam.

There is a truth which comes through the dialogue between the three monotheistic faiths. That's not to claim that I possess the entire truth or that anybody else present possesses it. I think rather that the truth possesses us in one way or another. It is breaking loose in amazing ways in our dialogue, ways that are totally unpredictable. We could describe what we're going to talk about today, summarize things; it doesn't matter—the truth breaks loose. That, I think, is close to what you're talking about, David, what you describe as the search, what we're really looking for.

SIDDIQI: Wilfrid Cantwell Smith, perhaps the world's leading non-Muslim Islamic scholar, made an interesting comment about truth. In

Arabic, there are three words for it: *sidq*, translated as truth; *haqq*, translated as truth; and *sahih*, also translated as truth. The first is used to speak of a person, like an honest and sincere person. The second is used to describe reality, the truth in terms of facts. The third is truth in terms of a correct statement, perhaps a grammatically correct statement that might be, in other respects, full of lies. As a Muslim, I do see sincerity, deep devotion and commitment in many people, be they Muslims, Christians, Jews, Buddhists, Hindus or something else. I am sure there are truthful and sincere people in all communities of faith. On the second level, the truth of reality and facts, I also see some truth and reality in other religious traditions. Islam talks about God's revelation that was given to all people. Since God is the Truth, then this true reality of God must be present among all human beings. On the third level, I do recognize that sometime we make grammatically correct statements and think that they are true but they are not true. However, we must continue our search for truth and sincerity among all people.

HUBBARD: Perhaps we could end this session on the theme of truth. I think we have all been enriched by the search for truth undertaken today and will never again be able to view the truth about our sister Abrahamic faiths in the same way as we used to.

CHAPTER FOUR

THE NATURE AND ROLE OF LAW
AND OF THE STATE IN EACH TRADITION

1. RELIGIOUS LAW IN THE THREE TRADITIONS

HUBBARD: In our fourth dialogue session, we'll consider the question of the nature and function of law in the three traditions. Dr. Gordis, will you explain the Jewish position, please.

GORDIS: Law, in Judaism, has played a very central role which has often been misunderstood—sometimes even distorted—in comparative religion discussions. It's misunderstood because it is viewed in isolation. Its centrality is pointed out, but not its relationship with other aspects of Jewish tradition. There is the distortion, for example, which suggests that Judaism is a religion of law and Christianity a religion of love. The best way to understand law in Judaism is to see it coming out of the interpretation of the Bible, Jewishly, with two strands of interpretation. These two, which are interrelated and intertwined, are *halakhah,* "the way one goes," the legal strand, and *aggadah,* the theological, ethical strand.

Thus, if one looks at a piece of law which superficially may appear to be technical in nature, one does not need to look very far behind to understand the ethical, spiritual or theological substructure. Those individuals, Jews or non-Jews, who would look at the law independently of that substructure risk distorting Judaism into a legalism.

On the other hand, those who look exclusively at the *aggadah*, the ethical and spiritual component, also engage in distortion because Judaism always reads from the general principle to the specific command of the tradition. Each of us, as a Jew, is commanded by our tradition to live life, worship God and relate to others in a certain way. That's why Judaism is not simply a set of generalized beliefs or feelings; but also a set of attitudes and commitments that are then translated into the discipline of practice. I'd welcome the chance to give a few illustrations of this intertwining, perhaps after the others get into the discussion.

HUBBARD: Alright, thank you. Dr. Grose, would you present your views.

GROSE: In Christianity, Gentile Christianity, the controversy set in at once between the church and the synagogue. Much of it had to do with the Pauline statements regarding the law—that it essentially was guidance until Christ came; and now its function is to convict us of our sins, but our hope and future is in the grace of God in Christ (Romans 3). So, as Luther described it, it's the law-or-grace issue. As one accepts Christ, one moves from the realm of law to the realm of grace.

That is pretty standard Pauline interpretation. I say "interpretation" because I'm not sure it's what the apostle really meant. A case could be made as follows for Paul in the way he handles the law-versus-grace issue: that the law is beneficial as a blessing for the Jewish people. As for the Gentiles outside the law, their only hope is Christ. To them the law is condemnation; but for the Jewish people the law has been, and is, beneficial. This is a line of thought taken up by some Christian authors.

Still, it remains in the general consciousness of Christians that the chief difference between Judaism and Christianity is that Judaism is a legalistic religion and Christianity a religion of grace. I don't see it that way. One of the ties that Christians have with Jews needs to be stated in this way: that Judaism is also a religion of grace. I will be specific. In the Mosaic covenant, the introduction to the Ten Commandments is a statement of grace: "I am the Lord your God who brought you out of the land of Egypt, out of the house of bondage. You shall have no other gods before me" (Exodus 20:2-3). That is, "I am the God of grace; therefore, hear me." "I am the God who gifted you with freedom in place of bondage, and I brought you out. Therefore, hear me when I give my commands."

GORDIS: I think it's only semantically true that Judaism is a religion of grace. For example, I don't view the phrase, "I am the Lord your God who brought you out of the land of Egypt" (Exodus 20:2), as a claim on the basis of grace. It's a claim by God as the God of liberation and, therefore, source of authority—a claim on the basis of authority and not, in my estimation, a claim of grace. The distinction between a religion of law and of grace has to do with the key to salvation in the two faiths. In Judaism, the key is essentially obedience to God's command. The deed, *mitzvah*, is what brings about and earns one a place in the world to come—in other words, salvation. That salvation is not contingent on an act of divine intervention; and, certainly, Judaism does not claim, as I think a pure religion of grace would, that the works of human beings are irrelevant to the process.

GROSE: I'm giving a Christian hermeneutic, you a Jewish one. From my perspective, where would the Israelites be without the gift of the commandments? That does not in any way alter the authority of Yahweh. But it's a dimension of Judaism I see, along with the fact that the future for the Jewish community is in obedience to the commandments. That future is salvation or a place in the world to come. I acknowledge, David, that this is inherent in Judaism. But what I've seen here is a light in the sky around the Mosaic experience. There's a Gift giver here who has the authority to bring this about. You had to have the gift at the outset so you could fulfill the commandments on the human side and thereby be in a positive relationship with your Maker.

GORDIS: This is true of the fundamental gift of life from God. Is that what a religion of grace means?

GROSE: I think the creation is, indeed, the supreme gift at the outset, though I have to qualify that matter as a Christian. Within this gift, the three Abrahamic communities understand their responsibilities and their God-given characteristics in different ways. In discovering grace in the Mosaic experience, I am acting as a Christian—taking my experience of what Paul means by grace and reflecting on it.

I would say, also, with similar perception, that Muhammad didn't earn his revelation. Certainly, he was already known as an honest man, an honorable man. But when he first received the revelation, he was minding his own business, so to speak. He didn't go out and say to God, "I want a revelation." Revelation came to him out of the blue (I'm talking in a vernacular way). I take that, also, as grace—grace for the Muslim community. I see this "gift-giving" as another element in the linkage between the three faiths, a vast area for further exploration.

The law, then, in terms of salvation and Christianity, functions to show us that we are in bad shape—law in the sense of the moral commands. And there is One who can deliver us from this "body of death," to use the Pauline phrase (Romans 7:24). To be translated into the kingdom of light, we still have to deal with what Paul calls the "old Adam" (1 Corinthians 15: 45-49). But we're also part of the new Adam, new humanity; and we're in a transition phase. The law is condemning us over here with the old Adam, and Christ is giving us life in the new Adam.

One of the problems with the fundamentalists is that they don't think they're in transition, they think they've made it. But notice what the Acts of the Apostles says about the day of Pentecost: " And the Lord added to their number day by day those who were being saved" (Acts 2:47). The whole thing hinges on the verb "being saved," being in the process. It is not something that was accomplished. When one makes it through the final judgment, then one is saved.

In the meantime, we can be thankful, as Christians, that we are on the path with Christ, the path He has opened for us. Herein is the grace question as compared to law—that Christians really have no right to say that they have Christ. They have the boldness by grace to say Christ has them.   It is a very important distinction. In contrast, the fundamentalists move over toward saying, "I have the Lord." That's dangerous stuff, and I don't think it's scriptural because we are *being* saved. "Being saved" is much more prevalent in the New Testament than "is saved."   So grace informs the pilgrimage toward ultimate salvation and we live in an environment of grace. It informs our relationship with our Maker, with our Savior and with all others. The law, then, is lived out by grace.

SIDDIQI: In Islam, law is spoken of really positively. In fact, it is a gift of God. It is an aspect of the divine grace that God has given us the law because He guides us in every aspect: in our spirits, our minds, our bodies; in our lives individually, as well as life in the family and the community. It is understood that *sharia*, divine law, is grace. Man cannot make a gracious law in a universal sense. Only God's law can be gracious for all. When God gives the law, it is good for all, because the law comes from the Compassionate One who knows everything. Since man isn't all-knowing, when he takes upon himself the authority to make the law, he harms himself—as well as others. So the law must come from God. The closer you are to the will of God, the better you are in your life, individually as well as collectively. There is no dichotomy made because the *sharia* is an aspect of the divine *ni'mah*, the divine grace. God is *El Hadi*, the guide.

The Qur'an (Surahs 2:35-39, 7:19-25) says that when Adam was put into Paradise, God told him he could eat where and when he wanted. But he wasn't supposed to approach a certain tree, although the name was not given. It wasn't the tree of knowledge, or an apple tree or any other tree; God just said don't eat the fruit of one tree. Then the devil came and tempted him and his wife, and they were asked to leave Paradise. But then God says, "When my guidance has come to you..." (Surah 2:38). So guidance was available to Adam in Paradise, but he did not fully believe in it. However, he finally realized that he truly needed guidance and must live by it to attain perfection. So God says, "If my guidance comes to you, whenever my guidance will come to you, whosoever will follow, there will be no fear for them, there will be no grief for them. But those who do not, they will go in hell fire, where they will live forever" (Surah 2:38-9).

The divine law is necessary for humans. The duty of the human being is to submit to this divine law, for Islam involves submission of one's whole being. In fact, the word "Islam" means giving every aspect of oneself to God, not holding back anything, putting oneself totally at God's disposal. In Islamic terminology *sharia* literally means the path to the source of water. Water is a source of life, so *sharia* is something that brings you life and takes you to its source. Another meaning of *sharia* is that it is a well-trodden path. It is not something invented, but has some kind of eternality in it. And it's not something imposed upon a person but something human nature itself recognizes as good. *Sharia* is related to *maruf* which is usually translated as virtue, but actually means something known to people throughout time as good.

Within human nature, there is some recognition of good as well as evil. God comes along and has to articulate and define this for us, so that virtue becomes established by the divine law. The law is not limited to one people but is for all peoples. In this sense, Islamic law is distinct from Judaic which is for one particular people. In Islam the law is for all mankind because it comes from the creator of the whole of mankind. Also, it establishes the universal values that are good for all people at all times.

GROSE: This has been an amazing chat on the subject of law. Although I yield to your wisdom on this subject, David, I think that the law in Judaism is also for all people. It is the fundamental wisdom for the human race, just as *sharia* is. Is my perception correct?

GORDIS: That's something I want to comment on. Law is such a vast and rich area that it could be broken down into lots of smaller questions relating to what both you and Muzammil have said. I thought I'd try to give a Jewish perspective on some of these. Let me talk about the origin and purpose of the law, its universality, its function in Judaism, its style and the question of authority. All these have been referred to and are somewhat connected. First, there's no question,

George, that you're right that the law is a gift to human beings. My only point is that there is a useful distinction between a faith that sees the role of salvation as dependent on the intervention of divine grace and a faith in which the works of human beings in response to commandments—which are God's gift—constitute the path of salvation. That, I think, is the core distinction between a religion of grace—Christianity—as opposed to one of law. Law exists in Christianity and grace exists in Christianity, and the same is true in Judaism and Islam. But their presence is not what's being argued.

SIDDIQI: The emphasis is the point. Muslims and Jews have emphasized the law while Christians emphasized grace.

GORDIS: Right. The question is, what is the purpose of the giving of the law in Judaism? Tradition tells us quite explicitly: *Lo nitnu mitzvot ela letzeref behemet ha briyot.* "The commandments were give only in order that man might be refined by them." (*Midrash Rabbah on Genesis*: 44,1). *Letzeref* is the operative verb and it has a double sense. Its fundamental meaning is to purify, refine, enhance. The law is the instrument of making people finer, better, nobler. But there is a secondary meaning of *letzeref* which is slightly homiletical but still very much etymologically correct: to bring people together. The two meanings in tandem provide a good idea of what the sense and the reason for the law is, Jewishly. It is a gift of God to the Jewish people, but—and George is right—beyond the Jewish people, with the purpose of refining and ennobling all people and bringing them together.

In Jewish tradition, there is a characteristic way of expression which conveys an idea by presenting what appear to be polar opposites, rather than by attempting a synthesis. Instead of asking, for example, "What is the truth—is God presented in the tradition as remote and untouchable or intimate and close?" In fact, the tradition contains both ideas because both have elements of truth. Likewise, the law is both particularly Jewish and universal. We have the principle of seven universal precepts, the Noachide commandments, which convey the fundamental principles of morality, behavior and civility and apply to all people—Jews and non-Jews.

The particularism in the tradition comes from a different notion: that, while the Torah was given by God, the authority to develop, interpret and apply the law—even to create the law anew—was given to human beings as well. And human beings are limited; no particular set of interpreters are qualified to know God's will in its entirety. Therefore, saying that particular expressions of law are Jewish suggests there are other interpretations which are binding on other people as long as the fundamental matters of morality are observed. These seven universal Noachide commands include the avoidance of cruelty to animals, the shedding of blood, idolatry, blasphemy, incest and stealing; and the establishment of courts of justice.[52]

SIDDIQI: Are you saying that other laws people follow are also divine?

GORDIS: Yes, they can be divine. People of other traditions who accept these broad Noachide principles have, for the Jewish tradition, a place in the world to come. They can acquire salvation. We do not have a doctrine of *Extra ecclesiam nulla salus est* ("Outside the Church there is no salvation,")[53] that you must be a part of the Jewish community to aspire to salvation. That's explicitly rejected.

SIDDIQI: So is it correct to say that it is the will of God for the Jewish people not to eat pork, but it is the will of God for other people to do so?

GORDIS: I would put it this way: a person of another faith is not expected to adhere to Jewish dietary laws.

SIDDIQI: You said this is a divine law, and the divine law is that it is God's will for the people to do something like keeping dietary laws...

GORDIS: I understand, but you have to let me formulate it in the way a Jew would. After all, the Bible itself gives permitted animals and prohibited animals.[54] Jews would prefer that people accept biblical injunctions.   Certainly the notion—which was not Jesus's but Paul's—that the law was to be abrogated,[55] is not something that Jews accept for themselves. However, observance of the Noachide laws does not include following the dietary laws except that one was not supposed to seize a limb from a living animal and eat it—that's cruel and morally offensive. But if a non-Jewish person adheres to the Noachide laws and does not obey the dietary laws, he or she can also be saved. The command to do something which is specifically and particularistically Jewish does not apply to the non-Jew.

The notion of particularity leads me to that of authority because yes, of course, God commanded the law.   However, even in Jewish tradition there are different ways of looking at that question. Unlike Islam, Judaism does not say that the law is completely divine and that any suggestion of a human role in making law is a departure from the divine. In Jewish tradition, the spelling out of the law through the process of *midrash*—and the application of law through the court—are separate human functions. As the Torah says, "It (the law) does not rest in heaven..." (Deuteronomy 30:12).

SIDDIQI: Islam also does not say that the law is completely divine. Human beings, too, have to make some laws and Islam gives them permission to do that. This is what Muslim jurists have been doing for the last fourteen hundred years and shall continue to do. I shall come to the point later about where and how and to what extent Islam allows human beings to make laws for themselves; but what I am talking about here is human autonomy, human beings' claim that they are totally autonomous. This is dangerous and this is arrogance. When a person thinks that I should live the way I want and make rules for myself according to my will and desire, and there is no force outside that should tell me what to do and how to behave, then the real problem comes. When human beings deny God the authority to tell them what to do, then the trouble begins.

GORDIS: Okay, it's not quite as polar to affirm the human dimension of law as it might be. In Judaism, it's not only not an offense, but it is affirmed. For example, you have the story that I shared in one of our earlier dialogues about the debate between Rabbi Joshua and Rabbi Eliezer ben Hyrcanus concerning the resolution of legal disputes (Babylonian Talmud, *Baba Mezia*, 59b). The moral of the story is that you don't pay attention to divine voices in making law. Instead, the authority to make and interpret law rests with human beings.

SIDDIQI: I think the point in your story seems to be that you have to take the text of the Torah seriously. This is the way I understand it, but I would like to hear your interpretation. In Islamic tradition, let me say, the rule is that you have the Qur'an and you have the *sunnah*, Prophet Muhammad's practice. Now if you want to make any law, you have to first look at these texts. You cannot introduce any ruling by ignoring the authoritative religious texts. If someone says, as some Sufi mystics used to, that he had a special vision, or he had a special inspiration and his inspiration told him that he can leave aside the rulings of the Sharia, then we shall say to that person, "No. The Law has come. It is with us and we cannot accept anything that contradicts the Law." This is the way Muslims also refused to accept some of the so-called *kasf* or *isharat*, the subjective experiences and visions of some Sufi mystics, when they contradicted the teachings of the Qur'an and Sunnah.

GORDIS: I wish I could tell you that, yes, Judaism and Islam agree on this, but it's not quite the case. There are substantive differences. For example, the principle of *lo bashamayim*, "not in heaven," is not that you have the text as it stands through divine inspiration. It's that the establishment of the law is now in the hands of human beings, human courts. This principle goes very far in the discussion of the law. For example, the Babylonian Talmud (*Gittin*, 32a) discusses a technicality of the law of divorce. The technicality is not important, but a principle is established. One authority asks, "Are you going to say that there is something in the Torah concerning which the Torah rules one way but because of an extraneous principle, *mipore tikkun olam*, `for the improvement of society,' you're going to go against the Torah?" And the answer is, "Yes," because the rabbis have the authority to do so.

SIDDIQI: Is this because that authority was given in the Torah, or they assumed it by their own will?

GORDIS: Yes. But, you see, it goes beyond the authority we could read about in the text. It even has the authority to negate the text. There are two poles of expression here; and the principle can't be reduced to an integrated, simple, declaratory sentence. Moses received the Torah on Mt. Sinai. On the one hand, we're told that everything that anyone is destined to say about a given text was already revealed to Moses on Sinai—every jot and tittle, every detail articulated by a faithful student was already received by Moses (Palestinian Talmud, *Pe'ah*, 13a). On the other hand, there's another midrash that talks about Moses on Sinai and says, "My God, he was up there for forty days, and we know from the Book of Job that the Torah is described as 'wider than the earth and deeper than the sea.' So how could Moses learn everything in forty days?" The reply is that, no, he didn't learn everything—only general principles.

SIDDIQI: This is an important point where there is a difference between Islam and Judaism. Rabbis probably took much more freedom in this matter, while Muslim *fuqaha'* (jurists) did not. This is also a classical charge of Islam on Judaism, that its rabbis made laws by themselves and then introduced them in the name of God.

GORDIS: Well, I don't know if they were doing so in the name of God; but there is no question that Judaism took very seriously the notion of a divine-human partnership. By the way, if you want to understand the tension between the law and instant access to the divine, then we ought to make reference to the mystical strain that exists in each of our traditions. Some of the philosophers were basically mystics in their approach.

One final observation on this point. Constantly reasserted in the tradition is that the authority for the legal process originated from Sinai, and that all that came after draws on the authority given to Moses on Sinai. The question always is: to what extent does one stress the divine authority more because one is aware of one's own human innovative character? When *halakhah* or legal interpretation is being created, one is trying to apply principles in new situations to reflect a new sensitivity. An example: the Torah says "...you shall give life for life, eye for eye, tooth for tooth, hand for hand, foot for foot..." (Exodus 21:23-4); but the legal system as a development from this says you don't do so. You don't take an eye for an eye or a hand for a hand. Financial compensation takes the place of the literal *lex talionis* or law of retaliation. The Bible dictates capital punishment, but in actual Jewish law this was legislated out of existence. So it will exist in theory but not in practice because the rabbis felt it was just not the way to punish. So the further they departed from the text, the more anxious they were to stress that what they were doing was based on divine authority.

SIDDIQI: Regarding human contributions to law in Islam, three points need to be understood. One of them is the role of the *yhihad* or independent reasoning on any matter where there is no text, neither in the Qur'an nor in the *Hadith* of the Prophet. Here scholars used reasoning, to arrive at what would be the will of God on a particular issue. Of course, they referred to the Qur'an and its value system, and the *Hadith*, and from there arrived at an answer.

The second point is that, in Islamic law, it is not simply that certain actions are either allowed or not allowed. Rather, Islam has divided things into five categories. Certain activities are obligatory, others are recommended, still others are prohibited. Then there are actions that are not recommended, and finally there are things that are left to a person's own decision and choice.

GORDIS: Permitted, but not recommended.

SIDDIQI: Yes, left to people's choice. This is the area in which legislators can work and make laws by finding out what is good for people; for example, whether they should allow driving at the age of 16 or 18 or 21, on the right or the left side of the road—thousands of examples can be given where people are supposed to make laws for themselves. The *Sharia* allows that; and these laws, once made, can be binding on the people when they agree to live in a particular society or state. This is because the choice is given to them and these matters are left to their own discretion. *Sharia* tells them, "Go ahead and make laws for yourself within this area, but make sure you do not cross the boundaries. Do not make permissible what God has prohibited and do not make prohibited what God has permitted.

The third area where the human element comes into law is that of public interest, which is called *maslaha*. The *Sharia* has given certain guidelines and parameters within which certain things that are not recommended may be allowed or certain things that are recommended may be disallowed in the best interest of the people. Here I can give you a recent example of organ donation. When a person is dead, in Islam it is not allowed to disturb the body of the dead. It should be buried with full respect and as soon as possible. But if someone's body organs can be used for another needy person, and due permissions are obtained from that person's will, then for the sake of *maslaha* it will be allowed to operate on his body in order to take the needed organ. Similar is the case with blood donation. Although consuming blood is not allowed in Islam, but for the *maslaha* or interest of a sick person, blood can be donated and received.

There is another area where one can even allow for oneself that which is prohibited for the sake of personal survival. Here, of course, one is not making a law, but is allowed to break the law to protect his or her own life. For example, eating pork or drinking alcohol is not allowed in Islam, but if one is going to die from hunger or thirst, then one is allowed to use these prohibited things just for survival. So we do have in Islam certain guidelines for making laws.

GROSE: Let me add a couple of things. First, the Apostle Paul did not declare for the abrogation of the law, as far as I know.

SIDDIQI: How about Jesus?

GROSE: No, Jesus certainly didn't. Neither of them declared for the abrogation of the law. Jesus declared that not one jot or tittle would change in the law until all was fulfilled (Matt. 5:17-18). What Jesus didn't accept was the rabbinic interpretations of the times. He kept breaking those left and right, including several understandings of the application of Sabbath laws. He healed on the Sabbath, for example (Mark 2:23-28, Luke 6:1-5). But as far as the Mosaic revelation, he said that doesn't budge.

Paul saw the law's function as convicting humanity of sin because we fall short of fulfilling what the law requires. It wasn't abrogation, so law continues in force in humanity; but its function is not the same. That's where Christianity differs from Judaism, as David so clearly explained. It doesn't have any saving power for Christians—it's a moral obligation and Christians will want to obey it because they love the Lord. It is still an obligation or commandment for the Christian community to follow the Mosaic law.

SIDDIQI: A commandment? Is it required of them?

GROSE: Yes. Jesus summarized the law in terms of love of God and of neighbor (Mark 12:28-34, Matthew 22:34-40, Luke 10: 25-8) and the rabbis made comparable summaries. It's a question of motivation. I remember visiting the Orange County mosque shortly after Muzammil's arrival to speak to the youth group. One of the group's leaders said, "If I don't obey the *Sharia* and all that God commands, I will go to hell." Then he asked, "Why do Christians want to do the right thing? Why do they follow God's law?" I answered, "Because of gratitude." I'm sure Muslims are grateful. Shall we talk about emphasis, in a way? It's a thanksgiving for the Christians to be moral. It's an expansion of the Christian central worship which is the Thanksgiving, the Eucharist,[56] the Lord's Supper.

GORDIS: Is that obedience to the Mosaic law?

GROSE: Yes, but not to all its later interpretations.

GORDIS: Well, how about Mosaic law as in the Torah?

GROSE: The Ten Commandments?

GORDIS: There's more in Mosaic law than the Ten Commandments.

GROSE: In Christianity, that's what it is. So it wouldn't include the other requirements of the Old Testament.

SIDDIQI: But George, you said that you recognize the whole Old Testament?

GROSE: Yes. This is interesting because in a way my view resembles the Islamic position on the Torah and the Gospel, since Islam affirms that part of the Gospel which conforms to the Qur'an. Christians don't follow everything in the Old Testament. The Church is selective, just as Islam is selective about affirming Torah and Gospel.

SIDDIQI: Islam is selective for a different reason. Islam is selective because it does not accept that the whole Torah and the Gospels as they exist now are authentic words of God. Islam is not selective because we accept whatever we desire to accept.

GROSE: Yes, so it is only a rough analogy. So we don't follow the ritual laws; Judaism doesn't either—there's no more temple. In part, Christians are selective about the Old Testament because Jesus is seen as the last high priest and himself the final sacrifice (Hebrews 7:23-28). We don't follow the food laws, so we're definitely selective.

GORDIS: This gets us back to Jerusalem, George.

GROSE: Okay. We're getting back there. But the Mosaic law, understood as the Ten Commandments, is in force in Christianity.

HUBBARD: But who makes a distinction between the Mosaic law understood as the Ten Commandments and the fact that it contains an immense amount of other material going way beyond the Ten Commandments?

GROSE: Give me an example.

HUBBARD: All the laws in Leviticus about clean and unclean foods—the fact that shell fish, pork and various kinds of wild animals are specifically prohibited (Leviticus 11, Deuteronomy 14).

GROSE: This is where I'm getting closer, I think, to what David was saying. Paul doesn't say, "Let's abrogate the law."   The effect of Pauline Christianity is that this part of Torah, concerning kosher and non-kosher food, is not binding on the Christians. We know there was a controversy between Peter and Paul about this. Peter, in one instance (Acts 10: 9-29), had a vision that everything—all kinds of animals, birds and reptiles— were good to eat. So then he started eating with Gentiles but was criticized by some of his fellow Christians. He replied that God told him everything He made is good, etc. This, in fact, is when Peter's mission to the Gentiles began. So there was, indeed, an abrogation of parts of Torah in the Christian community. But what has been maintained is the Ten Commandments. So the dietary laws are not binding on the Christian community.

GORDIS: Nor the entire religious calendar.

GROSE: You've raised a very significant issue, David. As Christianity began to spread among the Gentiles, and no longer the Jews, events in the life of Christ and the Church created a new calendar as part of defining a new people of God. The new Christian festivals included the birth of Christ (Christmas), his baptism, transfiguration, death (Good Friday), resurrection (Easter), and Pentecost—which replaced the Jewish feast of Weeks or *Shavuot*—when the Holy Spirit was bestowed on the Church. And the Christian day of worship is now the first day of the week because that's when Jesus's having risen from the dead was discovered.

Further, circumcision was not binding because it has no significance in Christianity, according to Paul. What mattered was a circumcision of the heart. Of course, Judaism would teach the same.

SIDDIQI: How is the heart circumcised?

GROSE: This is a metaphor for the action of God on the heart because of and through Christ.

GORDIS: It's in the Prophets?

GROSE: Yes, Jeremiah 31:33. That is, if you really belong to God, your heart has been marked. "Heart" is a metaphor for a person's essential being, the seat of emotion and will.

SIDDIQI: Explain in what way you metaphorically do that. Do you take a physical circumcision idea and say that now it's only acceptable metaphorically?

GROSE: No.

GORDIS: It's bypass surgery.

GROSE: It's bypass surgery. Very good! The circumcision is the sign that one belongs in God's covenant. That's how it began in Genesis (17:9-14). God commanded it as a sign of His covenant bond with Abraham and his descendants. The Christian perception is that Christians are covenant people through Christ, so that baptism takes the place of circumcision. So, in a way, baptism is a Christian circumcision.

SIDDIQI: Some Christians even leave that off, too.

GROSE: Some even leave that off and take an entirely spiritual view, such as the Quakers. So the circumcision of the heart is something like in Islam, where you do the ritual acts, all of them. You're always there when you should be and you pray all the prayers. But what about your heart? Is it inward? I believe this inward sincerity is called *inan* in Islamic Arabic. That's what the prophet Jeremiah meant, too, and this would fall into that category.

SIDDIQI: Do you mean that Jeremiah and other prophets said that you shouldn't offer sacrifice?

GROSE: No. They don't say you should not do it.

SIDDIQI: They say do it, but understand the meaning. Similarly, Islam teaches that you do the law, but do it with faith and inner meaning.

GROSE: Yes. Christianity was reaching into the Gentile world because Judaism already was identified as a circumcised people. So dropping circumcision partly involves the emerging of this new religion that is not going to be identified with the old religion or the prior religion.

GORDIS: Do you think the gentilization of Christianity and the repugnance of Gentiles to engage in circumcision are at all relevant to its propagation among Gentile Christians, as distinguished from Jewish Christians?

GROSE: Discontinuing circumcision may have been a factor in conversion. So you don't have to be circumcised to become a Christian, while to become a Jew you do. But, because Paul himself was circumcised, it was not an issue with him personally. He was looking at the mission of the Church and perceiving the Church as a new covenant people on new terms. But the terms of the covenant are now established by belonging to Christ. This bears on the law- grace question, that it's not a physical act which establishes your life in the community. Of course, you could raise the same question about baptism. Still, there is the point that's it's not by being outwardly circumcised that you become what you should be.

SIDDIQI: I'm sorry. If I understand Paul correctly, he saw the circumcision of the flesh as something very unnecessary, a burden for the people, not a gift from God. He taught that this was a special burden that was put upon the Jewish people. And why give this burden to someone else? So, in a sense, he had a very negative feeling about the Mosaic law.

GROSE: No, not about the law but about its function. He was attacking what he understood as "works righteousness," a term used in

Christianity. For example, a Christian might say about others, "Oh, they are `worksy.'" That is, they're working too hard at their religion and not relying on God's grace. So, to live by grace— which is what the Christian is expected to do—alters the equation. Circumcision, no circumcision—it doesn't matter. It's different, however, with the Christian basic Torah, the Ten Commandments. So with Paul, there is no break with the moral law as seen in the Ten Commandments. I think that is what Jesus was also affirming, although he didn't get into circumcision and some other matters. But the moral law as revealed to Moses is as much a part of Christianity as it is of Islam or Judaism.

However, the function of the law is different. From its prominence in Judaism with its dietary laws, etc., the Jew derives a place in the world to come and an awareness of obeying God. And it's much the same in Islam. The Christian's bond is different because his perception is that he cannot fulfill that bond, try as he may. One Christian insight is that if you break one commandment, you've broken them all. So even if somebody isn't outwardly doing something wrong but has coveted in his heart, it's the same as if he were stealing or murdering or committing adultery. So, in this kind of perception, everybody is a sinner, everybody needs the grace of God. Christians say it's found abundantly in Christ. So the law doesn't have the same function in Christianity, but it has the same God-given reality as law in Judaism.

GORDIS: I'd like to summarize what I've been trying to say in response to George's last statement. The law's function from the Jewish perspective—other Jewish scholars might differ, but I think this is a fair summary—is instrumental. Those who view law as ultimate are engaging in distortion. In other words, the mechanical fulfillment of the law as an ultimate end is not the Jewish idea. Rather, the law is an instrument for the enhancement of human beings and of the world.

That's why, for example, we have an almost identical parallel for situations which are not covered by precedent or text. Human beings—scholars—engage in the use of human reasoning, and analytical and moral discernment, to try to arrive at an understanding of what the law ought to be for those situations. That's why we have, in the legal system itself, categories for abrogating the law and changing it on the basis of such things as *tiqqun olam*, "making the world a better place." Or on the principle of "precluding hatred between peoples," or "for reasons of establishing peace and harmony," the law can be changed. All of this is a demonstration that the law is instrumental. If it becomes non-contributive and non-constructive to the enhancement of the world, an impediment to progress, then it needs to be changed. The way it is changed is through the divine-human partnership. Human beings are God's instrument for reasoning and for moral judgment. As they become increasingly sensitive and aware of standards of right and wrong, they have an obligation, Jewishly, to make certain the law reflects the best that is within them. That's not a declaration of autonomy, it's the way Jews perceive it.

SIDDIQI: Is this Orthodox belief?

GORDIS: There are some in all groups who would agree—David Hartman and Eliezer Berkovits, for example, are Orthodox scholars who write exactly in this direction.[57] It's a non-fundamentalist position but within a very centrist and authentic Jewish tradition. At the moment I'm claiming that it's mine, and I don't want to claim it's universal. But it's an established and quite authoritative position within Judaism. The bottom line is that to argue Judaism is legalistic, as distinguished from this kind of synthesis, is a distortion. The place of the law in Judaism is in the concretizing of principles and values through specific behavior expected of human beings.

Take, for example, the commandment, "Thou shalt not steal" (Exodus 20:15). That's wonderful. Everybody agrees one shouldn't steal. But unless you can translate that into the specifics of what it means to steal—or when the laws of stealing come into effect and what the penalties are for stealing—then preaching about "thou shalt not steal" is meaningless. Unless it's embedded in a language, in a discipline and a tradition which give substance to the command not to steal, it's likely to be lost.

It is similar with marriage. To see the marriage relationship only in terms of the formal rituals and ceremonies associated with it is to lose the sense of the relationship between husband and wife reflected in those formal foundations. To do so, robs that relationship of its content, its values and its magic. The *kethubah* or marriage contract has been criticized by some as archaic, irrelevant and legalistic; but this is an inadequate understanding. The *kethubah* simply says that when two people come together, if it's a genuine relationship, there are responsibilities which remain even when things get tough. That's why the relationship has to be reduced into law to protect both partners. So that the law, from the Jewish point of view, is not the whole picture but it is the concretizing and embodiment of the values and beliefs which guide human beings to make the world better.

The fundamental purpose of obedience to the law is not to earn someone a place in the world to come. Judaism has the notion of a world to come and salvation and messiah; but the stress is on doing the best one can in this world and leaving what will happen in the world to come basically to God. We really don't have access to know about what happens after death. That's for God to know and for us to pray for and aspire to. What we can know and do is try to make our lives better and the world better. One of the instruments we have for this is the law.

SIDDIQI: What caused Reform Judaism to renounce a number of laws?

GORDIS: Not only a number of laws. Reform Judaism rejected the authority of Jewish law down the line. Reform is a very dynamic movement, and I'm talking primarily about classical Reform. It said that Judaism, as it developed after the prophets, was essentially a product of external pressures on the Jews, and that much of what was created—especially the Talmud—was only important in its own time and place, and should not be viewed as authoritative. What really characterized Judaism, according to classical Reform, was the fundamental insight of ethical monotheism—God being beneficent, being one, and requiring adherence to ethical principles. What it amounted to, in the view of most historians, was a watering down of Judaism in the sense of adjusting and accommodating to a German-

Christian and an American-Christian environment while maintaining some appearance to Americans of Mosaic persuasion.

SIDDIQI: Was this a Christian influence in Reform Judaism?

GORDIS: A Christian and an assimilating influence. Reform itself has now moved far away from those nineteenth- and early twentieth-century traditions, includes a great deal of Hebrew in its worship and is very Israel-oriented. The Reform movement includes very extensive observance of Jewish law, a category that is no longer anathema. There are now those in the movement who debate questions of Jewish law and a whole literature of "Reform responsa" (responses to questions about the interpretation of Jewish law) by such people as Solomon Freehof, a Reform legal scholar, and Walker Jacob.[58] So Reform, after its initial antinomian phase, has moved very far back into an engagement with Jewish law, although it has not yet accepted the law's authority.

SIDDIQI: Islamic law is also going through a considerable discussion among Muslims. There are liberal voices coming from Muslims, some of them deeply influenced by Western thought. They are calling for changes and reform in the *Sharia* laws related to family. Some of them are asking for a complete ban on polygamy or restrictions on its practice by creating difficult procedures for receiving a license for an additional marriage. In some countries one has to convince the judge why he has to have another wife. Divorce laws are also under discussion. Here again, some people are suggesting more involvement of civil courts. Similarly, there are suggestions of reinterpretation of the Qur'anic laws of inheritance by giving more share to women than what they believe the *Sharia* has given.

Some criminal laws of the *Sharia*, such as the stoning to death of adulterers, cutting off the hands of thieves and capital punishment for homicide, are being criticized by some Muslims and many non-Muslims. Also, there are new economic issues—banking, interest, insurance, etc.—and such bio-ethical issues as test tube babies, surrogate motherhood and organ transplants. So law is a very living and lively subject in the Islamic community. I'm pleased that these discussions are going on. Whatever their outcome, I hope every one will keep in mind the ultimate objective of the *Sharia*: the establishment of justice and felicity for humankind. There is no good in a law that cannot bring justice to all people.

George, would you at this point add something on Christian perspective, and especially on Catholic tradition and its approach to Canon law.

GROSE: I've been dealing only with the New Testament period. I will do what you've requested, Muzammil, but first I need to get more perspective here.   I said that Christians maintain the Ten Commandments as part of their faith and spiritual obligation. But they've done what you have both described—made adaptations that are still in the spirit of the law.   Christians made a huge adaptation in replacing the Jewish Sabbath with the Lord's Day. They still see it as a commandment to observe one day out of seven. There used to be "Sabbath Laws" in the United States—nothing was open on Sundays, that kind of thing.

GORDIS: Or "blue laws."

GROSE: Yes. Sunday is called the Lord's Day because it's when Jesus rose from the dead. In that sense, every time you go to church on Sunday, you're celebrating Easter, the resurrection.   The early Jewish Christians observed both: on the Sabbath they went to the temple to pray; then they worshipped on the Lord's Day. (Acts 2:46.) But Gentile Christianity dropped that quickly and went on with the Lord's Day.

Another observation: Christians are almost oblivious to or ignorant of the whole body of Judaism. They know the Jews only as people of the Old Testament. Judaism is not taught in the Church, not preached about or discussed. Christians do the same with Islam; but they know Islam is different, has a different holy book, etc.   They think they know about the Jews because they have the Old Testament. This is a widespread mistake, and even most Christian seminaries don't teach

Judaism.

GORDIS: They don't teach Judaism past the birth of Jesus. It's only taught as a prelude to Christianity.

GROSE: Exactly. Seminaries may teach intertestamental writings (such as the Apocrypha, Pseudepigrapha and Dead Sea Scrolls) preparatory or related to the Christ event, but not Judaism itself. David, when would you say Judaism began—about 200 B.C.E.?[59]

GORDIS: The rabbinic movement began then. The systematic editing of the Hebrew Bible was probably completed in the fifth century B.C.E. with Ezra and Nehemiah. Then comes the beginning of the rabbinic period, and we know the Bible was being interpreted by rabbinic scholars in the third century B.C.E. Some of this interpretation is reflected in the Septuagint or Greek translation of the Bible. The Bible itself was canonized around the first century C.E.

GROSE: By this time there's no longer the temple, which was destroyed by the Romans in 70 C.E. Authority moves to the rabbinate and they guide the congregations throughout the Jewish world. So that's rabbinic Judaism.

GORDIS: Pharisaic Judaism.

GROSE: That period was formative for Judaism along with the biblical period; both formative, not one above the other. But Christians have obscure notions of the period based on the New Testament—a period that included the completion of the Hebrew Scriptures, and the growth of congregational life and Pharisaic Judaism. And Jesus, in many ways, was of the Pharisees. Nevertheless, the whole history of the Jewish people after the coming of Jesus is seen as an anomaly, something out of its proper time.

I remember when I first became aware of my own ignorance of the Talmud. I had a Jewish colleague who kept talking about the Noachide law which I'd never heard of. I looked in the Bible, and Noah hasn't got any law; but my colleague talked about it as if it were in scripture. Then I learned that, indeed, the Talmud—where the Noachide laws are spelled out—has quasi-canonical authority. A Jew must utilize Talmud along with the Bible. A Jewish lay person does this, as well as a scholar or rabbi.

I cannot speak with authority on Catholic canon law; but, when Christianity became the official religion of the empire, Church law developed and, with it, the Roman law which the Church inherited. So we have Roman law informed by Church law, a situation that goes on throughout the Medieval period on the European continent. Today, in the United States, Canon law applies to the Catholic Church. It doesn't apply to the Presbyterians or Baptists, since every church has its laws.

Interestingly, the Presbyterian Church, in its own governance, is like our federal government. That is, we have a legislative body, the General Assembly; judicial body, the permanent Judicial Commission; an executive branch, the Moderator and the Stated Clerk. So it's quite clear that there are historical antecedents in Calvinism to the American form of government. The founding fathers, the religious ones, believed that, in this way, they could approximate the will of God on a given issue for the country. This was behind, in part, the bicameral legislature. While the House members represented the country by population, the states were to have two senators irrespective of their population. The theory behind the Senate is that its members are not supposed, necessarily, to respond to the electorate in making decisions, but to try to ascertain, according to their own insights and conscience, what is the will of God on a given issue. Now, that's how the country got started, the original design.

2. THE CHURCH-STATE QUESTION

HUBBARD: George, what you've said provides a segue to our second topic on church-state separation or, conversely, whether religion and state ought to be yoked. Let's go back for a moment. Before the Reformation, there was simply Christendom in Europe, which had Church Canon law plus civil law; but they worked together. This varied to some extent from country to country, but religious and civil law were certainly entwined. Then the Reformation comes along and the Church's absolute religious power is broken, leading the way to the Enlightenment and the whole notion of church-state separation in the United States, France and elsewhere.

I'd like to move from there to the situation in the Muslim world. Muzammil, it seems that, in some ways, the Muslim world reflects the yoking of church—mosque, actually—and state. In Iran, for example, the Qur'an is enshrined as the official arbiter of civil law. Do Muslim scholars think the model of mosque-state affiliation is superior to the American model of church-state separation, or can one even speak in an either-or way?

SIDDIQI: First of all, from the coming of the Colonial Period to the Islamic world in about 1800—with Napoleon's presence in Egypt—and up to the 1950s, most of the Muslim countries had separation between religion and the secular law of the state. Civil law was much more Western law, whether British, French or whatever. So in many Muslim countries, the governments were not operating as universal laws under the *Sharia* but under British law. The situation has basically remained the same in the Muslim world with most countries having a dual legal system in practice. On the personal level, Islamic laws are in force and in most countries there are *Sharia* courts that handle these issues. Some countries also apply *hudud*, that is, the criminal laws of Islam, to a certain degree. So they would punish the adulterers, lash those who are found consuming alcoholic beverages or cut off the hands of those who are convicted of stealing.

But the whole legal system of these states, their economic system, political system, educational system are not Islamic. There is no caliph ruling these states. Rulers are, generally, not elected by free elections; they are either hereditary rulers or they come to power through military coups. Many rulers consider the public funds as their personal property and use them as they wish. People have very little to say on who runs the government and how. Muslim countries are divided on ethnic, racial, tribal, linguistic and nationalistic lines. These are not the principals of an Islamic state. So I would say that there is a de facto separation of religion and state in the Muslim world.

Compared with this state of affairs, of course, the American model is by far superior. Here government is democratic. People are free to choose and dismiss their representatives. Religions are also free to preach and practice. The government does not interfere in people's religion, although religious people are free to express their opinions on political issues. In the Muslim countries today, governments are quite free to interfere in religious matters, but religious people are not allowed to criticize political leaders and governmental authorities.

The second part of your question is whether Muslims should think of separation of church and state and adopt it as a model for their governments. I do not think that can be done because Islam has its own political system which guarantees the religious freedom of all people without separating the religion from the state. On the issue of religious freedom, I believe there is need for more *ijtihad*, that is, further elaboration and refinement by Muslim jurists. However, as you know, even in Western societies the separation of church and state did not come until Western humanism succeeded in secularizing these societies. In Medieval Europe, society was not secular, so the Church was involved in state affairs. In order to secularize a society, you have to privatize its religion. You have to say that religion is a private matter and it is something that a person does with his solitude, between him or her and God. A state should have its own rules and should function on those principles without any reference to God or a higher authority.

But Islamic law is comprehensive and covers all aspects of life. It deals with economy, politics, education, international relations, etc. How can one privatize this religion without reducing it considerably? Muslim societies have refused to become secular in spite of all the attempts and pressures from inside and outside during the past two centuries. People do not consider religion as a private matter. So how can one establish a secular state among Muslims?

HUBBARD: I'd like to make a distinction between a secular state and a pluralistically religious state. That is, there are many countries—for example, India, the United States and Canada—where different religions compete quite sincerely. There may be secular humanism there as well, as in this country, but the U.S. has many sincere believers—Buddhists, Christians, Muslims, Jews, and others. Now even if, in the United States or India, every individual in these countries were avowedly religious in some manner, there couldn't be a religious state in the way you envision, Muzammil. There would have to be some kind of church-state separation so that these religiously diverse people could compete equally and be protected. There's a difference between a merely secular state and a religiously pluralistic one. Does that distinction make sense to you?

SIDDIQI: Yes. I understand the distinction and I see that pluralism is working quite well in the United States. But it is working because people have agreed to privatize their religion. When the question of public policy comes up, people do not do what their religion teaches and they keep their religious values to themselves, their families and their churches. For example, should Catholic senators and representatives sponsor a bill allowing abortion? Their religion says "no," but in their role as public officials they have to say "yes" and keep their religion to their private convictions. So there is a conflict. Suppose there is a Muslim sitting in a public office making laws for a state contrary to the laws of Islam, such as legitimizing homosexuality. What should he do otherwise?

So there seems to be two options: one is what the secular countries have accepted. That is, make everyone's religion a private matter. Thus all people will be equal. Mind you, here, too, there is no absolute equality, because the majority often prevails. Their religious customs and traditions receive much more prominence than those of the minorities. So some people become more equal than others.

The other option is to see how the religious values can be implemented in a society, how to accommodate the variety and multiplicity of religious principles and expressions, so that I can say that I am Muslim, privately and publicly, and you, David, can say that you are a Jew, privately and publicly, and George can say that he is a Christian, privately and publicly. It is not easy to accomplish that. Muslims are struggling with this idea in Muslim countries: how to have a modern Islamic state with Islamic religious values without diminishing the freedom and dignity of non-Muslims living in that state. Muslims, however, have not accepted the idea of the secularization and privatization of religion on a theoretical level, although—as I told you—on the practical level they are doing the same thing more or less. There is only one Muslim country that accepted secularism, both in theory and practice, Turkey; but even there, this experiment did not succeed, because the people in general were not ready for it.

GROSE: Iran also attempted this and it failed.

SIDDIQI: Yes. During the time of the Shah it was tried. It did not work there because people refused to privatize their religion.

GORDIS: May I jump in at this point? I think the question you've posed, Ben, is a fruitful one. We Jews have experienced many different political situations. One was that of being a small minority, marginal to a homogeneous society, in a country which was predominantly Muslim or Catholic. The situation of a diverse society argues for the principle of pluralism; and, in that sense, the United States is historically unique. Jews have also lived in a secularized society, such as post-Emancipation France where, after 1791, they were granted full civil rights. And you have the experience of Jews living in a sovereign Jewish state today. Each of these presents its own issues.

To focus now on the nature of the American experience, it's neither that which says religion should be privatized, with the public domain staying secular; nor is it a society in which the religious law and practice of any one group should prevail. It can't be that because which group would you choose? And it chooses not to be that because it feels that religion, generally, and government, are enhanced because religious rule does not prevail. But there is a third possibility: that I participate in public life as a Jew and as an American; that you, Muzammil, participate in public discussion as a Muslim and as an American; and George as a Christian. We are concerned to shape the society out of the totality of our experience. It includes our Jewishness, or our Islamic character, but also our participation as Americans in general. When we look at an issue—abortion or capital punishment or governmental spending priorities (for example, national defense versus feeding the hungry or building homes for the homeless)—we bring into perspective quite explicitly those things which come out of our tradition. I can speak as a Jew, just as I can speak as a student of Western philosophy and as a child of the American democratic tradition. I bring these sources together and synthesize my position.

However, when I talk to another committed Jew, and I assume as a Muslim talks to another committed Muslim or a Catholic talks to another Catholic, we talk differently—though not to mislead—from the way we talk to someone of another faith or from the way we talk in a political forum. Because when a Catholic talks to a Catholic about abortion, it is perfectly proper for that Catholic to say to the other Catholic that abortion is sin, since killing a fetus is murder; and the Pope has said that abortion is murder and must not be tolerated. It's even legitimate, I think, for that Catholic to come into a public forum in the United States and say, "I am a Catholic and I believe that abortion is murder, it's criminal, and therefore my conscience does not permit me to support it."

However, in presenting this position, it's not satisfactory for that Catholic to say you should accept the position because the Pope or Catholic teaching says it's murder. The Catholic cannot argue for the position out of an appeal to an authority which is not generally accepted. He or she has to argue the position in ways which are open to discussion, disagreement and refutation. In other words, positions stemming from the viewpoint of one of our religious traditions should be introduced into the public market place of ideas, but the form and the language in which they are presented must involve a translation into the give-and-take approach required in a diverse society.

SIDDIQI: That's understood. A market place of ideas. But we're talking about specific laws.

GORDIS: I'm talking about abortion.

SIDDIQI: Whose laws are they going to pass?

GORDIS: Abortion law has to be shaped by the society.

SIDDIQI: You cannot have both. Abortion is either allowed or it is not allowed.

GORDIS: But who is going to decide that? The American electorate through the representative, political, legislative processes.

SIDDIQI: The majority, then.

GORDIS: Yes, the majority; and in the way our process works minority interests are protected as well. For example, members of the House of Representatives are elected on a proportional basis from each state while senators are not. I'm saying that the process by which laws are enacted is enriched because we hear from Catholics on their position. They may try to persuade non-Catholics to their view, but they can't do so by simply stating the Pope's position. They may try to convince me that, in fact, fetuscide is murder. And I might reply, "Well, abortion may be an evil, but it's not murder. Let's talk about it, be influenced, and then let's shape the society." All of this means that their Catholicism and my Judaism don't have to be left at home. However, my participation is not based on the assumption that we come together only to see who is more powerful and whose position will prevail.

Is this give-and-take, pluralist society elegant? No. Is it satisfactory to everyone? Not really, because everyone understands that on certain issues we may prevail and on many others we may not, especially in the case of smaller religious groups. I would argue that our system of church-state separation is a noble experiment, and it's different either from the privatization of religion or from secularization. We are one of the most religious societies in the world today, far more religious than societies which have an established religion. That's what makes America unique. To draw a parallel, there is a debate in Israel between those who affirm religion and those who reject it. The latter group would argue that the same church-state separation pattern should prevail there. Others argue, "No, this is the one little place where Jews can live as Jews, which means under Jewish rule and law. There are plenty of other places where pluralism can prevail."

SIDDIQI: The question now is, who is a Jew?

GORDIS: Who is a Jew, and who is a rabbi, and who is an authority? That's why you have the ironic situation today in the Arab-Israeli peace talks that one member of the Palestinian delegation is a fringe Orthodox rabbi belonging to the *Neturei Karta*. That's a sect in Jerusalem which rejects the notion of Jewish sovereignty and favors a Palestinian state. These people feel that establishing a Jewish state before you actually have Jewish rule means forcing what really must come through ultimate or divine salvation when Jewish sovereignty is genuinely established. Since the present State of Israel is one which has opted for a pluralist model, the situation is just as you described earlier, Muzammil. You have a Jewish court, a Muslim court, a Christian court; and marriage, divorce and personal status are left to the religious groups. But the government of the state, even though there is some impact from Jewish law, is secular law and draws on British, Turkish and common law.

This rabbi doesn't want that—for him, it's an outrage. Therefore, he would rather put himself in a very uncomfortable situation and be part of the Palestinian team. He and his little group did, in fact, commit treason against the state by acting as informers to what, from the Israeli point of view, was the enemy during Israel's 1948 War of Independence. This cost a lot of Jewish lives. Yet the State of Israel, ironically, supports them.

In the United States, Jews have historically supported pluralism because they felt most secure under it and also felt that a diverse country works best when it's pluralistic. This noble experiment may not be the best way for a homogeneous society—for a country that is 100 per cent Muslim or Christian—that opts to rule itself in a Christian or Islamic fashion. Not every society has to be pluralistic, and there isn't one form which is ideal for everyone.

GROSE: You two have given very fine expressions of the church-state problem and you, David, of this noble or elegant experiment in religious freedom. It's an experiment I hope will last, a real contribution to the world.

I think also about the four of us working on this dialogue. I don't claim to have the truth. I do claim that the truth has reached me, but for me to have or control the truth is quite a different story.

SIDDIQI: You know the truth has reached you?

GROSE: That's right. I know who I am. I'm a Christian because I was reached by that truth. I've no doubt whatsoever about that— no anxiety, no reservations, no uncertainties. But I don't have the whole truth about salvation. I have offered, as has each of you, the truth I possess so that, in the interplay, we have a shared trust. We are not worried about the truth and are confident the truth will out. That's part of the perception, too, in a democratic society. We are confident that, somehow, God is leading this country. That doesn't mean we do everything right, but He overcomes what we do wrong. This, I think, is a very biblical-Qur'anic point of view: that God is working to get His will done in spite of us—or with us, as the case might be. We can either be with Him or against Him or sitting on the fence. But whatever, He will get it done.

To have truth imposed through the government on the society at large is another question. That means that truth must be defined, and each religious community defines it. But one definition doesn't match another so the controlling group, whoever they are, dominates the others in any kind of theocracy. Islam has faced up to this in a way the West hasn't through the "Covenant of 'Umar" that defines the status of minorities.[60] In the West, we never got around to defining the status of minorities. In that sense, in that way, Islam did a better job.

HUBBARD: Are you referring to the *dhimmi*, the minority monotheists of other faiths whom the Muslim majority protected?

GROSE: Yes.

GORDIS: When you say "a better job," would you prefer that the Christian majority in the United States define the role of the minority? Do you think that's desirable?

GROSE: No, I don't. But I'm talking about the period of medieval Christendom when Christianity was the official religion and religious minorities had no rights.

SIDDIQI: I agree that, historically speaking, Islam did much better in dealing with its minorities than Christendom did with non-Christians. Under Islamic rule, Christians and Jews were not equal but they were protected legally and had their own status.

GORDIS: My sense is the situation in the United States is so remarkable because, despite the large Christian majority, the founding fathers refused to think in terms of majority-minority and to make the minorities subservient.

SIDDIQI: I accept that and I agree with you that religious minorities have done quite well in the United States, but there were other types of minorities that did not do so well. I refer to the problem of race and color in the United States.

GORDIS: Yes, but these were the exceptions that proved the rule and represented a retreat, rather than an advance.

GROSE: We have a mixed system in America: along with Calvinism there were a large number of rationalist or Enlightenment thinkers in the period when the Constitution was adopted. John Locke, the major theoretician behind it, was a skeptic on religious matters; and he wasn't alone.

GORDIS: True, but remarkably even the large number of founding figures who were strongly committed Christians refused to place into the language of the founding documents the notion of a Christian country. In my view, that is what is divine about these documents.

3. RELIGION AND RACISM

SIDDIQI: Can we talk a bit more about the experience of Blacks in the United States?

GORDIS: We've had plenty of racism. I'm only talking now about a limited issue.

SIDDIQI: I think racism occurred because religion was not central. Even though the slave owners said they were Christian, actually religion didn't play a prominent role—race did.

GORDIS: Let me even go farther. I think the disaster of the Blacks in this country took place because religion sanctioned it. The interpretation of scriptural passages which talk about a slave caste and ownership of one person by another, when viewed as immutable, became a warrant for preservation of the institution of slavery. Had religious interpretation moved to the point where slavery was rejected—as interpretation did, for example, in Judaism—things might have been different. But Judaism didn't prevail.

SIDDIQI: Judaism said you could not have a Jew as a slave, but you could have a non-Jew (Leviticus 25:39-46).

GORDIS: Yes, technically, that's the case. But generally that never was operative. Jews never owned non-Jewish slaves.

SIDDIQI: What about the United States? Jews never had slaves?

GORDIS: They did, as did Christians and Muslims. I'm not talking about that, but about when Jewish law prevailed. Let me not lose my train of thought here. In the rabbinic tradition you have a statement: *Ki li b'nei Yisrael avadim, velo avadim leavadim*, "God says slavery is abhorrent because human beings should be My slaves." (Babylonian Talmud, *Kiddushin*, 226). So people should be slaves of God, not slaves of other slaves. But that was not what happened. Because the Hebrew Bible allows for slavery, sermons from the colonial period in

America defend slavery by quoting scripture. So religion became a co-conspirator, along with racism, that allowed the practice to go on.

GROSE: These biblical quotes came from both the Old Testament and the New.[61]

GORDIS: Right. I would even say that the outrage committed against Native Americans was also given biblical sanction through the mentality of the conquest of the land. You came and you conquered, just as the Israelites conquered Canaan. This was not true religion but a distortion, an abuse.

GROSE: There was a book, in fact, entitled *The Almost Chosen People* which intimated that Americans were something like the chosen people. If this is the case, Americans are entitled to the promised land. Others, such as Native Americans, better take note and surrender.

GORDIS: This shows how pernicious is the notion that any group of people—if it's a majority or not doesn't matter—views itself as the chosen, the elite, the bearer of the truth and takes upon itself the right to judge the humanness, the rights, the status of any other group. When this happens, what you're asking for is bloodshed and suppression.

SIDDIQI: Maybe we should have a discussion sometime on the chosen people.

GORDIS: Yes.

GROSE: Absolutely.

HUBBARD: George, why don't you finish?

GROSE: I would go in the direction of the present discussion. I've spoken of what I'm convinced is a very positive contribution of Calvinism to American society, the separation of powers in the Constitution. It's kept us out of a lot of difficulties for all its unevenness of operation. But, at the same time, the Calvinists brought in strongly the doctrine of election. Who are the elect people? The

European Christians who came here to establish the first settlements. So the Native Americans or the African Americans or whoever else may come, don't participate in this election. This is still affecting the thinking of some Americans.

GORDIS: I'd like to make a radical proposal on the chosen people doctrine: get rid of it. No matter how it was originally intended, it's been pernicious and destructive, and continues to be so. If we all got rid of the notion that we have claims to the truth, that we are the elect—which means everybody else is somewhere beneath us in some sense—then religion could bring people together and suggest the commonalities we have.

HUBBARD: I wish more of us were God-choosing people, rather than people who thought they were God-chosen.

GROSE: Let me finish by saying I find no way to abandon the biblical doctrine of election or chosenness. Granted, it is a mystery; but I find it throughout the Hebrew Bible and New Testament. I even find it resonating in the Qur'an as God brings to Paradise those whom He will. Speaking as a Calvinist, I see election associated with the sovereignty of God. Those Christians of free will persuasion may come at this differently and agree with you, David, but I would refer to the Heidelberg Catechism which begins as follows: "What is your only comfort in life and in death? That I belong—body and soul, in life and in death—not to myself but to my faithful Savior, Jesus Christ."

Finally, Christian theologians—Augustine, Wycliffe, Luther, Zwingli and Calvin—have taught there is a visible and an invisible Church. The invisible or true Church is known only to God. The visible one contains both reprobate and elect—the "wheat and the tares," as Jesus said. Since the true Church is invisible, some Christians may find themselves on the outside and, mysteriously, some Jews and Muslims on the inside. I believe this teaching should be more widely known.

HUBBARD: We need to conclude this session, though David and Muzammil may want to return to your final comment later, George.

CHAPTER FIVE

THE MEANING OF PEOPLEHOOD IN EACH TRADITION AND ITS RELATIONSHIP TO CONTEMPORARY ISSUES

1. PEOPLEHOOD IN THE THREE FAITHS

HUBBARD: I'd like to ask each of you to state concisely what it means to be a member of the people: the Jewish people, the Christian people, the Muslim people. Dr. Gordis, will you start us off, please.

GORDIS: There's no word which can describe this peculiar group that constitutes Jews other than "people." Sociologists and social historians have tried to characterize it according to one of the usual formulations: religious group, national group, ethnic group—none of them works. So it's almost by default that one uses the term "people." It's because, beyond the religious ties that bind them together—beyond common aspirations, history, language, culture, land— there is something greater than any of those parts which holds them together. That's why the unnatural state Jews lived in for two millennia—scattered, removed from their land—has not caused their disappearance, unlike many other peoples.

To be brief, there's a trinitarian formulation in Judaism which comes out of Jewish mystical literature, from the *Zohar*[62] that is very widely quoted: "The Holy One, blessed be He, Israel (meaning the Jewish people) and Torah are one." This grouping is a unity. "Torah" means the entire body of tradition: legal, ethical, historical, philosophical and ideological. The spiritual dimension comes from the sense of a special relationship to the Divine. And the people itself function in time to use the instrument of Torah to realize the divine plan. All three represent a single whole, a single continuum. That's really what peoplehood means to Jews.

In the contemporary Jewish community, the term "people" has come to suggest that Jews connect to Jewishness in a variety of different ways. A substantial number of Jews connects through the religious tradition, but there are many Jews who do so through one of the other dimensions of Jewish peoplehood: through the Jewish communal experience, through the land of Israel, through the sense of moral obligation that leads one to support and sustain the community without reference to theology. So, in one sense, the notion of people synthesizes the various dimensions of being Jewish. In another sense, it's a descriptive term which suggests there are multiple dimensions to Jewishness. An individual Jew may be characterized as part of the Jewish people by referring to one or a few of these dimensions without choosing to enter into all of them.

HUBBARD: Very concise. Thank you. Dr. Grose, turning to Christianity, what are your thoughts?

GROSE: In the early days what emerged was an intense fellowship. It was said about the Christians, "See how they love one another." This spirit was described by the Greek term *koinonia*, fellowship. In the formation of the Church on Pentecost day when 3,000 people were gathered in, this was said of them: "They devoted themselves to the apostles' teaching and fellowship, to the breaking of the bread (Holy Communion) and the prayers" (Acts 2:42). If Holy Communion is seen as the center of Christian worship, it is an act of fellowship. It's where the divine reaches out to the people and the people to the divine. Then you see, we've got a community really built on the Holy Supper which was initiated by Jesus.

In his letters, the Apostle Paul regularly addresses the churches he founded: "to the saints of Philippi," "to the saints of Colossi," and so on. In later Christianity, "saints" became a separate class within Christianity, but not at the outset. All Christians were saints, that is, those set aside for God's purposes, as if they were all ordained. They all belonged to God through Christ; therefore, that's what it means to be holy. It was an imputed holiness: we are good because of the goodness of God toward us, not because of an intrinsic good.

On a contemporary note, during World War II Dietrich Bonhoeffer was a major figure in Christian thought and a Christian martyr.[63] His book *Life Together*[64] describes two types of community, one "spiritual," the other "psychic." "Spiritual" is clear enough, referring to the Christian community; but what about "psychic"? In the community at large, what he calls the psychic community, everybody relates to one another in one fashion or another, usually, he thinks, by exploitation—"You scratch my back, I'll scratch yours,"—which is so characteristic of political life. By contrast, the spiritual community is a fellowship in which people sacrifice for each other and care about each other more than themselves. He then describes something very important: in the psychic community, the world, people relate directly; in the spiritual community, they relate through Christ. Now, that's not indirect, but it's not direct. It is through Christ that we know one another, respond and love one another, care about one another, work with each other, and so on. So Bonhoeffer has defined in modern times what it is to be in Christian community.

In a more historical sense, we have the phenomenon of Christendom, a religious type of political reality, with remnants in Catholicism to some extent or any place where there's an established church. Here there was no separation of church and state. Christendom can be roughly tracked from Constantine to the present day in its remnant forms. Constantine legalized Christianity in 313 and his successor Theodosius made it the official religion of the empire in 392.

In some ways, to me, Christendom is analogous to Islam which, as a total life experience of the community, doesn't have an analog in the

West at the present time. Western religious groups are separate from governmental groups in our pluralistic society. Christendom was pervasive—everybody was a Christian. In the feudal system, for example, all the serfs and other people who belonged to the lord of the area were baptized. To be a living person in that area was to be a Christian and to be baptized. This type of community—where every village, town and region was Christian—is not the same as how the Church began with its intense fellowship of mutual devotion and caring. Before the Reformation, within the period of Christendom, we see this in the monastic movement with its devoted fellowship. Francis of Assisi is a marvelous example of what was going on in the monastic movement by way of an intense, loving community, a recapturing of the original experience of the Christian faith in the "see how they love one another" mode.

HUBBARD: When does the period of Christendom end, as you see it?

GROSE: It hasn't ended, because we have these remnant phenomena. Wherever the Church is sponsored by the government, Christendom still exists. So long as the Catholic Church has those hundred or so acres of Vatican City, that's Christendom. If they give up that property, then perhaps Christendom is over and we're in a post-Christendom period. Also, so long as the British monarchy has anything to do with the installation of the Archbishop of Canterbury, we have the remnants of Christendom.

With the Reformation, the rediscovery of this community life again emerged in a Protestant form. All branches of the Reformation—Anabaptist, Lutheran and Calvinist—had dimensions of this rediscovery of *koinonia.* One group that had a profound effect on western Christianity was the Moravians from whom we get the term "pietistic." These Czech and German Christians had a powerful sense of caring about each other and a highly developed life of prayer.

From this group John Wesley, the founder of Methodism, got some of his spiritual life. Wesley, newly ordained in the Church of England,

was sent to Georgia as a missionary (1735-37). The voyage back to
England was marked by a terrific storm at sea. Most of the passengers
were terrified, except for the Moravian missionaries, who prayed and
sang hymns throughout the storm. All of this affected Wesley with the
sense of the intensity of the *koinonia* and contributed to the growth
experience of Methodism and the Methodist Church. So I see
Christianity in terms of peoplehood in two ways: one is the real thing,
when there is the fellowship of mutual caring and the response of
God's love in this caring. The other is more objective as a political or
regional entity which is normally called Christendom.

HUBBARD: Thank you. Dr. Siddiqi, may we have your thoughts on
peoplehood?

SIDDIQI: In Islam, there is more a concept of community than
peoplehood. And it is a community of faith. From here the concept
of *umma* comes which was introduced by the Prophet when he
migrated from Mecca to Medina. If you look at pre-Islamic Arabia,
Arab life was very much based on tribalistic divisions. Muhammad
emphasized that your allegiance is not to the tribe, but to your faith.
The coming of Islam involved a breaking of the tribal system. It
manifested itself very beautifully when the Prophet established a
special brotherhood between the people of Mecca, who were called the
"migrants" and the people of Medina whom he called the "helpers." In
this way, a whole community was established.

When the Prophet came to Medina there was also a Jewish community
there. And there were also some people who did not accept him as a
prophet of God—the polytheistic Arabs. In the first constitution
established for the state of Medina, he said that the Jewish people are
an *umma*, as are the Muslims. So there is a community of faith. Of
course, family and tribal identities are not denied, but it's said that we
have created you into families and tribes so that we may know each
other. Actually, the superiority or the inferiority is not based upon
tribe or color or race, but on God-consciousness. "The noblest of you
in the sight of God is the most pious among you" (Surah 49:13). The
community is the community of faith. During the Umayyad Dynasty,[65]

unfortunately, Arab-consciousness emerged; they didn't give non-Arabs entering Islam the same status. But this was immediately challenged and was corrected.

In the *umma*, the community of faith, there are many groups: people of different languages, colors and tribes. So it's not that these distinctions are somehow obliterated; however, the primary commitment of the Muslim is not to his tribe but to his faith. Because it's the community of faith, anyone who accepts the faith becomes part of the community. So the *umma* has the possibility of growth, and more and more people can become part of it. In fact, in the Qur'an "*umma*" has been used in a very interesting way with several meanings. On the one hand, we find that Abraham, one person, is called an *umma* in the Qur'an (Surah 16:120). On the other hand, you will find that the entire humanity is an *umma* (Surah 2:213). So the concept is dynamic; all people can be part of it. Moreover, we find that among the Muslim people some are much more conscious of this, so it is said, "Let there be from amongst you an *umma* who invite to all that is good and forbid all that is wrong" (Surah 3:104). Still, all people are part of the *umma* and their primary allegiance is to their faith. Its mission is to communicate the message of God, to live by the command of God and to establish justice. The Qur'an (Surahs 4:135, 5:8) says "You become the upholders of justice and stand as witnesses for God."

HUBBARD: How does the idea of the caliphate relate to the *umma*? Is it the political wing of the *umma*? After all, the caliphate lasted until the fall of the Turkish Empire in 1924.

SIDDIQI: The *umma* started to organize itself so that everyone would live under the *sharia* under the law of God. The *sharia* is not just a matter of rituals, worship and dietary laws; or matters of marriage and divorce. It encompasses every aspect of life, including the political. So the Muslim people had to choose someone who would represent the *umma* after the Prophet died. There had to be another head of the community, the caliph. This caliphate continued until the colonial period after World War I with the fragmentation of the Muslim world and the secularization of Turkey. Kamal Ataturk[66] abolished the caliphate with one stroke, but the idea still exists in the minds of the people. After the caliphate was abolished, there was a caliphate movement in India that functioned for many years. And there were different ways that people used the term *khalifa*. Some made it a spiritual concept, and Sufi[67] orders started calling their sheiks "caliph." In any case, the basic idea of the caliph is to head the *umma* and see that it fulfills the basic rules of the *sharia*.

GROSE: I'd like to add something about the Greek term *oikumene*. In our time, it's taken almost to mean "universal" or "interfaith," but it doesn't mean that. It's the inhabited earth. *Oikos* is house in Greek, *mene* earth. The understanding of it in the Church's inner life corresponds to that of the *umma* in Islam. *Oikumene* is a missionary term which is analogous to the dynamism of the *umma* and also is centered on the message of the faith. Paul in Romans (10:9) summarizes this message: "...if you confess with your lips that Jesus is Lord and believe in your heart that God raised him from the dead, you will be saved."

SIDDIQI: Is the term *oikumene* used in the New Testament?

GROSE: No, it's post-New Testament but used very early by the Greek Fathers of the Church. Similarly, the words "Trinity" and "canon" are not in the Bible, either, even though they're Greek terms. So *oikumene* really is a term used to describe the mission, the ecumenical movement to the inhabited earth to which the gospel is sent. It's a paraphrasing of the end of Matthew's gospel, to go and baptize the nations (Matthew 28:18-20) or the beginning of the Acts of the Apostles: "You shall be my witnesses...to the end of the earth" (Acts 1:8).

2. THE CONCEPT OF CHOSENNESS

SIDDIQI: At the conclusion of our last session, David, you suggested we stop using the concept of chosenness. I wonder if you could give us an idea of how the term was used, historically speaking, by the Jewish community.

GORDIS: The Hebrew term for "chosen people" is *am sigulah*. The best way to look at the notion of chosenness historically—and to understand the distorted sense in which it's been misunderstood and misrepresented—is through the simple formulation in the blessing a person recites when honored by being called up during a service to read from the Torah. One blesses God and says, "Praised be Thou, O Lord our God, Ruler of the world, who has chosen us from among all peoples and given us the Torah." But the Hebrew word *ve* ("and") really means "...<u>by</u> giving us the Torah." So the prayer doesn't simply say Jews are chosen, but relates chosenness to the giving of the Torah. In other words, the Jewish people has viewed itself as having been privileged to be the instrument through which Torah was given to people.

GROSE: That reminds me of something. I am in the midst of a research project for the Lilly Endowment entitled, "A New Hermeneutic for Ishmael." In the Foreword, I placed this quotation from Moses Maimonides in his *Mishneh Torah:*[68] "It is beyond the human mind to fathom the designs of the Creator. Our ways are not His ways, neither are our thoughts His thoughts. All these matters relating to Jesus of Nazareth, and the Ishmaelite (Muhammad) who came after him, only serve to prepare the way for King Messiah and prepare the whole world to worship Him with one accord." And Maimonides goes on to explain that these other two communities have carried the Torah to the far reaches of the known world.

GORDIS: One of the principles of Maimonides is the function of the other monotheistic communities as instruments of bringing Torah, in the philosophical sense of monotheism, to the world. It's also interesting that in Jewish ethical literature there are two incompatible accounts of the selection of the Jewish people to be the recipients of the Torah. Remember that, in the strangely Jewish way we've talked about, Jews do express things in polarities rather than by synthesizing.

One story (*Midrash Rabbah, Exodus*, 2,5) says that God went around to different nations, and He said to one, "Will you accept my Torah?" These people said, "Well, we're interested; what's in it? God replied,

"You may not murder," and so forth. They said, "No, we can't take it; that's the way of our people—they are pirates" and whatever. So God went to the next people and said, "Are you interested in getting the Torah?" They said, "Yes, we are, what's in it?" He said, "Thou shalt not steal." They said, "Well, I'm sorry, we can't take that because our pattern is that we help ourselves to each other's property." Then God went to Israelites, and they didn't ask, "What's in it?"; they said, "Naaseh ve nish'mah, we will do and we will hear," in the sense of accepting and obeying. So the Jewish people, according to this account, were chosen, but in the sense of being self-chosen because they responded to God's offer. It was an act of the coming together of God's will with the Jewish people's will to accept the Torah.

The second account (Babylonian Talmud, Shabbat, 88a) is really quite fascinating: When God approached the Jewish people about giving them the Torah, He overturned a mountain, suspended it in a threatening position over their heads and said, "If you accept the Torah, fine. If not, this mountain will drop down on and bury you, and that's the end." So here it was not a matter of choice because God, essentially, forced the acceptance of the Torah on them.

In either of these cases, of course, the notion is that an act of free will is not simply free without a reference point. It is an act of freedom in a context.   There is a phrase that sums it up beautifully in the rabbinical literature: "The only truly free person is a person who's engaged in the Torah." One is free to accept obligation—freedom isn't license—and that's where these two stories come together. Going back to the notion of chosenness, it never means superiority or privilege. If anything, it's a notion of duty. It's for the sake of bringing God's word and God's message to humankind. In prophetic and rabbinic literature, and traditional historiography as well, the idea of having been chosen represents a burden, not a privilege.

The passages in Isaiah (49:1-6, 50:4-11, 52:13-53:12) which are known as the "Suffering Servant" passages—and that are viewed christologically by traditional Christian interpreters—introduce the notion that the Jewish people suffers because it bears this very special responsibility and is held to the highest standard. That's why, historically, while the traditional way of explaining Jewish tragedy is with the phrase, "We were exiled from our land because of our sinfulness...," Jews were not foolish enough to think they were more sinful than other people. But they understood that somehow, in God's plan, they were to be held to special account because of special obligation. And they suffered because of it. The distortion that entered the picture was that Jews had a sense of superiority because they were chosen and were better than everyone else. This is not the way the concept was ever meant to be understood. It's caused so much pain and distortion that I'm not the first to say that the term "chosen people" should be discarded.

For example, the Reconstructionist branch of Judaism, begun by Mordecai Kaplan, actually removes the term from the liturgy. For example, the very blessing that I quoted before, "Who has chosen us by giving us the Torah," has been changed by the Reconstructionists—because of the risk of pain and distortion in keeping it—to a different blessing: "Who brought us close to his worship and gave us the Torah." They just take out "Who has chosen us..." every place it appears in the literature. Not because the concept itself is offensive, if one understands how it was meant, but because of the way it sounds to those who choose to misuse it or those who simply don't understand that it has nothing to do with superiority.

SIDDIQI: Recently, in a dialogue with a Jewish rabbi and a Christian priest, the rabbi was mentioning that chosenness is within our bones, within our flesh; that even if a Jew doesn't accept the Torah, he's still a chosen person.

GORDIS: That's already an interpretation.

SIDDIQI: He was giving much more a concept of chosen race rather than a community chosen for a message.

GORDIS: I think it's a distortion. One of the things you referred to earlier is a very interesting notion: How does one enter the Jewish community? You talked about the diversity of the Islamic community and, of course, Christianity is diverse, as is Judaism. Despite the fact that we talk about peoplehood with all of its different characteristics, there's only one way to enter the Jewish people if one is not Jewish—through the study and acceptance of Jewish faith. It creates all sorts of contemporary problems because there are people who want to be Jewish or marry a Jew, or have committed to the Jewish people, Jewish ethnicity, Israel, etc. but are not believers. We know there are plenty of Jews who aren't believers, so why must a person attest to a faith in order to become a Jew? Because it's the only way in.

SIDDIQI: Even if you reject the Torah, you are still a Jew.

GORDIS: Yes. The Talmud says, "A Jew, whether or not he sins or goes astray, is considered a Jew." Did I ever mention to you the conversation I had with Cardinal Lustiger, the Archbishop of Paris and a very influential European churchman, on the subject? He is of Jewish ancestry and still considers himself a Jew, speaks Yiddish, has been very interested in Jewish affairs. He was making the point that he considered himself Jewish and quoted the same *halakhah* that a Jew remains a Jew no matter what. There were a couple of other people in the group, and one said, "Yes, but Cardinal Lustiger, how come, of all the Jewish traditions, all the aspects of *halakhah*, this is the only one you tend to quote and to follow?" So he said, "I think I am not the only Jew who does that, either." He's a very warm person and very supportive of Jewish interests in France.

SIDDIQI: So what makes a Jew a non-Jew?

GORDIS: Well, here one has to be a little bit nuanced. If a person apostatizes, adopts another faith, one no longer has the privilege of Jewish participation. For example, one can't go into a synagogue and be called up for an honor at the Torah.[69] It's kind of misleading. One remains Jewish because all the liabilities, the commandments, of being Jewish remain upon you. But, if you have adopted another faith, you will not be granted the privileges of Jewish participation.

By "liability," let me give you an example. A marriage between a Christian and a Jew has no standing in Jewish law. Therefore, if that marriage is dissolved, there is no requirement for a *get*, a Jewish divorce document. However, if an apostate Jew who has accepted Christianity marries a Jewish woman and that marriage is dissolved, a *get* is required for the woman to remarry.

SIDDIQI: The marriage of a Jew and a non-Jew is not recognized?

GORDIS: It has no standing. It is neither valid nor invalid; it doesn't exist in Jewish law.

SIDDIQI: So the new secretary general of the United Nations, Bhutros Bhutros-Ghali, who has a Jewish wife—his marriage has no standing?

GORDIS: That's correct. That does not mean their children are not Jewish—because she is Jewish, their children are Jewish; but the marriage itself has no standing. Intermarriage is a very widespread and much discussed phenomenon, apparently because the recently completed National Jewish Population Survey shows a very high level of intermarriage. There are some in the Jewish community who say that rabbis invited to officiate in a marriage between a Jew and a non-Jewish partner ought to participate. Otherwise, they are pushing that couple away from the Jewish people which is small and needs everyone. In fact, some of them call these "mitzvah marriages," marriages in fulfillment of a command. Other Jews say, "Absolutely not, you can't do that."

I don't perform intermarriages, but when a couple comes to me who are about to intermarry, I will do everything I can to bring the non-Jewish partner—if he or she is so inclined—close to Judaism. I will teach them, put them into a class, invite them to come to the synagogue, and so forth. When the time comes for the wedding, I will explain to them that to convert to Judaism is a serious matter, not to be taken lightly; that if you want to become a member of the Jewish people or raise your children as Jews, you are welcome, but you must become Jewish formally before a Jewish wedding is performed. For a rabbi to participate in something which doesn't exist Jewishly makes no sense. What I would prefer you—the couple—to do, I say, is to marry civilly so that, according to the state, you are married; and then let's pursue our discussions. You pursue your study of Judaism; and at the time when you want to have a Jewish marriage—because now you desire to become Jewish—then be converted to Judaism and I'll perform the marriage. But to call on me simply as a kind of a public relations gesture to officiate in a marriage when it doesn't exist in Jewish law, doesn't make any sense. I would attend the wedding as a guest, however.

SIDDIQI: If you recommend that they go and have a civil marriage, aren't you, in a sense, telling them to go and commit sin?

GORDIS: No, there is nothing sinful about that.

SIDDIQI: It is not recognized by the Jewish law, and it is against the Jewish....

GORDIS: Something which is not recognized is not necessarily sinful. It simply doesn't exist. That's not sinful.

GROSE: This is very similar to Christian thought. There are certain institutions founded by God at the creation of the world. The family—marriage—was one, the state was another; and so all humanity has some form of marriage which is blessed by a kind of general blessing. But only Christians can have a Christian wedding.

GORDIS: It wouldn't make any sense otherwise.

GROSE: It wouldn't make any sense. Once a couple came to me, and the woman said she'd like to be married in the Presbyterian Church. I said, "Are you Presbyterian?" "No." "What is your church?" "I don't have a church." I talked to the man and he didn't have a church connection at all, either. I asked why they wanted to be married here. "My mother was married in the Presbyterian Church, and it would mean a great deal to her if we were married here." I said, "That is no reason. You go and have a civil marriage." So we all have our ways of drawing a line and saying we cannot do something, or saying that, at a later date under other conditions, we can.

GORDIS: This is a parallel situation.

GROSE: Yes, a very important one. I think the chosenness thing is worth looking at. I think of the saying of Jesus which has comforted so many: "Take my yoke upon you" (Matthew 11:28-30). What is Jesus' yoke? It's a covenant yoke, it's got to be that. The Torah is understood as a yoke, isn't it David?

GORDIS: Yes, the yoke of the Torah, the yoke of the commandments.

SIDDIQI: Islam also teaches a concept of chosenness. God says in the Qur'an speaking to the believers, "You are the best community (*umma*) chosen for the benefit of humankind; you command what is good and forbid what is evil, and believe in God" (Surah 3:110). Here, however, it is clear that the *umma* is not a race; anyone can become a Muslim and join it. The chosenness is also for a mission and not in itself. As long as one fulfills the mission, one is chosen, otherwise one loses this honor. But some Muslims misunderstand it and think that they are the best regardless of what they do. In the Qur'an it is mentioned that Abraham fulfilled God's commands and God told him that He would make Abraham a leader. The Arabic word for leader is *imam*, which has a very special meaning and one can even translate it as "a chosen leader." Then Abraham said, "And (is this true) of my children, too?) God said, "But my promise is not given for the wrongdoers" (Surah 2:124).

GROSE: I think our discussion relates to how the sense of being Jewish changed, partly because of the young science of anthropology, where everybody got categorized and grouped under different headings and sub-headings. That's a nineteenth-century phenomenon in the West. So when the Nazi movement came, it labeled Jewishness a race. This was part of the Nazi ideology with no foundation in fact, but it drew from this anthropological development of categorizing not only flora and fauna but also people. So we need to reconvey that we're dealing here with three spiritual communities—Jews, Christians and Muslims.

I see a very big problem in Christianity on this point. Christian historians are now studying the roots of the Church of the East and view these Christians as Arameans. Who's an Aramean? Abraham was an Aramean, according to Deuteronomy (26:5). It's hardly an ethnic description but it covers a region inhabited by certain peoples who then developed a language, Aramaic, from which Arabic may have come and is closely related to Hebrew. So we have these Aramean or Arabic Christians. I know a very prominent one, a pastor in Nazareth, who believes his ancestors were among the early Christians. Once, after the Lebanese civil war began in 1976, a Jewish colleague of mine said, "I don't hear anybody being concerned about the Maronite Mid-East Christians. Don't you Christians care about those other Christians over there?"

Later, while teaching a course on the Crusades at the University of California, Irvine, I learned what happened in 1099 when the Crusader army took Jerusalem. They were there to take it away from the "infidels." Their own chronicler said the tunics of all the soldiers were drenched in blood that day. They slaughtered everybody. One family got out: the governor who bought his way out. Not another living soul survived that massacre—no children, no women, no old people, nobody. Now, who was in the city? The Jews went to a synagogue where they were slaughtered, burnt. But also, as far as I can tell, Christian Arabs were killed, perhaps because the Crusaders couldn't tell the difference between Christians and Muslims, but nevertheless, why couldn't they? Why didn't they say in advance to their commanders, "When we get in there, make sure you find out who the Christians are." Nothing like that was done, they killed everybody. To the Crusaders, they were either Muslims or Jews. They couldn't be Christians, because they all looked the same, more or less.

So that's similar to not giving a damn about the Maronite Christians.

We care about Mid-Western Christians because we're from the Mid-West, or whatever. This is ethnicity gone awry, and I don't know that it's just a Christian phenomenon. One of the benefits of this dialogue is that it confronts Christians with respecting and welcoming those who are not Christian. That, in turn, will have an effect on the internal problems of Christianity when it gets racial.

GORDIS: I must say I react with a degree of ambivalence to your point, and I'm using it to make a different point. I myself use a different formulation from the one of chosenness which I discard. I'd like to substitute the notion of uniqueness: each of our traditions is unique in its particularity but universal in its humanity. There's a certain pernicious quality that one would expect of those Christian Crusaders. It's like saying, "Okay, we're going into a town to see if the inhabitants are ours. If so, we'll protect them. Everyone else we're going to slaughter." So my reaction to that well-known Crusader story is this: Look at the bloody record all we religious people share. When any one of us had the chance, we became an instrument for spilling blood. Particularism—as a fulfillment of our own religious tradition—should be put aside in favor of a universalism that sees the humanity in the other.

Now, let me illustrate what I hear from the story. You ask why the Crusaders weren't caring about those of their own religious tradition. Of course, we assume that it was okay to slaughter the Jews and Muslims who were the enemies. But even within ourselves, we are allowing that particularism, even to the degree to which it makes sense—and we all understand what you were saying, I'm not criticizing—to work in a negative and damaging way. Somehow, together, we have to face the reality of how religion has functioned. In the case of Jews, Muslims and Christians, when any of us has had the sword in our hand, we've lost sight of the universalism.

So, in terms of chosenness, I would say the formulation that we should try to teach and share together is this: each of us represents, in our particularism, a unique contribution to the world and to God's plan. Jews have their function in bringing Torah and standing witness in

their way; the Christian witness exists; Islam refreshed and renewed
and broadened the teaching to a wholly different world and continues
to do so. But, Muzammil, when you talked about the brotherhood of
Mecca and the brotherhood of Medina, I said to myself, it's wonderful;
but we also need to talk about the brotherhood of humankind.

SIDDIQI: I believe that Islam also teaches the universal brotherhood,
the brotherhood of the whole humankind without any distinction of
color, race, language or even creed. The brotherhood of the people of
Mecca and Medina was a model, and on this pattern other types of
brotherhood were supposed to be developed. Muslims in their history
very often followed these teachings both on the individual as well as
collective levels, but sometimes they failed in understanding and
applying the universal aspects of Islam. I must say that the
nationalistic and exclusivist structure of the Muslim world today is
contrary to the noble universal teachings of Islam. We do have to
improve ourselves in this respect.

GROSE: Many times I've been tempted to give up this work among
the three faiths. But we belong to each other, and once this was
disclosed to me, I can't leave it. Our linkage means that we are a
family, and that is a powerful message. This doesn't even get into the
question of whether or not we are a family with other people who
aren't Jews, Christians or Muslims; but at least, we three are. Each of
the three communities desperately needs to understand this because
they all have the "we-and-they" tendency which you've described so
clearly. I want to make two further comments about what you said.
First, if we say "uniqueness" in preference to "chosenness," that doesn't
necessarily refer to God's initiative. This doesn't exclude uniqueness,
but chosenness does mean somebody did the choosing. Second—and I
didn't want to bring this up at all because I feel it's a secret, like an
invention that is not yet patented. But I feel that inherent in every Jew
is the Muslim and the Christian; inherent in every Christian is the
Muslim and the Jew; inherent in every Muslim is the Jew and the
Christian. Without moving away from the uniqueness there's a paradox
or something going on here, but it's very real. There's a profound
correspondence to one another, and to say we have commonalities
doesn't really touch it. Maybe you can help me come up with a term

for this.

HUBBARD: You're almost saying there's a mystery in the union of the three or the interaction of the three, aren't you?

GROSE: We can say "interaction" and teach an objective university course on it, but when I say "a profound correspondence," I mean something deeper which I don't understand. What each of these communities forgot when they got to be exclusive was Who had called them into being. That's how they got to be destructive. They took half the gospel. They were walking, breathing heretics in each case of fanaticism, wherever it occurred, in any of these communities.

GORDIS: The most heinous sin is when human beings not only assume the mantle of the divine but then attribute the basest of their motives and behaviors to God. They blame it on God.

GROSE: It's terrible, and we see this over and over again, historically, which calls for the prophetic ministry in each of the three faiths. In both World War I and II, the Germans were praying to God, and the French, the British, the Americans—all praying to God in the name of Jesus Christ, and then going out and killing each other. This is a form of madness.

HUBBARD: Look at the recent war between Iraq and Iran.

GROSE: Yes, and it's very clear, isn't it, that Muhammad said there would be no attacks on Muslims by Muslims. That's a moral outrage. And we've got the Catholic-Protestant conflict in Northern Ireland which goes on and on. It reminds me of what the distinguished twentieth-century Protestant theologian Paul Tillich said: that there's the God we worship and the God beyond that. The God who's caught up in all our rituals and suppositions and habitual ways of doing, and "the God beyond God."[70]

GORDIS: That's the real one.

GROSE: Yes, and once in a while He says, "That's enough!"

GORDIS: I want to respond to your request, George, for more understanding on the nature of the correspondence between the traditions. I can't think of a term, but I wanted to suggest a comparison from physics: sympathetic vibration. It's a characteristic of matter that it will resonate at the same frequency with other matter. One might suggest, metaphorically, that what you're getting at is that these three peoples—because of something in the existential nature of their being—resonate at a common frequency.

GROSE: I like that. And there's another term that relates but is a little more objective: a universe of discourse. We know what one another means, at least up to a point, and we can apply that to this kind of interaction.

3. THE PEOPLES OF THE BOOK AND OTHER RELIGIONS

SIDDIQI: This is because the three traditions, being so proximate and coming from the same area in the Middle East, share a lot with each other. Of course, I see a great importance in the three understanding each other. On the other hand, coming from India as I do, I think we should not just look at it from that point of view. There is humanity living on the other side—Buddhists, Hindus, the Chinese and people of other religions. We have something in common with them, too. Not as much as we have between our three faiths, but a great deal.

GORDIS: There should be more of this dialogue with the other traditions. Some of the things we can be most enhanced by are dimensions of spirituality—spiritual techniques and attitudes—that are more characteristic of the Eastern religions than of our own traditions. So, while the commonalities exist much more among us, we do have this community of spirit with the others. That's all the more reason for us to make that membrane which surrounds us more permeable, not less.

GROSE: That's marvelous, what both of you said. To me, this relates to chosenness and uniqueness, also. I don't think the Hindus think about chosenness. That's not their way of thinking. Nor the Buddhists. But I think we must come to terms with our own family relationships.

SIDDIQI: I think the concept of election exists among the Hindus and Buddhists, too. They see themselves as the ones who are compassionate and that they are those who bring good to the world. They do have those ideas of chosenness or uniqueness whether they think about the divine or not.

HUBBARD: All of this is important, but it's going to get us off in another direction.

4. PEOPLEHOOD AND SERVANTHOOD

GROSE: We've got this family situation which we're seeking to work through, and I offer a thought: the matter of servanthood, which is so real in Judaism, Christianity and Islam. Jesus said the greatest is the servant of all, and the Suffering Servant passages refer to the Jewish people as understood in Judaism.[71] And a Muslim is a servant of God (*abd-Allah*). So everybody's got this theme.

GORDIS: In Jewish history—partly for historical reasons but probably for reasons of principle as well—there's very great distrust for anything like a secular authority in the form of a king. The principle that's given is, "The Jewish people should be servants of mine," God says, "and not servants of other servants" (Babylonian Talmud, *Kiddushin*, 22b). Kings are only God's servants, too. You shouldn't have an intervening secular authority to which the Jewish people are subservient.

SIDDIQI: The Qur'an says about Jesus, "He was no more than a servant: We granted our favor to him" (Surah 43:59).

GROSE: I think that would almost fit into the New Testament in a way that I've alluded to before. In Paul's Letter to the Philippians, the Son of God "did not count equality with God a thing to be grasped, but emptied himself, taking the form of a servant, being born in the likeness of men" (2:6-7). Both the terms man and servant are found in that same passage. So the servanthood theme is very strong.

D.T. Miles has written[72] that evangelism is only possible when it's looked at in the following way: when one beggar tells another beggar where the bread is. So the first beggar, who knows where the bread is, remains a beggar. That kind of lowliness needs to be encouraged among the three faiths, an extraordinary lowliness which is only possible where a person has been touched by God. To put it another way, I don't think I have the truth; the truth has me. I don't think I know the truth; the truth knows me. I don't think I've been given all the truth. I believe it exists in Christ; but the fact that I don't know Christ fully means I don't know all there is about it. Many Christians fall into the trap of saying that Jesus is my savior without thinking about other people. There's a hymn that illustrates this: "In the Garden." "I walked in the garden alone, and nobody was there but just Jesus and me." I think that's the most narcissistic, self-centered, isolationist, non-fellowship song I've ever heard in my life! I've never used it when I was pastor of a church. But people love it at funerals—"And he walked with me, and he talked with me."

SIDDIQI: It may be okay for the dead person; he can be alone. But the living people have to seek community. I agree with you that we should try to be possessed by God and should not claim that we possess Him. That is actually the meaning of Islam, "submission to God."

GROSE: I believe that Jesus has claimed me. I'm his person; but I'm not his only person and I don't feel I know all there is about him, nor do I fully understand what he said and did. But he's my focus and always will be.

GORDIS: Can I put in a good word for that hymn? If it existed in isolation, I'd have the same reaction as you, George . But hymns and prayers are part of a complex, and there are moments when one needs to be able to feel and express that sense of aloneness, that notion of a private relationship with God. If one puts it into the context of the totality of spiritual experience, some of which involves community and connection, then one can see it as one dimension of the search for God or for Jesus. Then it becomes much more powerful. There's a principle in the Talmud: When you have a difficult problem, the way to solve it is to "go out and see what the people are saying" (Babylonian Talmud, *Berakhot*, 45a and elsewhere). The very fact that people are moved by the hymn—and these are not evil people, not people trying to write anyone else off—means that it's responding to a certain need they have. Perhaps, instead of forbidding its being sung, the hymn ought to be placed in a context which says, yes, this is one dimension, but it's only one.

SIDDIQI: That's very interesting. There's a story that once Prophet Muhammad was sitting, and a Bedouin came and he asked him a question. He liked the Prophet's answer very much, so he prayed for him and said, "Oh God, have mercy on me and Muhammad, and do not have mercy on anyone else." So the Prophet said, "You limited the Most Spacious One." The prayer should have included everyone; but the man limited it. Sometimes people make mistakes sincerely.

GORDIS: At the risk of belaboring it, I want to make the suggestion—if we're seeking commonalities for what one would want to say to the larger community in this time and place—that the shared notion of servant is one that could occupy an important place. One of the characteristics of the world, mainly because of remarkable technological advances, is a sense of the almost infallibility and absolute power of human beings. And it's anticipated in all our traditions. In the Hebrew Bible people are warned against saying, "My strength and my power accomplished all this" (Deuteronomy 8: 17). I did it, I didn't need God for it.

This leads to the question: Why bring a child into a synagogue or church? The child may not be able to understand, so what is it that the child is going to get from the experience? When asked that question, I say that a child is going to learn from seeing that there are adults coming together. And, instead of putting themselves in position of ascendancy where they are masters, they place themselves in a situation where they are worshipful of something above and beyond them. In that sense, this notion of "walking humbly with our God" (Micah 6:8) could help us stress to human beings what it means to be dependent. We don't have the power to go it alone. We are interdependent, both as individuals and as communities. Because we understand interdependence, we have the responsibility to empathize with the other who is dependent upon us, just as we are dependent upon him or her. The whole atmosphere of relationships could be transformed if there were truly a sense that we are not the masters of this world but, at best, partners with the divine. In fact, we are small and puny....

HUBBARD: I wish that international business leaders had some sense of that, especially now that there's a global economy and a sense that pollution—and almost any problem you can think of—is systemic to the world as a whole.

GROSE: Another thing is funding. Several years ago, I spoke to a large corporation about a contribution to our work. The officials replied that it just doesn't fit into their corporate interest. Corporate giving follows corporate interest.

HUBBARD: The same is true of national interest. It was in our national interest to go into Kuwait in Operation Desert Storm but not to go into Tibet which is suffering from the long Chinese occupation.

GORDIS: Or to give haven to these Haitians who are dying or being killed while we debate about how temporary their quarters are going to be in the marine base at Guantanamo Bay, Cuba. So much in our experience is designed to make us feel big. How much of it is designed to make us feel small?

HUBBARD: Perhaps we ought to return to our main topic of the relationship of the three peoples.

GROSE: I find that I have no trouble affirming Judaism and Islam along with the resurrection of my Lord. I don't have an intellectual problem with this any more. On the one hand, I think it's absolutely true that Jesus died and rose for the sins of the world. On the other, that does not undercut even partially the validity of Judaism and Islam as far as I'm concerned. I don't think I know what all of that means to me at the moment.

David, you asked earlier whether we validate one another's communities. We validate one another as friends, but we're looking at issues that affect billions of people. In what way can we validate one another religiously? We may take the servant role in the sense of saying, "I'll help you all I can, but in reality you're absolutely wrong."

GORDIS: This is where most people of good will are—which is better than where the rest of the world is.

GROSE: Right, but it is still condescension at this point.

SIDDIQI: When I read the Qur'an, something holds me and puts a certain demand on me that it doesn't on you. I may very humbly associate with you and help you; but at the same time I see that what holds me, what grips my soul, is not yours. What touches you from Christ doesn't touch me the same way. Last week I was in a dialogue program and somebody said that Muslims don't take Jesus as the savior and don't have a savior. I replied that he was wrong, that we take him as a savior and we take Muhammad as a savior, but in a different way. Christians take him as a savior who died on the cross and took away sin. I take him as a savior in his inspiring personality. I am inspired by his life and actions, and this inspiration heals me, moves me and helps me to understand certain problems. I see this as a very saving act, but not in the sense of somebody's taking sin on the cross and dying for us. It doesn't make any sense to me. If it makes sense to you, fine.

So there are certain things we see in our traditions. I see the Qur'an as being the word of God. It speaks to me that way, but you don't see it

that way.   When you read the Qur'an, you may see that it is an
inspiring word or you just take it as a great book for Muslims; but you
don't think it makes a demand on you.

GROSE: My own sense of God's transcendence has been powerfully
affected by my reading of the Qur'an.

GORDIS: Could I suggest that what we are really talking about is a
stepwise progression?   The first step is that we remain in isolation
from one another. That means I not only have the truth, the truth holds
me. But everyone else is wrong, and I have nothing to do with anyone
else. They have nothing to say to me nor I to them, except perhaps to
try to make them the same as I.

The second step is for me to understand that my tradition speaks with
a truth which is very real, palpable and ineffable; but I understand that
others don't read it in the same way.

The third step to ask is, What are the implications of that? How do you
read my sacred text? How do I react to the fact that you read the
Qur'an in your way? It's not just that I don't read it the same way you
do, but am I moved to a special relationship with the Qur'an? The
members of a faith-resonating community read the Qur'an differently
from the way either of us would read Shakespeare. In other words,
there is something for me in reading the Qur'an, and even in reading
the Hebrew Bible, which is different from what you find. While you
may make different assumptions than I, I'm moved and enhanced by
that reading.

It's not simply that George reads his Christianity his way, and that I
can't pretend to understand when he talks about Christ's having come
to take away the sins of the world. If you ask me if I accept that or
not, the answer is no; but that's not what's important here. What's
important is the degree to which I, as a Jew, am changed and affected
by the reality of Christianity, which is the reality of George and other
Christians. That's important and stimulating to me. It's also important
to me that Islam not only exists, but that you, Muzammil, and other
Muslims find that kind of truth in Islam. It's important because I know

you and know you're not a scoundrel or a fool. You're a spiritually alive human being, and your spirituality is rooted in the experience of Islam. That cannot leave me unaffected, even if I don't read the Qur'an as you do.

GROSE: To take a specific example, I've been helped by the Servant Song in Isaiah 53 which Judaism takes one way and Christianity another: that it refers to the Jewish people as the Servant and, on the other hand, to the Christ. I can't explain fully how living with the passage both ways has helped me, but it definitely has.

I'm also aware and sense a little bit of what the Qur'an does to a Muslim. I know some people who have talked about their life in Islam and say, "I couldn't be anything but a Muslim. When I hear that call to prayer, I know. That's my life, that's who I am." And some have talked about the quality of the recitation of the Qur'an. There are some people in the world who are trained and whose lives are devoted to going around reciting the Qur'an. It's a powerful, haunting experience that reminds me somewhat of a cantor singing. I heard a cantor once in a synagogue in the District of Columbia who wasn't just a good vocalist but was conveying something. It was a magnificent experience that I'll never forget.

GORDIS: It's "the God beyond God."

HUBBARD: Before we move on, gentlemen, would you like to say anything further on the subject of how we are moved by one another?

SIDDIQI: We have reached a greater appreciation of each other—we have to believe that—resulting from greater knowledge. This could also have certain effects on our behavior towards each other. Certainly, we do make judgments because our traditions sometimes make judgments and this is the way we understand them. But we can sometimes suspend judgment so as to recognize each other's humanity and spirituality. By this appreciation for each other, we can see others' problems, can be moved by their pain and should be willing to help and suffer for their sakes. I think that's also part of what our faith demands from us.

GROSE: When we were together at the mosque in Orange County nearly a year ago, I said something I hadn't planned on ahead of time: "I call upon Christians to love Jews; I call upon Christians to love Muslims." This needed to be said, just like a husband and wife need to say they love each other. It's only for me to say this about Christians, and I don't want to overstep myself by even suggesting anything for Jews and Muslims. But I feel called upon to ask Christians, "Do you love Jews? Do you love Muslims?"

GORDIS: To say, "I love Jews, I love Christians and I love Muslims," I think is an easy abstraction. Of course, it's the translation into behavior that matters.

GROSE: I want to tell you, I haven't heard anybody else say it. Somebody ought to articulate it once in a while for openers, that's all. But few even think in those terms because people say loving fellow Christians is hard enough!

GORDIS: We all could give parallel formulations of that same idea from our own communities.

GROSE: One of the neglected doctrines of Christianity is the doctrine of the Holy Spirit. But I think that I'm moving on a matter of the doctrine of the Holy Spirit in this way: I believe and find that God speaks to me through the Qur'an, as he does through the Hebrew Bible. It's not to me just a proposition. Notwithstanding that I don't read the Qur'an the way a Muslim does, or the Hebrew Bible the way a Jew does; yet, I'm being addressed, spoken to. That's very real to me.

GORDIS: Do you make a distinction, George, between the Hebrew Bible, which is part of Christian scripture, and the Qur'an, which is not? Do they affect you in different ways?

GROSE: Somewhat, just because I am very familiar with the Hebrew Bible, the Old Testament. I'm less familiar with the Qur'an.

GORDIS: It's only familiarity? It doesn't have anything to do with authority?

GROSE: I'm at the place where I find a great similarity in the authority between the Hebrew Bible and the Qur'an.

SIDDIQI: I think the point David is making is that the Old Testament is part of the Christian Bible.

GROSE: It's in the same cover.

SIDDIQI: So already you admire it as part of your scripture.

GROSE: Indeed, it is my scripture as much as the New Testament, which, incidentally, is a very Calvinist position.

SIDDIQI: So you read the Old Testament not as an outsider, but as a person who believes that it's part of your own tradition.

GROSE: Yes, but I am fully aware that Jews read it differently— not everywhere, but in certain important places. Yet, in many places Jews read and understand it the same way. We accept the same biblical scholarship now, and thank God for that. So, as far as interpretation goes, there are many parts that are the same.

GORDIS: You read it in your way and we read it in God's!

GROSE: One of the problems we face in our interfaith work—and one of the reasons for my special interest in Ishmael[73]—is that we have the Hebrew Bible within the covers of our book but not the Qur'an. That's a historical fact. Helping Christians appreciate the Qur'an—as they already appreciate, in their own way, the Hebrew Bible—is one of our tasks. Clarifying Ishmael's position in the Book of Genesis ties it to the Qur'an and gives the Qur'an a somewhat different status than it would have without this tie. Ishmael is more than just a link to the three communities—Isaac and Ishmael as Abraham's sons and so on—because Abraham and Ishmael bring the Qur'an to the Bible. The opportunity for Christians is to see a little more in Ishmael than they thought was there.

GORDIS: That's a very beautiful point, George. I think for the Jewish reader of the Hebrew Bible, it is important and enhancing to read the story of Abraham and Ishmael in the Qur'an. One of the dangers of reading the Hebrew Bible in isolation is seeing Isaac in isolation and forgetting or becoming insensitive to Ishmael. One's sensitivity and humanity towards him as part of God's plan is enhanced if one reads the story of Abraham, Isaac and Ishmael in both the Hebrew Bible and the Qur'an.

GROSE: Yes, it's mutually enhancing. As a Christian I cannot say the Qur'an is canon, while I can say the Hebrew Bible is. We've got the two covenants in the one Bible for the Christians and we don't have the Qur'an included, so we have an issue we must face. But until Christians come to appreciate Ishmael more, they probably will not appreciate Islam more. If we come to a more positive reference about Ishmael, then we will have a more positive view of the Qur'an as a body of spiritual literature from the standpoint of a non-Muslim.

SIDDIQI: You've made a very important point, George. It will be deeply enriching for all three of us to read the Hebrew Bible, the New Testament and the Qur'an. I said before in our previous discussion that Muslims look at the Bible as part of the divine revelation. We believe that the Qur'an is the continuation of the same revelation given to Moses and Jesus—peace be upon them. Let me add here another point that is, perhaps, worth noting and emphasizing. Whenever the Qur'an speaks about Jews and Christians, it does not speak about them as some kind of strangers or aliens. It speaks of them as God's people who were addressed before by Him through His many prophets and are now being addressed by His prophet Muhammad. The Qur'an sometimes praises and sometimes criticizes them. The Qur'anic criticism of the People of the Book is taken by Muslims in the same way that you take the criticism of the Prophets of Israel for their people and of Jesus for his people.

5. PEOPLEHOOD AND LAND

HUBBARD: Now that we've talked about peoplehood and some of its implications, I'd like to ask you what land and sacred space means to each tradition. David, how does land relate to Jewish faith and understanding?

GORDIS: One has to understand that the central story, the central defining myth of Jewish history is that which is contained in the story of the Exodus. It combines two things: the Exodus from Egypt and the establishment of the Jewish people through the giving of the Torah, which is the spiritual becoming of a people and a nation; and through entering the land of Israel, which is the physical becoming of a people and a nation. The story begins with the Exodus, but it ends only with the parallel themes of Sinai, Torah and entering the land of Israel. One must understand that, for Judaism and for Jews, the natural state and the object of national aspiration is to be in the land of Israel; and that to be away from the land of Israel is the unnatural state of *galut* or exile.

How exile has come about is for the historians to describe. Traditional historians, depending on the period, will link the separation of the Jew from his land to the results of sinfulness, being wayward; but it is always linked with the assurance by God that the Jews will return to their land.   There are many examples of this, most from Second Isaiah—chapters 40 and on in the Book of Isaiah—and from the latter part of the book of Jeremiah. For example, Jeremiah reassures the people, first of all: "A voice is heard in Ramah, lamentation and bitter weeping. Rachel is weeping for her children." Then God's voice is heard and He says, "Keep your voice from weeping, and your eyes from tears; for your work shall be rewarded...they shall come back from the land of the enemy" (Jeremiah 31:15-16). There's never been a time from the destruction of the Second Temple in 70 C.E. that Jews have not been in the land of Israel, though often as a very small group. But it's been a central theme always in Jewish tradition that the exile is unnatural, it's punishment; and that Jews will be linked again to the land.

This theme manifests itself in the liturgy. In the central prayer of the service recited three times a day, and four times on the Sabbath and holidays, we have the notion of returning to Jerusalem and rebuilding it. In the grace recited after every meal, there is the idea of rebuilding Jerusalem and restoring us to peace. The prayer for peace in the evening service, which starts with "Let us lie down in peace," ends with, "who spread the tabernacle of peace over Israel and over Jerusalem." So Jerusalem and the land of Israel are central. The legal formulation goes as far as to say that a Jew who lives outside the land of Israel is "as if he is without God" (Babylonian Talmud, *Kethuboth*, 110b). That is a characteristic exaggeration which is part of the rabbinic style. It's similar to the saying that if one leaves out one of the ingredients of the Sabbath spice mix, one is deserving of death. Obviously, that's not what it means—and neither does the saying about living outside the land—but it's as if one is without God if this dimension of land is excluded. Why? It's another case of a kind of tension within the Jewish tradition between a particular sacred quality of the land of Israel generally for the Jew—and Jerusalem in particular—and the universalization of Jewish faith.

In the time of the Second Temple it was clear that the community, which was under Roman domination and control from 63 B.C.E. to 70 C.E. when the Temple was destroyed, was in decline. You had in that period the development of the synagogue, the *beth knesset*, within the Temple complex. The synagogue was for prayer while the Temple was for the sacrificial service. What's the difference between them? According to Deuteronomy, the sacrificial service can be performed only at the Temple of Jerusalem. Prayer can be said anywhere. So the synagogue and the synagogue service have become instruments for the universalization of the Jewish faith. Yet, the Jewish worship service includes large sections which relate directly to the sacrificial service, and expresses the aspirations—even among those who don't look for animal sacrifice to be restored—for a reconstitution of the centrality of Jerusalem for all of world Jewry. For though God is everywhere—that's part of the tension I mentioned—God dwells in the city of Jerusalem, which is `ir hakodesh, "the sacred city," as Jews address it.

So the link to the land has physical, existential, emotional and spiritual dimensions. It is clearly present in the legal literature and is a dominant theme in the liturgy in a daily, oft-repeated way. It's a central feature of that composite we were talking about as peoplehood—peoplehood and land. If one understands this, one begins to fathom some of what many see as a kind of hypersensitivity in the Jewish community, where we sometimes think Jews overreact to some threats and dangers. The reality of having a Jewish presence and a Jewish existence in the land of Israel, after two thousand years of separation and denial of it, is the fulfillment of a central aspiration of the Jewish community. But it is always considered terribly fragile. It's tiny when one looks at the map. So no matter what the news about the Israeli army doing this or that, there is an exaggerated but exquisite sense of fragility and danger, and the possibility of the loss once again of this object of the aspirations of so many years. That simply is part of the Jewish psyche. There is a sense of insecurity that, after what has happened to the Jewish people, the world would quickly take the land away again.

This helps explain some of the policies of one or another Israeli government which someone might disagree with. It explains, for example, why the non-recognition of the State of Israel by the Vatican—even though there are contacts between the two—contributes to that sense of insecurity. The mighty Catholic Church is saying to this tiny Jewish state, "You're not really legitimate."[74] It also explains the sensitivity about this piece of land which other people have an interest in and a legitimate claim to. But you can understand the reaction of insecurity among Jews when the conflict over the land is translated into a sense of, "You don't belong here; you are illegitimate."

HUBBARD: Thank you. George, from your perspective, how do land and sacred space operate?

GROSE: I alluded earlier to Christendom, the well-defined Christian lands of Europe and Byzantium. Everybody knew where it stopped and started. For a long time, in the medieval period, there was no real sense of mission in terms of carrying the gospel to others who were not Christians, except for the Crusades. The Christians weren't much aware of Asia; their world was the Mediterranean world.

In terms of the spirituality of Christianity, there's the major theme of the heavenly Jerusalem, particularly in the Book Revelation (Chap. 21). It's very real to Christianity that when the kingdom comes it will resemble or partake of the earthly Jerusalem, but it will be glorified in all ways and have a river of life and tree of life; and by the leaves of that tree all the nations will be healed. That's the ongoing spirituality with regard to Jerusalem, but it is based on the historical Jerusalem.

Then, from the eleventh to the sixteenth century, there are the Crusades, one after the other, to recapture the Holy Land from the Muslims. The first was authorized by Pope Urban whose army was the main one. This tradition continued in the Spanish experience. If a knight fought the Saracens in Spain, that counted as being on a Crusade because the knight was recouping part of Christendom which had been taken away by the Muslim conquest of Spain in 711. All of this continues the Christendom theme.

There is also the theme of the mission to all of the inhabited earth. It was not so much a matter of government control as an outreach to all nations on the basis of Jesus's commission of the disciples in Matthew (28:16-20). That passage doesn't say the alteration of all nations so that there's one nation. Therefore it doesn't quite correspond to the *Dar al-Islam* (Abode of Islam) theme. Catholicism corresponds more to this idea as it developed, but in the early days of Christianity it wasn't a question of whether Paul went in his missionary work to Spain or Crete as political entities. He wasn't thinking of having one political entity; that wasn't what early Christianity was about.

A comparison can be made between Muhammad and Jesus in this regard. I don't think Muhammad could have said, "My kingdom is not of this world" (John 18:36) or, "Render unto Caesar the things that are Caesar's and to God the things that are God's" (Mark 12:17) or, "They are not of the world, even as I am not of the world" (John 17:16). There's a holistic sense in Islam that is different from Christianity.

These sayings of Jesus continue to be part of the spiritual reality of Christianity, even though medieval Christendom was more like Islam than anything I can think of. Still, the sayings have a reference elsewhere. Also, one reason why things happened as they did in Jesus's last days was that he did not fulfill one type of messianic aspiration. He didn't throw the Romans out, even though there were zealots, so-called, who had hoped he would. Some scholars even think Judas Iscariot was a zealot who turned against Jesus at the last minute when he realized that he wasn't going to do that after all.

In Christianity, there are at least two views on the State of Israel. Liberal Christians are not so much concerned about it as are very conservative and fundamentalist Christians. Fundamentalists see Israel's establishment as a fulfillment of the biblical prophecy that the Jews would return to the Promised Land, and they think this will eventually lead to the return of Christ. Liberal Christians value Israel as the place where Jesus walked.

Christians aren't too concerned about who controls the Holy Land. I don't have a particular preference myself, but I think that Christians on the whole would prefer that the Israelis control this land rather than the Muslims.

Ben and I were privately discussing the question of two peoples, one land; and I pointed out that really it's three peoples, one land because the Christian Arabs are there. They may still be the majority in Bethlehem and are in Nazareth, so it's their land also. So there's really a three-fold land claim, whatever the form the political entity might take or be called.

HUBBARD: Thank you. Muzammil, what are your thoughts?

SIDDIQI: In Islam there is sacred time, such as the month of *Ramadan* when Muslims fast from dawn to sunset, and the time of *Hajj*, the pilgrimage to Mecca in the month of *Dhu'l-Hijja* which every Muslim is enjoined to make once in a lifetime if possible. These times are sacred because during them certain divine revelations took place. They are set apart from other times.

In the same sense, there are places that are sacred not because they are sacred mountains or rivers or deserts, but because certain manifestations took place there. Mecca is the locus of the manifestation of Abraham who came there and built the Kaaba. Prophet Ishmael lived there, Prophet Muhammad was born and preached his message there.

Jerusalem is the locus of those great prophets of God—Moses, Jesus, David, Solomon and others. David Gordis referred to the drama that took place there. However, it is not looked at by Muslims as a Jewish drama but as part of Islamic history. Muslims take it in a very deep sense that Jesus is their prophet, as are Moses, David and Solomon. So the whole land had a special meaning and is part of the Islamic understanding of divine revelation. There is also the story of the *isra'* and *mi'raj,* the night journey of the Prophet from Mecca to Jerusalem and his ascension to heaven. The story brings Jerusalem and Mecca together in Islamic understanding. So the city has a deep spiritual meaning for the Muslim and is set apart from other cities, as the land is set apart from other lands. The Qur'an calls it Al-Ardal-Muqaddaseh, "the holy land" (Surah 5:21). Jerusalem is called *al haram*, a sacred place, a term also used of Mecca.

The second issue is the difficulty Muslims have in understanding the Jewish claim to the land, the idea that "God gave us (the Jews) this land exclusively." What about the others who are living there? It was not an empty land but was inhabited by many other people. Why are they deprived and disinherited? Rabbi Kalir[75] in one of his books says, "God determined a land for His chosen people, even before the people were there." I ask, "Was it an empty lot. What about the rights of the people who were living there already?"

There is a recognition in Islam that Jews should live there, come and visit there, have their synagogues and schools. The Jewish community lived there and so did the Christians with the variety of their churches. Most of the Christian shrines you referred to, George, were built during the time when the land was under Islamic control. None of them were taken away except for a very short time during the reign of the Fatimid caliph al-Hakinin in 1009 C.E. Some historians have said that Pope Urban used this as a pretext to start the Crusades. There were economic and other reasons—not just spiritual reasons—for the Crusades, although the lack of access to Christian shrines might have been one of the causes that instigated the whole thing.

GROSE: Pope Urban had religious reasons, not spiritual ones.

SIDDIQI: Yes, so he used these, though there may have been other reasons as well. But Christians and Jews do have a right to their holy places. Remember that the Jewish temple was not destroyed by Muslims and didn't exist when they entered the city. They took it as a sacred place where a mosque should be because it was considered by Muslims the mosque of their prophets David and Solomon. It was not seen as a temple.

When Umar, the second Caliph, entered Jerusalem in 638 and the city was surrendered to him by the Christian patriarch Sophronius, Umar asked where the Mosque of Solomon was. There was nothing there, and it is reported that a man named Ka'b al-Ahbar, who was familiar with Jewish history, guided him to the spot. Umar found that the place was not very well kept and was a dung hill where people used to bring their horses. He cleaned it with his own hands. And so Al Aqsa Mosque was built there later.

The other mosque on the site, the Mosque of Umar (Omar), had a different origin. When Umar went to visit different churches in Jerusalem, he entered the Church of the Holy Sepulchre at the time of afternoon prayer. So he said he wanted to pray. The Patriarch said to him, "This is a place of prayer; if you want, you can say a prayer here." But Umar felt that maybe later some Muslims would claim the church because he, the Caliph, had prayed there. So he went outside a short distance and prayed in the courtyard, and there they built the Mosque of Umar.

HUBBARD: On the matter of Arabs and their rights in the land of Israel: if the rights of the Arab inhabitants of Palestine had been safeguarded, would there have been a problem in principle on the part

of Islam to a Jewish state? I think all of us would agree there were
certainly problems of various kinds, including injustices to the Arab
population, during the period of Israel's formation. But is the idea of
a Jewish state in itself a problem for Islam?

SIDDIQI: In principle, I do not think there is any problem for Islam
whether Jews live there as a community or form a Jewish state. After
all, ever since the Islamic conquest of this land, Jews lived there
alongside Muslims. They had their places of worship, their schools,
their businesses and all other community activities. They prospered
and enjoyed their lives with safety and security. It was Arabs and
Muslims who protected them and gave them the autonomy to organize
their lives. But now the situation is very different. First of all, this
state came into being with force, without the will of the native people.
Secondly, it is very powerful and has more weapons and military
power than its neighbors, all of whom feel its threat. It is a minority
that challenges the majority that lives all around her. It has expelled
the natives, the Palestinian people from their homes and lands and
gives them second-class status. All this makes it very unacceptable.

If Israel were to exist not as a threat, not as a major military power,
and the rights of Palestinians were recognized, then I do not think there
would be any major problem for her to exist in that area. Arabs would
be more accommodating and not mind Jews living among them
administering their own people and enjoying their own holy and
historic places as they like.

Now, it is the reverse, really. Israel is saying that it will see whether
to give any rights to Palestinian people. It wants Palestinian people to
live under its authority and protection, with no army and no power.
The Arab demand should be different. Instead of talking of
eliminating Israel, they should be saying, "Why don't we protect Israel,
rather than the other way around? We are the majority here; we shall
let the Jews live among us as protected people, as they lived before"
(during the period of Muslim control of Palestine).

GROSE: This relates to the so-called Covenant of Umar where
People of the Book are *dhimmi*, protected people in a Muslim land. But

there's another question here that I've often wondered about. The implementation of *Sharia*, as I understand it, was the real drive behind Muslim expansion—not conversion, particularly in Iraq and Persia. I recall a situation in Persia where a Zoroastrian community decided to convert to Islam and headed for Baghdad. The caliph then called out the army and drove them back.

SIDDIQI: *Sharia* is, of course, very important, but Muslims did not force all of its laws on non-Muslims. They were allowed to live by their own religious laws. As late as the Ottoman period[76] there was a *milla* system for non-Muslim communities which were given full autonomy to administer their affairs under their own religious laws without any interference from the ruling state. There were also other patterns of governing the non-Muslim citizens of Islamic states in different parts of the Muslim world at different times.

GROSE: But when the Muslim rulers got to a new country, they were not preoccupied with converting the population to Islam. Their preoccupation was administering the country according to *Sharia*. They wanted God's law to be the law of the land to guide the common life of everybody—and that included whoever else was there, under certain provisions. Inasmuch as the state of Israel is not under *Sharia*, even though it respects the family law of both the Christians and the Muslims, Israeli sovereignty is not a problem. The Israelis are not applying *Sharia* but other laws.

SIDDIQI: You're right, George. Muslim rulers generally did not coerce into Islam the non-Muslim citizens of their states, because of their respect for the Qur'anic injunction. "Let there be no compulsion in religion..." (Surah 2:256). They did, however, administer their territories by the rules of the *Sharia* which were sovereign. With the coming of the State of Israel into the area, there is no sovereignty for the *Sharia* because the Palestinian people have no sovereignty.

HUBBARD: I think what George means, though, is that during Jewish history you had Jews living all over Europe and the Middle East. They applied Jewish law to themselves in their own setting, but didn't care about what was going on outside.

SIDDIQI: The Muslims have done the same thing to others. They didn't apply *Sharia* to everybody. The Jewish community lived according to the Jewish *halakhah,* the Christian community according to its own laws; but Muslims have to live now in Palestine without any sovereignty.

GROSE: I see tension between national sovereignty that is not applying *Sharia* and national sovereignty that is. That's one of the reasons for tension between Arabs and Israelis.

SIDDIQI: Yes, this is an area of tension. There is "national sovereignty" which was recognized in Islam even for non-Muslim minorities living in Islamic states up until the Ottoman period. Here every community was allowed to live by its own religious laws, almost to the point of accepting a state within the state. But then there is the concept of sovereignty in the current political sense of the word, and that is also included in the *Sharia.* It is in this sense that tension arises.

What needs to be recognized is that there are other people in the land who are not foreigners and should not be expelled. They also have rights. So the difficulty Muslims face is the Jewish claim that, because this land is considered sacred, it's all theirs and nobody else has any right to live there; or, if they do, they must live under Jewish control. And this despite the fact that Arabs have been living there for a long time—even before the Jews and Judaism arrived on the scene.

GORDIS: In certain ways this brings a lot of different elements of our discussion together, even though we, by and large, don't deal with political questions. The Mid-East conflict is one of the saddest and most tragic chapters in religious history and the history of relationships between people. Not because it's so much worse than other kinds of conflicts, but because its where the three faiths, in one way or another, interact. Here some of the worst elements in all of our traditions come forth, rather than the best.

One of the reasons this takes place is because of the really poisonous intersection of nationalism and religion in the Mid-East. Both have positive elements. The expression of nationalism is very good and useful, culturally stimulating, etc.; but it also has dangers in it. Likewise, along with the good, and potential good, of religious faith, it has the possibility of engendering and bringing out some of the worst hatreds and the spilling of blood. That's why, in some of our earlier conversations, I stressed the fact that each of us has an obligation—as we talk to our own people—to concede the point that all of our traditions have ennobling elements in them and dangerous ones. So what are we going to choose to underscore and make the driving force behind what we do together? We don't live in an ideal world. In an ideal world, in my book at least, we would do away with nationalism altogether; it is more harmful than useful. After all, we are all human beings. There must be better ways to organize people.

From the purely Jewish point of view at this moment, many Jews— besides myself—would agree to that. But they and I would also point to the present historical reality, after so many of the Jewish people were wiped out in our lifetime and when there is no other corner of the world where Jews are the masters of their own fate. They need a place where they can live and determine the relationship of their old traditions with current realities, and develop in a natural way as a people. In light of this, Jews shouldn't be asked to be the pioneers of post-nationalism. Let other places see the collapse of nationalism first.

But I have no doubt that if those of us who are sitting in this room were given the authority to resolve the existing conflicts, we would do so successfully. After all, it's that same old question: how does one relate to the other? Everything that you said, Muzammil, was correct. You and I are friends and would continue to be; and that would be the spirit which would help us get out of this turmoil.

Unfortunately, the historical record on the part of all of our people is a very sorry one. The record of the Crusades, for example, which in some Christian history was a great time of glory and the expression of faith, was also a time of ugly persecution, murder and intolerance against Jews and Muslims. That's why when we hear about, for example, a Crusade for Christ, or the American Red Cross Crusade, it turns us off.

But when you talk about the notion of coexistence, Muzammil, unfortunately I recall the time, for example, when Jews were denied access to their holy places in Jerusalem. Every Jewish site was obliterated.

SIDDIQI: It only happened after the creation the State of Israel, not before that. Islam's record in this matter is quite good.

GORDIS: Okay, that's exactly right; but at the time of the creation of Jordan, when it was under the British control, there was access.

SIDDIQI: There was access during the whole Muslim period.

GORDIS: Sure. But what happened after that period, was that the tombstones on the Mount of Olives were used to pave roads and the Jewish quarter of the old city of Jerusalem was obliterated. The atmosphere for the notion that peoples could coexist was not helped by that, to say the least.

In an imperfect world, what is the best one can hope for, at least at an interim stage? How is one going to overcome this dehumanizing and demonizing of the other? First, there have to be contacts, interrelationships. You know, Muzammil, that I don't support all Israeli policy.[77] You know that I am in favor of territorial compromise, though it must be consistent with the security of all parties involved. There must be a solution which gives the Palestinians authority, sovereignty even, over the territory where they live. They have to have self-determination, and there needs to be a very close link between Jordan and the Palestinian state—whatever it's going to be called—and Israel. With economic cooperation, people start to associate with one another. It would take time to evolve, and let's hope and pray that it's going to come out that way.

The other aspect of the problem is that there are many Christians and Arabs in the State of Israel. So far Israel has done quite well—not perfectly, but quite well—with the non-Jewish population. There is a high degree of freedom and autonomy for them in terms of family law. They participate in government, there are Muslim and Christian members of the Israeli parliament, the Knesset. Now an imperfect world is good, but not good enough. What I am concerned about is the danger that the situation's going to get worse, not better. That's why I think it's so urgent that there be progress in the current Arab-Israeli peace talks. This isn't just another conference but a historic opportunity. If we lose it, there won't be the status quo; it's going to go downhill, get worse and worse.

So there is great risk involved here, and the way we relate on the Middle East is really all put to the test. I experienced this recently when the Wilstein Institute,[78] which I direct, did a survey of American Jewish leadership—the people most committed to Israel—about the peace process. The survey was widely reported in the press in Israel, England, the United States—all over. Prime Minister Shamir was even asked about it. The survey found that these Jewish leaders want what you and I want: territorial compromise for the sake of peace, if there can be security guarantees.

SIDDIQI: But security not by taking more land.

GORDIS: No, not by taking more land.

SIDDIQI: How much land will Israel take? The security comes from letting the neighbors feel secure. But, instead, Israel has so much military power and so many arms.

GORDIS: But it works both ways. Look at the geography of Israel[79] and at President Assad of Syria, who is now being created as another Saddam Hussein through the courtesy of our own President,[80] and then put yourself in the position of an Israeli liberal, not a Likud member.[81] And by the way, the majority in Israel also don't support Shamir's position; they support territorial compromise. But put yourself in their position. These Israelis feel that the United States is now, for whatever reason, anxious because of the deterioration of the Soviet threat, to cozy up to the Syrians. They look at the fact that the United States was very active against Saddam Hussein in Iraq but didn't say a word when Assad took over Lebanon. And no one is saying a word about the military buildup of the Syrians who are developing, with the Chinese, atomic capabilities as well. So the Israelis have very strong feelings of insecurity, certainly no less than the Palestinians have. And let's remember, the Palestinian charter—even to this very day, and they refuse to renounce it—calls for the destruction of the state of Israel. This is not something which is....

SIDDIQI: What the Syrians, the Egyptians and others see, is that the Israelis have been armed to such an extent that now they can move any side at will and bomb any city they want to. And this is what they are doing. They also have atomic bombs which are not called "a threat." But the Syrian buildup and the Iraqi buildup are considered threats, although the Iraqis never used the bomb against Israel—they used it against their own people. Iraq fought Iran for eight years and used all kinds of weapons, and our country was behind it.[82]

GORDIS: Muzammil, what cities has Israel bombed? The one place where there was a chance for peace was with the Egyptians. That led to the giving up of the Sinai Peninsula by Israel and the establishment of a peace treaty that has lasted. There's no military action on the border with Egypt and there are diplomatic relations between the two countries.

SIDDIQI: There is bombing going on in south Lebanon.

GORDIS: There were incursions from both sides of the Lebanese border, and I'm against that. I was against the Israeli invasion of Lebanon when that took place in 1982. On the other hand, in retrospect, the bombing of the Iraqi nuclear reactor near Baghdad was not a bad mistake. Did you have any doubt that Saddam had every intention of using the bombs that would be produced there against Israel?

SIDDIQI: People like Saddam and Assad—that's another story. Who makes them and keeps them in power? And who does not allow genuine democracy to emerge in the Middle East? This is again the whole game.

HUBBARD: It's a Big Power game.

SIDDIQI: It's a Big Power game, that's true.

GORDIS: Muzammil, I've sat in Palestinian homes in the West Bank with Muslim and Christian Palestinians. However, the Israelis did not permit the development of an indigenous Palestinian leadership with whom to be able to negotiate. I've said that to Israeli leaders myself. I know Shamir and Peres.[83] I've sat with them as we are sitting now. They don't like me because I've said this. However, when you ask, "Who creates the Assads and Saddam Husseins?", it is Big Power. But what does that do to the Israelis' feeling of security? They feel increasingly isolated when the Big Powers, after the experience of a Saddam Hussein, are now doing the same thing by creating an Assad. Then, when the United States summons the Israelis to a peace conference, they don't have much of a feeling that they're going to get a fair shake. That's why they're reacting the way they are.

SIDDIQI: The Big Powers see that Shamir and Saddam are the same thing and are supporting both of them so that the Middle East will remain in turmoil.

GORDIS: I don't think they're the same thing because I don't believe Shamir ever threatened to destroy Syria, to wipe Iraq off the map, or Lebanon. I don't think it's fair to say they're the same thing. I don't think they are.

SIDDIQI: But what is he doing to the Palestinian people, especially with the Israeli settlements in the West Bank?

GORDIS: I think that his feeling is—and I believe he's wrong about it, though you can make a good historical case—that the land of Israel goes up to the River Jordan. I believe the State of Israel accepted the principle of partition when it was established, and that's the basis on which peace can be reached. That's why I'm for territorial compromise. I am opposed to Shamir, but I think there is a difference between saying he uses the historical claim differently from me and saying he is a Saddam Hussein or an Assad. Assad claims that "greater Syria" is to include Lebanon and all of geographic Palestine up to Egypt. Saddam says, "I am going to wipe this Zionist incursion off the map." We may not like Shamir, but not all people we don't like are the same. I don't like Shamir, but that doesn't make him into an Assad or a Saddam Hussein.

SIDDIQI: Did Saddam Hussein ever use his weapons against Israel?

GORDIS: Yes, when first he had a chance. In the war with the United States, Operation Desert Storm, he was throwing SCUD missiles against Israel which was not even involved in the conflict.

SIDDIQI: That was to show the Palestinian people, who were supporting him in the Gulf War, that he was able to do something for them. But I don't think he meant to cause any real damage to Israel.

GORDIS: If you were the prime minister of the State of Israel and knew Saddam Hussein—at the same time he was fighting the United States and other Arab armies—was heaving these missiles into Israel, would you say he does not represent a threat? Is there any doubt in your mind that, if he could have put an atomic warhead on that missile, he would have sent it to Israel?

SIDDIQI: I am sorry to say that Israel will remain under the threat as long as the Palestinian people's rights are not recognized.

GORDIS: I agree. And the Palestinians will remain a threat as long as they and the other Arab states don't come to terms with the fact that Israel is going to stay and must stay. So you and I are in agreement about that.

GROSE: You are talking in two opposite ways: one is the situation we're in; the other is the position of David and Muzammil as persons, their own political positions, which are similar. The political realities out there are not so hot.

HUBBARD: Well, let's conclude on that point.

CHAPTER SIX

HOW THE DIALOGUES
AFFECTED THE PARTICIPANTS

1. THE OVERALL EFFECTS OF DIALOGUE

HUBBARD: This is our final session—December 15, 1992. In the five previous dialogues, we've grappled with various questions: our assessment of the founding figures of our own and the others' traditions, our theological commonalities and differences, the meaning of sacred scripture for each of us, the place of law and grace in each faith, and the meaning of peoplehood and land.

This time we want to look at how the experience of dialogue has affected each of us and changed our assessment of the beliefs of the others.

GROSE: The truth question is real to all of us because in our own faith and faith communities, we find the truth. The truth comes to us, addresses us, and we know there's such a thing. Otherwise, all we are is socially conditioned people, and religious truth is just a humanistic expression. So the truth question is a real question, which we've been working with these past months. This is not to say that the way the truth has addressed me is the only way it can come forth. The point is that there is truth. That's a theological position, not a history-of-religions matter of looking objectively at various phenomena. It's saying the truth has reached me—and each of us knows that—and through that truth I reach out to all of you. It's because the truth has addressed me that I reach out to Muzammil, and to David and Ben. It's through the truth that has found me that I know and love you guys. That's what's prompted me all along, and I think you would speak similarly.

HUBBARD: Okay, we're trying to get a handle on how we've changed, how we've been affected by these sessions, what the experience has been like for each of us. We're going to go around now and get other ideas. Dr. Gordis, would you reflect on the experience, please.

GORDIS: For me, there have been structural consequences as well as more profound things. By "structural" I mean the very fact that our joint project has created the opportunity for us to come and talk together. Lives are busy; and projects which in theory one thinks are very good, one never gets to. The fact that we have set aside the time for these very intense human encounters is significant. In certain ways that's the most overwhelming reality for me. We are together now in a way that we were not together before. Because we come out of respective traditions, those traditions have come together in a way they would not have without this opportunity. In a way, the process has worked perfectly in that we understand each other better, and yet still come from very different worlds and respond differently.

I listened carefully to George's formulation of this a moment ago. Even at this point, while I understand his comfort level with that formulation, I'm not comfortable with it. I come at it very differently, so even now after our previous discussions, it is important that we understand each other. My sense of truth and of faith is one which doesn't find the notion of "just a humanistic expression" to be something negative. Rather, I find a human expression—even a humanistic expression—to be fundamentally positive. For me the search for truth within my own religious tradition, too, is an expression of humanism. It says that human beings are equipped, through their intelligence and their power of making moral choices, to engage in the search for truth and to discover the divine presence in that which we've received. Yet, we never receive revelation in pure form because it's revelation to human beings. The constant struggle of a religious community and a religious person, from my point of view, is to attempt to come closer to understanding the nature of truth and of the divine, and the nature of our obligations; and to try to do better than we're doing in that search. In that sense, the truth is not something which is given and complete, but always partial and incomplete. That's humanism in the sense that, as human beings, we are partners of God in the process of creation and the process of world improvement and transformation.

Which leads me to reflect on the nature of faith. I think, if I haven't misunderstood our discussions, we do still have a different understanding of what the word faith means. But it's important, at this stage, to reiterate that the lines which cut across us are really a matrix. There is not simply Jew, Christian and Muslim but different approaches within those communities. Within the Jewish community are those who would express themselves in ways which are closer to your way, George, than mine. So we have to be cautious, even as we move to the end of the process, not to presume to speak for the entire community of any of our religious traditions.

There are those who would take a literalist or fundamentalist position within Judaism and say the tradition holds the truth and they speak out of it. I am not comfortable with that notion. For me, faith is a constant tension between that which I feel I know with every fiber of my being and that which I am uncertain of. My religious life is a process of exploring and bringing together those two dimensions, so that the language you used, George, is very different from what I would choose to use. I come to you, and to Muzammil and Ben, as partners in exploration and discovery, together seeking for truth. I would use a different language and my frame of reference is different from yours. I don't proceed from the notion that my tradition tells me the truth, and out of this truth I come and relate to you with love. I find truth in my tradition in which I am at home, but I seek truth also in my relationship with each of you for I see you are involved in a parallel process. My process has been enriched and strengthened by what we have engaged in together, by the learning, by the exploration.

GROSE: What I said, David, and what you said come together in supporting one another. You described as a hazard, though you didn't use that word, the fact that we have the truth. That's a very misleading statement. I don't think we have the truth; the truth has us. It is spiritually very dangerous to think that we possess some aspect of God. We don't; aspects of God reach out and claim us. That's quite different. So then we cannot say—I can't say—I've got the whole truth. This is a very important clarification. We sometimes hear Christian fundamentalists say, "We've got the truth." I can't say that. I do know that the truth has me, but the truth that has me is not fully known to me.

So I go out on the search which you describe and it's a different casting, I think, of the same search. To put it in Christian terms, it's a pilgrimage. We all go to our holy places and we have the spiritual search, which in Islam is the *jihad.* It's a struggle to find the path of God, God's footprints in life, His messages and clues. I think we're a bunch of detectives, in a way. I enjoy that; it's a special blessing.

SIDDIQI: I found our meetings here very constructive whether we take David's approach to truth or George's. I see myself kind of in both positions. On the one hand, I realize and have deep faith that the Qur'an is the word of God, that Muhammad is the Prophet of God who speaks on behalf of God and tells us what the truth is. But, at the same time, as a human being, I'm not the Prophet, I'm not the Qur'an. I have to understand both the text and the message of the Prophet, and I also have to understand how it has worked in history with the Jewish and Christian communities. So it has been very instructive and useful to sit together with the others.

David says he is not speaking on behalf of the whole Jewish community, and George and I don't claim to speak on behalf of our whole communities. Still, because we are coming from academic backgrounds, we have some understanding of what other people in our traditions think and feel. So the dialogues have been very useful in finding our commonalities and also seeing where and how we differ, and how we can relate to each other in spite of our differences. They also have helped us see the possibilities for developing an understanding of humanity where all people can work together and live in peaceful coexistence. Our three communities of faith, living in the twentieth century and moving toward the twenty-first, must ask: With the varieties of understanding of truth, and of claims for truth, what is the future of humanity? That is the basic issue that we should keep in our minds.

2. RELIGION'S MIXED ROLE IN HISTORY

GORDIS: Could I just pick up on that last point which I think is very important. If you look at the record of religion in human history, it certainly is—to use polite language—an uneven record and, in many ways, a very bloody one. Religion has made great achievements, insights and contributions but it hasn't been an unmitigated triumph of the human spirit. Religion, after all, doesn't mean God. Religion is how people organize themselves, almost expropriating God's language and God's message to do to each other what they want to.

I agree with you, Muzammil: the fundamental issue the world faces is related to the basic question of how one deals with the diversity and variety of conceptions of truth. And almost every other issue—economic problems, poverty, the conflict and wholesale slaughter which so outrage and pain us—is part of that question. How, in other words, does one deal with the otherness of the other? It's a question which has come up constantly in our discussions. It seems to me that if we sit back fairly and look at all of our traditions as a whole, the whole world of religion, one would have to come to the conclusion that religion has been more a part of the problem than of the solution. It's contributed more to the bloodshed and the divisiveness than it has to a positive conditioning of people in dealing with the otherness of other people. What I would like to see happen in our process, as a modest beginning, is for us to contribute to transforming religion into more of an instrument for solution than a part of the problem.

SIDDIQI: My point is that there are so many other things, not just religion, that have been part of the problem.

GORDIS: Oh, I don't say it's exclusively responsible.

SIDDIQI: Economics has been a part of the problem, too, and politics.

GORDIS: Let me be more precise because you are right. I certainly don't believe that all the problems of the world are caused by religion. However, I'm not an economist or a military expert; I'm a religious person, and my heart and soul are preoccupied with the religious vocation. My overall sense is of disappointment in reflecting on religious experience in terms of what potential it has to contribute to how people relate to each other and what it has actually done throughout history.

SIDDIQI: Look at the situation in Bosnia today, for example. Is the whole problem because of religion, because of the Muslims and Orthodox Christians there? Or look at what is happening in India.[84] Is this simply because of Hinduism and Islam, or are there some other issues as well?

GORDIS: Muzammil, I am not saying that all the problems of the world are the fault of religion. I am saying that religion overall, in terms of how it's indoctrinated and conditioned its constituents, has not been very successful in equipping individuals to deal with the otherness of the other in a positive way. That's a long distance from saying that religion is responsible for all these problems. I'm saying that religion has the potential, as we look towards the future, of doing much more in the way of healing than it has done.

SIDDIQI: But many religious people don't practice religion, they simply talk about it. We talk about loving our enemies and we don't. We talk about doing justice to others and feeding the hungry and the poor. If we don't do that, if we simply talk about it, then how can the problems be solved?

GORDIS: Precisely.

SIDDIQI: So the problem is not with religion, the problem is with our lack of practice and implementation of the religion that we talk about.

GORDIS: That's what I am saying. Religion is not the teaching; it's the experience of what people have used religion to do.

GROSE: We're talking at a couple of levels here. I see religion as a cultural expression full of all kinds of flaws, as history is. I don't defend Christianity; I defend Jesus Christ and his revelation based on how it has affected me. I find I have little grounds for defending Christianity as a cultural phenomenon.

SIDDIQI: Do you mean you don't defend Christianity or Christian people?

GROSE: Oh, I defend Christian people.

SIDDIQI: Even when they do wrong?

GROSE: Well, that's another question because we defend even the enemy in a sense.

SIDDIQI: Defending that is justification?

GROSE: No, no, I don't justify...

SIDDIQI: But there is Christianity and there are Christian expressions of it? There is Jesus and the scripture and so forth, and then the Christians' expression of their faith in their lives. And then we have to make a distinction between the two.

GROSE: It's their belief and how they carry it out. So I cannot defend how Christians behave collectively, institutionally; I don't defend the Church. These are matters that other Christians may not agree with me on. I've heard fellow Presbyterians say the Church can be equated with the kingdom of God. I don't think so, even though the Church is the expression in history of the Christian faith. But I can't defend the Church because it is locked into all kinds of historic ambiguities and terrible tragedies, as well as tremendous beauty, joy and love. It's a mixed bag. With all due respect, I think Islam and Judaism as historical communities are also a mixed bag—I'm speaking very candidly—in their cultural, historical expression. So I cannot defend everything the Muslims have done, or the Jews or Christians. I can't and I won't.

SIDDIQI: I also say this, that Islam is not what Muslims do. Islam is what Muslims ought to do.

GORDIS: We're talking about two different things by religion. I'm not talking about religion in the abstract as religious teaching. When I'm critical of the record of religion, I'm talking about it in a phenomenological sense. That is, what religion—in the complex of beliefs, people, institutions and practices—has done and the impact of these religious phenomena on the world. Just as with the impact of nationalism on the world, there are positive and negative factors. As a religious person, I am not proud of what religion has done generally to equip individuals to deal with others who are different from them.

I think we have to distinguish two things. One is religious hypocrisy which, thank God, we're all blessed with! There are plenty of hypocrites who put on the mantle of piety and preach love to the poor, the enemy, the friend; and they're the most degenerate kind of people. We all have them and know them. Hypocrisy is not new and it is ugly. The Hebrew prophets talked about hypocrisy; all of our traditions talk about it. It's a central and noble message. There is that wonderful scene of Jeremiah standing in the temple court as the people come out after a special occasion (Jeremiah 7). He said: "Will you steal, murder, fornicate, etc.; and then go back into the temple, go through the motions and fool yourselves by saying, 'Look, I'm saved?'"

Therefore, overcoming this hypocrisy is one thing I hope we can be more successful with in the future.

But there is another dimension, that of religious ideology, a theme that I fear I've belabored over the course of our discussions. I believe that each of our traditions contains within it two faces: the face of openness, tolerance, understanding and empathy towards someone who's different; and also the face of susceptibility to a divisiveness that causes hatred and animosity through claims of exclusiveness towards the truth. And these are poisonous. From an ideological point of view, I would hope that our efforts not only serve to overcome religious hypocrisy, but also to underline the truest elements of our religious traditions which are desperately needed in our fragmented world. These elements can help in bridging, not abandoning, one's own beliefs.

This is a fundamental issue in the world now. People criticize the Germans and others for not taking refugees. The United States takes some, but mostly it's the European countries who are not doing so. Why? They want to maintain the homogeneity of their own society, and consequently people who are ethnically different have no place to go. Doesn't religious tradition have something to say about the otherness of these people and the compassion one ought to extend to them? I think religion has to emphasize that voice, rather than the notion that the presence of someone who is different defiles our space or our world.

GROSE: I've seen something in my own life and church, and in the other communities, that we need to pull together on: the issue of idolatry. It's idolatry when the Serbs engage in ethnic cleansing because they are idolizing themselves. As I've quoted Luther before: "The human mind is a factory for idols." We keep generating things we put in place of God. Christians may look down on the others; or our nation may not want certain other people here. It's xenophobia partly rooted in a tremendous insecurity, and the insecurity is overcome by means of idolatry. It's hit our three communities hard.

SIDDIQI: I feel there are two problems that create exclusivity and the degeneration of the moral and ethical values that religion teaches. One is pride and arrogance, where people sometimes think they have everything and others nothing. It's a kind of misplaced self-esteem; when it degenerates into arrogance and pride, then one cannot give the other person a chance to say what he has to offer and share.

The other problem is fear of the other, that the other is going to take over what I have—whether it's money, power or position—and this leads to confrontations. The Muslim community feels afraid of what the Jewish community is going to do. The Jewish community fears the Muslims, the Arabs. The Christians—the Serbians, for example—are afraid of the Bosnian Muslims; the Bosnians of the Serbians. Now we're seeing the same thing in India between the Hindus and Muslims. Even though the Muslims are small in number,[85] the majority community somehow is afraid: "Maybe these people will get married, everyone will have four wives, their numbers will increase, and they'll overcome us."

3. RECONCILING THE "MISSIONARY IMPULSE" WITH DIALOGUE

HUBBARD: It seems to me that what you've all been saying relates to the question of the "missionary impulse." In many religions—Judaism is somewhat different in this respect, but certainly in Christianity and Islam—there is a tradition that says, "Go and make disciples" or "Bring the message of Prophet Muhammad." This is a natural impulse when one is proud of one's tradition and has the words of one's founder, Jesus or Muhammad, urging one to go forth and evangelize the world. But how does one balance it with the realities of personal freedom and the fact that the world is probably never going to be all Muslim, all Christian, all Buddhist or whatever else?

GROSE: Even all Jewish.

HUBBARD: Or all Jewish, certainly. There's not too much of an argument about that at the moment.

GORDIS: We have a slightly longer way to go!

SIDDIQI: Personally, from a Muslim point of view, I believe that whatever you realize as truth, you have to share with others. But there is no compulsion, no coercion, in terms of religion; it's a free choice. If people want to become Muslim, I feel very happy; if they don't, this is their choice. I don't think Islam has given me the mandate to go and force people to become Muslims. The Qur'an says again and again to the Prophet that you cannot force people to become Muslim (Surahs 2:256, 10:99). Most of the people, even though you who may like them to, will not become Muslim (Surah 12:103). Still, the message has to be communicated. Missionary work in Islam consists of being a witness to mankind through your own practice, through living according to the commands of God; and being willing to share this message with others and then leave it up to them. So missionary work is not using all kinds of overt and covert methods of converting people, but leaving it to people's own free choice.

GROSE: Christian mission has gotten a bad name sometimes, but not always rightly so. We know many examples of missionaries exploiting the situation, taking advantage of other peoples; but, at the same time, the Christian mission has helped a lot of people. I think there are instances of some coercion in Islam; but that's not Islam, even though some Muslims have done this. There are a few instances of fanaticism, like the Almohads[86] who took over in Spain after the great Umayyad period. They were pretty rough people who wanted to expel others and weren't that different from the Inquisition-minded Christians who followed.

I think I've cited this before, but I remember one instance where I was pressed during a public dialogue by Christians in the audience with regard to what was I doing to convert my non-Christian colleagues. I resorted to the Bible, noting that the Christian has a mandate to witness—just as the Muslim does—to share the truth, the insights and the love that has been given to us. The only valid conversion, I think, is something God does in the heart, so none of us can compel that. There are forced conversions. At various times, people have been baptized who weren't interested in being baptized, or children were baptized without permission of their parents. But the reality of Christian faith is God's work in the heart, and I think the same is true of Judaism and Islam. No other human being can compel that. Thus, witnessing, as such, is not compulsion; and that's what we've been doing. We are witnessing all the time in other places and ways in our families and our lives; but as we work together, the four of us, it is, indeed, a witness. And we are demonstrating to each other that we can do it in ways that bless one another, as well as ourselves.

HUBBARD: David, do you want to comment on this?

GORDIS: I think there is a genuine tension between the spirit of what we are doing here and the missionary function. I think the formulation that both of you made, Muzammil in a somewhat fuller sense, is the best that one can do with it. People feel so strongly committed to their own tradition that they want to share, without compulsion, with others who might be engaged by it.

However, in a religious tradition which either explicitly or implicitly still says, "*Extra ecclesiam nulla salus est,*" ("Outside the Church there is no salvation"), that doesn't work, that's not God's work in the heart. It states that either you're in or your damned. There is still the inquisitorial thrust in organized religions and it's an unresolved problem.

GROSE: I would concur that we have to bring these questions forward. In my work representing The Academy—when I deal with my Christian co-religionists or, more particularly, Christian officials in the Church—I sometimes can't tell the difference between the most liberal of the liberals and the most fundamentalist of the fundamentalists when it comes to reaching out to Jews and Muslims. They're all saying, in house, someone's too liberal or somebody else too fundamentalist. But when you come to the relationship to the other two Abrahamic communities, it doesn't make much difference. The other two faiths are outside the house.

GORDIS: That's what I meant. So one of the functions of our coming together ought to be to stress within our own traditions those impulses which are positive rather than those which are negative.

SIDDIQI: I think salvation is the work of God and very often, instead of leaving it to God, we try to give it ourselves. That's where the problem comes. There is also a misunderstanding, sometimes, of the religious texts which speak about God's judgment. People use these as if they also could judge.

GORDIS: This is idolatry: by making gods of themselves, human beings play God.

SIDDIQI: There's a nice story about someone who went to a zoo with his son who said, "Father, buy me this animal." The father said, "No, it's going to eat a lot; and I don't have the money to feed it." There was a sign that said, "No feeding." So the son said, "Buy me the one that says 'No Feeding.'" The sign, of course, was put there for the visitors, not the animals; but the son misinterpreted it. This is very often what we do when we read our religious texts: we take something written for God and say, "Maybe this is written for me."

GROSE: It's the right of God that we take for ourselves. I relate the idolatry problem to whether or not the truth possesses us or we possess the truth. If we think we possess the truth, we become idolatrous, fanatical and destructive. It's just as bad as if a husband says, "My wife is my possession." This is one of the big feminist issues. Or the wife could say also, "My husband is my possession." Or I could say, "My children belong to me," when we know they belong to God. It's trying to be God, when we're not. And that's where we're in agreement, profoundly, in what we're trying to do.

I have something I think I'd better say so that I don't miss saying it later, even though it may not fit exactly into just what we're talking about. Recently, I was driving to dinner in Los Angeles with our good friend, Dan Ninburg.[87] I said, "Dan, when I look you in the eyes, I see also a Muslim and a Christian." Now, I'll put it in another fashion also. We are dancing in the shadows of our own becoming. I see in the eyes of my friends not only who they are, but also the others who are there with them. When I look at Ben's eyes, I see a Christian and a Muslim, also; when I look at Muzammil, a Christian and a Jew; when I look at David, a Christian and a Muslim. When I look in the mirror, I say, "What do you know?" I see something very profound here, and I can only put it in these very poetic terms.

SIDDIQI: For a Muslim, there is no problem because we already recognize Jesus and Moses. It's already there!

GROSE: But as a Christian, I have been confronted with this problem. My way of expressing this is not, well it's not prose, it's sort of mystical.

HUBBARD: Is it a convergence somehow? Are you saying you see the religions, at least on some level, converging?

GROSE: No, not converging, not identifying. It reminds me of an incident with a Lebanese student I taught several years ago who was Muslim and whose mother was a Jew. After one class session, he said, "Dr. Grose, you're a Christian." I said, "Yes." He said, "You're a Jew." I said, "Yes." He said, "You're a Muslim." I said, "Well, that, too." He was groping for something, and I've reflected on it over time. It's a mystery. But we are dancing in the shadows of our own becoming. Something is coming, but I don't see it as a merging of the religions. We are emerging, each of us, as we develop as human beings. I see it in the way of the Muslims and the Christians and the Jews. We are not now what we may become. And that's the basis for some hope.

4. THE IMPLICATIONS OF THE DIALOGUE FOR SOCIETY

HUBBARD: Now, on the question of hope, let's look for a minute at some possible solutions to the problems you've talked about: the ideology that gets entwined with religion, the way religion becomes idolatrous or hypocritical. How can the sort of work we're doing make some difference to these problems? How can it make it such that we will, in fact, approach one another differently in the future?

GROSE: I've got a letter here from a student in my UCLA course on Jewish-Christian-Muslim dialogue, Jean Hubert. Born and raised a Catholic, he says that suddenly his Catholic faith means a hundred-fold more to him. We need each part of our community to be able to say something like, "What do you know! I mean I never knew how much more the Hebrew Bible and the Qur'an could mean to me because of my friendship, love for and association with Jews and Muslims. I'm making new discoveries every day. Look how God has blessed me." Or if Christians could get to the point of saying, "My friendship and contacts with the Jews and Muslims have helped me tremendously in my faith in Christ and in trying to live a Christian life." Perhaps Jews and Muslims could make similar discoveries.

We're not there yet as communities. Some people are fearful of dialogue between the three; some see this as an exotic activity; but, for others, there's a deep-set repugnance for coming together in any meaningful way. But if we could help them see the powerful blessing that inheres, then I'd even say there could be a revitalization of society, a new dynamism.

SIDDIQI: This is so important—The Academy's work is a model that should be presented to others. When I talk about our work to the Muslim community, whether in Lebanon or the West or India, they often say, "Well, you people are living in America. You have political stability there and are economically quite well off, so you have the luxury of being able to sit down and have a nice discussion. You don't have all these suspicions and fears that we're going through." My answer is that it's true the model for dialogue can be developed here because it's easy to do so. But it is very much needed in these other areas, too, because some of the reasons for economic problems and political chaos result from religious strife. It works both ways: interfaith dialogue can promote political stability and the economic well-being of nations; at the same time, economic well-being and political stability can assist dialogue. Justice on the political level has to be done, and on the economic level.

But interfaith dialogue could help remove the suspicion and fear that, for example, are causing the current strife in India between the Hindu and Muslim communities. The two communities are going to kill each other and destroy the whole fabric of India. It is so important that they come together, but they fear each other based on economic problems. People are out of work, and Hindus fear that the Muslim community is going to take away jobs; but Muslims feel the same way. So The Academy's work is important as a model developed to bring communities together.

GROSE: We are in a beneficent atmosphere in the United States for this sort of dialogue. As Jesus said, "To whom much is given, of him shall much be required" (Luke 12:48). Still, there are problems. A church in this area made a $500 grant to The Academy last spring, but the pastor thought they could do considerably more than that. I talked to the chairman of the church board who handles the bequest from which we were seeking funding for *The Abraham Connection.* He said the board members thought it was an interesting philosophical enterprise but not that close to their concerns. They didn't get it! In our time, Christians handle many things well, but in reference to other religions—on the basis of a passive hostility—they often don't respond. Is it a studied non-response?

We are kind of avant garde in this work. God knows, and you know, that many times I wanted to give it up. It's been hard for me personally in various ways. But there is tremendous hope for what we can accomplish, isn't there?

Turning to the Bosnian crisis, we surely ought to be doing a lot more. In our time, Bosnia's what's left of the interposing of at least two of the Abrahamic communities—maybe a third in small numbers; Jews are there, too. Muslims have been in Europe for a long time, but we forgot about that because the Turks got stopped outside of Vienna.[88] So here we have now the interaction of the Christians, the Serbian

Orthodox, and the indigenous Muslims right in the continent of Europe. It's a test case, and we're flunking. Still, The Academy might be able to help in some way by providing a model. W.A. Visser t'Hooft, the first Secretary General of the World Council of Churches, told me in 1975 that he thought what we were doing would contribute to "the concrete historical situation." He wasn't just going to let us be a traveling bunch of dialoguers.

Everything we do is related to the political and economic spheres. It's my conviction that one of the ways, if not the chief way, to untangle a problem is to get at it religiously. It's the entrance, the access to the problem, the way to cut the Gordian knot. In Christian terms, I would say, with the Apostle Paul, that "We wrestle not against flesh and blood but principalities and powers" (Ephesians 6:12). So, as we draw on our deepest spiritual resources, we are counteracting the forces of evil. It's not just stupidity out there, but evil, too, using stupidity. That's a Christian way of looking at it. We're engaged in a great war, and we've found allies.

HUBBARD: Let's get David in on the conversation.

5. THE FUTURE WORK OF THE ACADEMY

GORDIS: I've been listening carefully. We shouldn't lose sight of the American dimension of our enterprise, that the dialogue is taking place in the United States. It is well and good to say that what we need is religious dialogue in the Middle East or Bosnia to solve the problems there. But maybe the problem is that in those places where it's necessary, it can't take place because of the nature of their circumstances. The blessing of American society is that dialogue can emerge in the midst of our pluralism and diversity.   It's the preconditions for dialogue that are absent in so many troubled areas.

This dialogue between the four of us is wonderful and satisfying, but by itself it's not going to transform the world; yet, that's really what we want to do in our own way. We happen to have this instrument for dialogue and change, The Academy. Unfortunately, there aren't too many other places where such work is going on. But the important thing is that it be done, not that The Academy do it. It's also a risk, a kind of idolatry, that we make The Academy the issue, rather than the process of dialogue. Nevertheless, attention must be paid to this fragile instrument, The Academy, not in and of itself, but because it's one of the few means for nurturing the process we want to see happening.

The next step is for the program of The Academy to be generalized so as to strengthen the activity of interreligious relationships. Specifically, that means we want to move students and faculty members to an appreciation of interreligious dialogue, then train them to establish dialogues. For that, they need to learn the techniques of group dynamics and leadership. They need curricula, reading materials and models for dialogue. We can also train lay facilitators from each religious community to do this sort of work. This is a concrete function I hope we will do.

We will need to prepare these curricular materials both for academic institutions and for community or continuing education. I also hope we will continue to go into churches, synagogues and mosques so that we can model interfaith activity where a greater concentration of religious people are to be found.

Finally, I think our credibility will very much depend upon sustaining a research function. There are issues needing further study, such as the tension between missionizing and religious pluralism, messianism, the nature of the scriptural canon, redemption and salvation, institutional versus personal religion, faith and doubt. So, along with teaching, training and research—the three fundamental activities of academe—we would add this notion of wanting to affect the real world. It's a facilitator function: we want to bring people together so they can be the consumers of the materials we've prepared and be influenced by the people we've moved in the direction of interfaith encounters. This, then, is a programmatic translation of what I would like to see happen as a follow up to these discussions and a confirmation of our work.

GROSE: These are important, tangible aspects, David. The

Academy's prospectus talks about fellows of The Academy, people given scholarships so they can spend a month, three months, a year being trained by us. We might give them a certificate or credit towards a Masters program. They, in turn, would train other people since we can only reach so many lay people at a time. Our insights, expertise and experience need to be passed on to others who in time will take over this work.

GORDIS: That sparks a thought: maybe we ought to put together a week-long program in the summer, perhaps between the end of the academic year and the beginning of the summer session, in Boston or southern California. If it works, we could do such a workshop alternately in the East and the West and bring together clergy, academics, religious educators, and religious counselors at colleges and universities. We would deal with the theoretical foundations of what we're doing, get people enthusiastic about it, and train them in the techniques for doing this kind of work.

GROSE: If we could make some kind of appropriate beachhead on these coasts, it would be a great idea.

SIDDIQI: I think it is an excellent plan to have a week-long program with ministers, rabbis, imams—ten to fifteen from each side.

GORDIS: Even if we had twenty-five people altogether, with a faculty of six or seven people, it would be terrific.

HUBBARD: And the book that will result from these dialogues, *The Abraham Connection*, could be the textbook for the conference.

GORDIS: The conference would have three functions: combine learning and study in the subject areas, train people to develop their skills in bringing what has happened here to more people, and provide an opportunity for sharing religious and spiritual experience with others. Through the experience, they would learn and be moved by the particularity of the other, and also share in the commonality of the three faiths.

6. OUR COMMON HUMANITY

GORDIS (contin.): George, when you say, "When I see Muzammil, I see a Christian and a Jew and a Muslim," I understand what you're saying. Myself, I see the other person's humanity and spirituality. I think we're saying something similar; you tend to put it in somewhat more mystical terms.

GROSE: It's necessary to say both because, when it comes to "humanity," we can say that about the Hindus and the Buddhists, as well.

GORDIS: I do want to say that, but I think what you're saying is that this is not simply an abstraction. You want to say that I see myself in you.

GROSE: It's another way of saying it.

SIDDIQI: Yes, it is important that we recognize our common humanity. As human beings, unless I try to see myself in you and you see yourself in me, we cannot relate ourselves to each other positively. Isn't it also the meaning of the dictum, "Love for others what you love for yourself?" We should also recognize that each one of us is striving to be human in our own way. Wilfred Cantwell Smith[89] put it this way, "There is a Christian way of being human, a Jewish way and a Muslim way..."

GROSE: To do what?

SIDDIQI: I was quoting Smith who said, "To be a Christian is to be a human."

GORDIS: I'd put it this way: for the Jew, Judaism is the best way we have of being human. It's not a special distinction for the Jew. The same would be true of the Christian or Muslim. I've had Jewish feminists come to me and say, "The first thing I am is a woman, the second thing I am is a Jew." I reply, "Well, that sequence is okay; but preceding your being a Jew and being a woman, how about your being a human being?" So the first thing to say is that you share humanity with others. Before mentioning those things which divide and set you apart, skip five lines, leave a space, and begin with what we share as human beings. So often, that's forgotten.

GROSE: This reminds me powerfully of something that Archbishop Scott[90] said during a dialogue with us several years ago. He quoted the famous sentence in John's Gospel: "For God so loved the world that He gave His only Son..." (John 3:16). He said it doesn't read, "God so loved the Church," but "the world." If He loved the world, which means humanity, then—as you've said so powerfully, David—we must let our humanity come forth. Our humanity, in God's intent, is what it's all about. We're not going to be more than human, but sometimes people are a little less than human! So we all need to be fully human. If we are, then we're in a right relationship with God.

You remember the play and film "Children of a Lesser God." I'm not thinking so much about what happened to it as a play, but just the title. We are not "children of a lesser god;" that's something we all agree upon.

GORDIS: Our dominant consciousness should be of ourselves as human beings because in all the fundamental ways—birth, life, death, pain, suffering, fulfillment, the challenges that life creates—we are all human beings, all in the same boat. We face the same dangers, have the same possibilities and challenges to make the world a better place, seek fulfillment, etc. This precedes the fact that we structure ourselves with different languages and vocabularies, and follow these parallel paths. But, to start with, we too often condition ourselves to fixate on the things that divide us. The divisions are real and can be constructive; that's what pluralism means. Yet, it's important that we not skip over the first reality, the reality of our own humanity.

GROSE: There is a Christian way of coming at this, that is, Christ is the new Adam. He came to reconstitute human nature as God had originally intended after Adam's fall and human history with all of its tragedy and sin. Paul exhorts Christians to "Have this mind among yourselves, which you have in Christ Jesus..." (Philippians 2:5). They are to be Christ-like because Christ is what humanity is supposed to be. That's a major element in Christian mysticism and among the less dogmatic of the Christians, such as the Quakers. They're big on, "How can we be Christ-like?" that is, how can we fulfill our humanity. What I have proposed, but also realized in the sense of knowing, is that there's something going on amongst the Muslims and the Jews that looks pretty Christ-like to me. This is part of what I mean by saying, "When I see Muzammil, I also see a Christian and a Jew; when I see David, I also see a Muslim and a Christian."

GORDIS: Isn't it instructive in terms of the Hebrew scriptures—and I think it's true of the Qur'an also—that creation is the creation of Adam, and Abraham is several generations down the line. We discussed in an earlier session the wonderful statement from the Talmud about why the world is created from a single human being—it's that no one has the right to say my ancestor is greater than your ancestor. We have the same common ancestor. We're talking about Abrahamic religions, but we ought also to be mindful that Abraham and Abrahamic religions are several generations past the creation of the world. Creation preceded the divisions, so our humanity precedes our differentiation. Sometimes we tend to forget that.

SIDDIQI: All human beings are brothers and sisters. They all proceed from the same mother and father. It is not only that their nature is one and the same, but they are also related to each other in blood. This is the Islamic position and is what the Qur'an says, "O people, pay heed to God who created you from a single soul and from it created its mate, and from the pair created many men and women. Pay heed to God and to the wombs that bore you; surely God is watching over you" (Surah 4:1).

GORDIS: If you look at it as kind of a parable, the world is created in a single soul. That's the first, immediate feature: one human being was created, one humanity.

SIDDIQI: There is another statement in the Qur'an that emphasizes the respect of the humanity of the other person in the strongest terms. It says that the killing of one person—without a just cause—is like killing the whole of humanity; saving the life of one person is like saving the whole of humanity (Surah 5:32).

GORDIS: The Mishnah makes the same point. Why were all people created from a single human being? One reason is to teach that a person who saves a single soul, it is as if he saved an entire world; and if a person destroys a single soul, it is as if he destroyed an entire world (Mishna, *Sanhedrin*, 4, 5).

GROSE: Martin Buber has had much influence on those who have gotten into dialogue in the twentieth century. It's his thought that God is in the midst when two people or more are interacting in an "I-thou" manner.[91] Dietrich Bonhoeffer speaks of a community of the world and makes a distinction between the world and the Church. The community of the world he calls a psychic community rather than a spiritual one. He says Christians don't relate to one another directly but through Jesus. To relate to one another directly is where the problems lie—problems of dominance, submission, exploitation, lust, greed, and so forth. It's a provocative thought, this interposing of Jesus Christ in a relationship which purifies it. I'm not sure about it, but I don't dismiss it; and it's not altogether different from Buber's idea that God is in the midst when there's dialogue.

As we work together, as we've done here and in our public lectures, a tremendous beauty breaks forth that goes past any aesthetic categories. It's not the same as the beauty of Sunday morning worship, though it's connected to that. I think we've all realized something of this. Yet, it has nothing to do with the melding of our three religions. In my lecture at the World Council of Churches,[92] I said, "It may be that the promises vouchsafed to Abraham are being held back until the Jews, Christians and Muslims find each other." Or, as we find each other, these blessings and dynamisms break forth. This is what we are being led to.

7. THE PERSONAL EFFECTS OF THE DIALOGUE ON THE PARTICIPANTS

HUBBARD: Let me follow that up by mentioning an experience that's happened to me a few times. When telling non-academic friends that I was collaborating in a book on Jewish-Christian-Muslim dialogue, the answer was, "What dialogue?" In other words, from their perspective it was useless to talk about dialogue between three groups that had been at odds for so long. Usually my friends would refer to the improbability of Jewish-Muslim dialogue in light of the many problems in the Middle East and the long-standing hatreds and tensions there. Of course, I would reply that this is precisely one of the reasons we're doing this work—we want to change that. So I'd like each of you to comment on how the dialogue has changed your own thinking about the other two faiths, and then how that has implications for the larger faith communities you are in.

GORDIS: George mentioned how the dialogue experience is different from Sunday and the same as Sunday. When we've had public dialogues on weekday evenings, I've thought to myself that I'd love to get the people at these events to have a chance to see Jewish Sabbath morning worship. And I wish people at Sabbath services in my community could be a part of weekday evening dialogues. Do you follow the distinction? One event, the public dialogue, involves observation and learning which does away with demonizing the other faith groups. The other, the worship service, involves being swept up into the experience. I want to see the kind of weekly worship that takes place in the mosque, the Presbyterian Church, the Catholic Church, etc. And it's important for people to see that dialogue is possible, that it takes place, that it's not sterile; that we can come together in something other than conflict.

To go to the personal question: certainly, I've learned a great deal through our discussions. I had read and studied the Qur'an years ago; and had studied Christianity, especially because of my specialization in Rabbinics and the fact that Rabbinic Judaism and Christianity developed in the same period. But that's a different kind of learning than what emerges through these discussion. So there is a deepening of understanding of the religion of my friends here which goes beyond the theoretical. It's religion *in vivo* not religion *in vitro*—experiential rather than theoretical. That's one outstanding dimension of the impact on me.

Second, I also shared, when we began these sessions, some of the skepticism reflected in the responses of your friends, Ben, when they asked, "What dialogue?" You'll remember from the initial discussions that I never had any question whether dialogue was a good thing to be tried; but there was skepticism as to whether it was possible, whether there was any reality to it. I'm convinced now that it is possible, productive and useful in terms of the growth of human experience. That's why I think we ought to make every effort to expand it.

The most personal dimension has been the chance to develop what I think are profound and deep relationships—which partake of both intellectual and emotional characteristics—with those who participated. To use a little of your language, George, there is a mystical element here. By mysticism, I mean those dimensions of experience which are not susceptible to articulation in prose, and perhaps not even in poetry. But they are a reality of interrelationships which transcend the every day. There's been something extraordinary about our coming together. A bond has been created, and a spiritual awareness and opening which I've felt transformed by. You know, we're all very busy. But there has never been a time when I've gotten up in the morning—with piles of other things to do on a day we were meeting—when I didn't anticipate it with exhilaration, rather than saying, "Oh, God, I've got to travel the freeway to Fullerton again." That's a great blessing, and I'm grateful to you for providing that.

HUBBARD: Thank you very much. George.

GROSE: A while back I was talking with my daughter about funeral arrangements when I die—what scriptures I'd like read, what hymns sung. And I said I wouldn't be satisfied with having Bob McLaren[93] alone handle my service because I've got to have Muzammil, Ben,

David and some of my other friends involved, too. So it will be part of my last testimony that I arranged for at least one Muslim and one Jew to stand in a Christian pulpit at my service. I don't say this in any dismal sense. Rather, when one dies, the memorial service tries to be a summation of one's life. I look forward to great things in the world beyond. I'm very optimistic about it.

SIDDIQI: You want to have a dialogue there, too!

GROSE: Why not?

GORDIS: The only difference is that in the world to come there will be Hindus!

GROSE: I remember a time some ten years ago when I felt very lonely and out of touch with my church. I really didn't have anybody I knew, as far as clergy in the Church, who understood what I was doing in my work with The Academy. What did I do? On the day marking Muhammad's birthday, I drove to the downtown mosque in Los Angeles and listened to a lecture about Muhammad. This was in my period of great loneliness, lasting several months or a year, when I felt quite out of touch with my own community. That loneliness has been much assuaged by my cherished friends I work with— principally, you here and the other board members who will be with us at lunch. And I'm also finding, thank God, some in the Church who understand what I'm doing. That's a great healing for me to know, and it has come sometimes as much from lay people as clergy.

I was a chaplain for four years at Whittier College, and sometimes chaplains are not seen as very important by Church authorities. The pastor is the only one who counts. I told one of my colleagues at the time, Dr. Abdelmuhsin El-Biali, that I missed preaching. He said, "What's the matter with you, George? You're preaching to us all the time!" This was the reality principle coming in and straightening me out. But I've also felt—in the work of Jewish-Christian-Islamic dialogue—as if I'm in a scouting party: "What do you know; there are the Muslims and the Jews out there. Wow! This is new territory, what's going on?" At first I asked myself, "Am I doing the right thing? As a Christian, should I be doing this?" That questioning's been overcome by me. But if Christians could all be called pioneers and keep looking for the promised land, they just might find Muslims and Jews in their parallel wagon trains. I'm using the western images because we are out here in the West. When we circle the wagons, let's hope it's not against one another but inclusive of one another.

SIDDIQI: George asked himself if he was doing the right thing, and I've done the same thing—ever since I got involved in Muslim-Christian dialogue twenty years ago and then later working with you in The Academy and as good friends. I always felt after sitting together—even though questions arose in my mind—that, yes, this is the right thing. It is important work, it should be done, and done more. Some of our suspicions and misunderstandings will disappear through these discussions. There's something wrong with me if I misunderstand you, so I should understand the other person in the right way. I think these meetings have been very useful.

Like David, I also studied and took courses in Judaism and Christianity; but I've found that having these extended conversations has deepened my understanding of the Christian and Jewish faiths. And the dialogues have done something else. Even though I still have problems with your theology, David, and yours, George, when I talk about Jewish or Christian theology, I see your faces as if you are hearing me. So, because you are my friends, I must speak accurately. I still express disagreements, but I do so in a way that is not going to misrepresent you. In a sense, when other people talk about Judaism, I see David's face, and I also say that I'm not going to listen to any misrepresentation of him—someone I sit with, eat with and talk with. And I see George's face when Christianity is discussed. So this kind of conversation, sitting together, can help us speak about each other in the right way. Even if we speak about our differences, we should say that this is our understanding; and we'll give the other person the chance to present his position.

The third thing I see—as David mentioned—is that there is greater scope for this work. I'm becoming more and more convinced that it's important for many people to be involved in dialogue. Of course, some in the Muslim community—with the tensions they see between Muslims and others in Bosnia and elsewhere—are taking the other side and becoming more exclusive and fanatic. They say, "Don't talk to others because everybody is against us, so we shouldn't be with them." That feeling is growing among some in the Muslim community. I feel this is not the right answer. We need to think about why the situation is the way it is and how we can improve it; for no community can live by itself. In this world we are becoming more interdependent, so it is necessary to have dialogue and discussion, and to have a better understanding of each other. Give and take, and compromise, will also be necessary—this is how we can work. I'm not saying compromise in matters of faith, of truth, but in many other areas that will make cooperation possible. So I see a greater scope for our work.

GROSE: In our society, much is being done by Jews and Christians working together on problems like homelessness or poverty. It's not well known that Muslims also care about and work on these problems. In fact, I've been desirous of having Muzammil appointed to the Human Relations Commission of Orange County where Jews and Christians have been very active. I don't think there are any Muslims on it, but that will come. So the three communities need to work together as a team on these social problems. And behind such efforts is our dialogue work or work like it.

HUBBARD: May the moderator add a few thoughts. First, when we began these meetings in the fall of 1991, I was on a sabbatical leave. You three were really my teachers during that period, and I've learned much.

Secondly, Martin Buber has said, "All living is meeting." That thought has guided me for a long time. "Meeting" means that you come together and share ideas with people you didn't think you'd be sharing with, and that you are forever changed and can never be the same again. I've had other experiences like this one, too. For example, I happen to be fairly active in the Planned Parenthood organization, and yet I often challenge the other board members to listen to the other side. Even though I think the pro-choice position on abortion is the right one, I tell them not to stop listening to the good, intelligent people on the pro-life side who have a different view of this issue. I try to dialogue with pro-life people because there is a dialectic that goes on when people of very opposite points of view get together, and it changes everybody for the better. Obviously, I think this is true here. Our three faiths have had centuries of tension. There have been periods of wonderful cooperation, such as the Spanish Golden Age,[94] but also periods of tragedy. Yet, the more we meet and listen to the other, the more we are changed. Something happens that makes the whole human situation different because of meeting. You can never be the same once you've listened to and experienced the other.

Furthermore, it isn't just a matter of intellectually listening to the other. You now see human beings who are good and caring, and have deep feelings and concerns. For example, I am aware that these dialogues have cost some of you something. Certain people have criticized Muzammil and George; David, I'm not sure in your case but...

GORDIS: There are so many things to criticize me about they may not know where to start!

HUBBARD: I see the problems you've had and I'm struck by another problem, what I call the problem of good. Philosophers and theologians wax eloquently about the problem of evil, but the problem of good is the other side. I'm amazed sometimes at the fact that there is such a well of goodness in humanity. True, there's another well full of stagnant, evil water; but there's a good well, too, and it amazes me how much genuine goodness, concern and devotion there is amongst people. I've seen it around this table— people who care and are dedicated put themselves into this work at the risk of personal criticism. That restores my faith in human nature. Human nature is always going to be staggering, struggling; but the problem of good will not go away. You can't dismiss that "problem," either, any more than you can erase the immense evil we see around us. So the work of dialogue between Judaism, Christianity and Islam is exemplary or paradigmatic for other areas, whether it's the one I mentioned of pro-

and anti-abortion people talking or it's people of different political or philosophical ideologies coming together, and so forth. This sort of interfaith dialogue experience is a powerful lesson for humanity. In that sense, it's been worth every second; and I think it's going to make some difference.

EPILOGUE

On March 4, 1865, in the waning months of the Civil War, President Abraham Lincoln delivered his second inaugural address—since called, simply, the Second Inaugural. "With malice toward none; with charity for all; with firmness in the right as God gives us to see the right, let us strive on to finish the work we are in. . . ," he said, concluding.

In the dialogue between Jews, Christians and Muslims we are given to explore the outer reaches of our humanity; to be exposed, now and again, to a splendor which leads us on. "Let us strive on to finish the work we are in. . ."

In the same Second Inaugural, Abraham Lincoln uttered these words: "Still it must be said, 'The judgments of the Lord are true and righteous altogether'" (Psalm 19:9).

As one day follows another in this our particular time of testing, we have confidence in the judgments of the Lord toward the communities of Israel, the Nazarene and the Ishmaelite—the Jews, the Christians and the Muslims—for these judgments are "sweeter than honey and the honeycomb" (Psalm 19:9).

Will we now draw together and "Dispute not...except on the best of terms" (Qur'an 29:46) and bring to flower a new civilization, the contours of which we can only dream about?

END NOTES

1.   John Calvin, Institutes, Vol. 1, p. 437. English Translation: Philadelphia: Westminster Press, 1960.

2.   A millennium after the patriarchal era.

3.   Genesis 22, where God commands Abraham to sacrifice his son but spares him at the last second.

4.   Jewish theologian, 1907-73.

5.   A description coined by Rudolph Otto in *The Idea of the Holy* (English translation: New York: Oxford University Press, 1957).

6.   "Torah," as found in the first five books of the Bible, means the "recital" both of what God has done for Israel and what they are expected to do in return. So "law" is not an adequate translation.

7.   The feast of "weeks" which occurs 50 days/seven weeks after Passover and commemorates the giving of the Torah to Moses at Sinai.

8.   The *hijrah* (migration) from Mecca to Medina in 622 C.E., year one of the Islamic calendar. 622 C.E. is 1 A.H. (*Anno Nigirae* [In the Year of the Hijrah]).

9.   See the First Book of Maccabees.

10. Third-century compiler of the Mishnah.

11. Second-century teacher and martyr.

12. Tenth-century Talmudic scholar in Babylon.

13. The "Eighteen Benedictions" or *Shemoneh Eserah*.

14. See Matthew 5:17

15. John 18:33, 39; 19:3, 19, 21.

16. Greek: *theotokos*.

17. There are now about one billion Muslims.

18. The list of books officially considered part of either the Hebrew or Christian scriptures.

19. The nineteenth-century founder of the Church of Jesus Christ of Latter Day Saints or Mormons.

20. As Dr. Siddiqi mentioned earlier in this chapter, according to Islam, Abraham, David and Solomon were prophets; and all had more than one wife.

21. Dutch-born philosopher, 1632-77.

22. Second century.

23. During the so-called "Golden Age," 900-1200 C.E.

24. For example, as discussed in Chapter One, Muslims do not believe Jesus was crucified and raised from the dead. See Surah 4:157.

25. In Christian bibles the prophet Malachi is the last book of the Old Testament; but the Hebrew Bible, though containing the same books as the Old Testament, puts them in different order. Thus, the so-called wisdom writings—Psalms, Proverbs, Job, etc.—follow the prophets.

26. For example, Genesis 1:26, "Let *us* make man in our image..."

27. New York: Schocken Books, 1961.

28. From the *Siddur*, the Jewish Daily Prayer Book.

29. A text seen as referring to events in the life of Jesus Christ.

30. Ibn Ishaq's definitive biography of Muhammad, *The Life of Muhammad*, (English translation: New York: Oxford, 1955) opens with the genealogy of Muhammad as descended from Abraham through Ishmael.

31. As quoted in Hans Kung's *Theology for the Third Millennium* (English translation: New York: Doubleday, 1988), p. 178.

32. Compare "Islam," the religion of submission.

33. Compare 1 John 2:2: "and he is the propitiation for our sins, and not for ours only but also for the sins of the whole world."

34. A tractate of the Mishnah concerning ethics.

35. Julius Wellhausen (1844-1918) argued that the Torah was a composite of four documents brought together in final form in the fifth century B.C.E. For a contemporary approach to the composition of the Torah, see Richard Elliott Friedman, *Who Wrote the Bible?* (Englewood Cliffs, NJ: Prentice Hall, 1987).

36. Jewish philosopher from Alexandria, Egypt (20 B.C.E.-40 C.E.).

37. See Isaiah 55:11: "...so shall my word be that goes forth from my mouth; it shall not return to me empty, but it shall accomplish that which I purpose..."

38. See, for example, Adin Steinsaltz, *The Thirteen Petalled Rose* (English translation: New York: Basic Books, 1980).

39. A founding member and Vice President of the Academy for Judaic-Christian-Islamic Studies.

40. They are called "minor" because their works are shorter. They are: Hosea, Joel, Amos, Obadiah, Jonah, Micah, Nahum, Habakkuk, Zephaniah, Haggai, Zechariah and Malachi.

41. Jewish writings dating from about 250 B.C.E. to 100 C.E.

42. This is the widely-accepted idea that the authors of Matthew and Luke had access to the Gospel of Mark and to a collection of Jesus's sayings called "Q" (from the German word *Quelle*, "source") when they wrote their gospels.

43. See "The Letter of Aristeas" in R.H. Charles, *The Apocrypha and Pseudepigrapha of the Old Testament in English* (Oxford: The Clarendon Press, 1977), Vol. 2. *Septuaginta* in Latin means 70.

44. For example, the *Didache* or *Teaching of the Twelve Apostles, The Letter of Barnabas* and *The Letter of Ignatius.*

45. For example, *The Gospel of Thomas* and *The Gospel of Peter.*

46. These were theologians of the second to the sixth centuries who defended and clarified the meaning of Christianity and early Church creeds.

47. Preeminent Jewish philosopher and Talmudist, 1135-1204.

48. The *Hijrah* occurred in 622 C.E.

49. The pilgrimage referred to is the *Hajj*, the visit to the Kaaba in Mecca, which Muslims are enjoined to make at least once in their lifetimes if possible.

50. Exegesis is the exposition, critical analysis or interpretation of a word or passage.

51. He died in 1898.

52. See the rabbinic commentary the *Tosefta*, Tractate *Aboda Zara*: 9,4.

53. A dictum of the medieval church.

54. That is, kosher and non-kosher animals; see Leviticus 11, Deuteronomy 14: 3-20.

55. See, e.g., Romans 10:4.

56. The Greek word *eucharisteo* means "I give thanks." See Jesus's words at the Last Supper which instituted the Eucharist: Luke 22:19: "And he took bread, and *gave thanks*, and broke it and gave it to them. . ." cf. Matthew 26:28, Mark 14:23.

57. See David Hartman, *A Living Covenant* (New York: Free Press, 1985); Eliezer Berkovits, *Not in Heaven* (New York: Ktav, 1983).

58. See Solomon B. Freehof, *Current Reform Responsa* (Cincinnati: Hebrew Union College Press, 1969); Walter Jacobs (ed.), *American Reform Responsa*, (Central Conference of American Rabbis, 1983).

59. "Judaism" here refers to the tradition which evolved out of ancient Israelite religion and stressed the oral interpretation of the Torah to adapt it to changed circumstances. It culminated in the production of the two Talmuds, Jerusalem and Babylonian, in about 450 and 500 C.E. respectively.

60. Attributed to 'Umar the second Caliph or successor of Muhammad. It granted protected status to Jews, Christians and Zoroastrians in Muslim-governed areas.

61. See, e.g., 1 Timothy 6:1-2.

62. The classic of Jewish mysticism written in the thirteenth century C.E. by the Castillian mystic Moses de Leon.

63. He was executed by the Nazis in 1945 for plotting to assassinate Hitler.

64. English translation: New York: Harper, 1954.

65. Damascus:661-750.

66. The leader who made Turkey a secular nation in 1923.

67. Sufism is the mystical dimension within Islam. It emphasizes mainly the spiritual aspect of the Islamic tradition.

68. Maimonides completed the *Mishneh Torah,* a 14-volume commentary on the Talmud, in 1180.

69. That is, saying one of the prayers before or after the Torah portion is read by the rabbi.

70. See Tillich's *The Courage To Be* (New Haven: Yale, 1952).

71. See, e.g., Isaiah 49:3.

72. In his book *The Preacher's Task and the Stone of Stumbling.* The Lyman Beecher Lectures, Yale University (New York: Harper, 1958).

73. See Genesis 16-17; Surahs 2: 125-29 and 19:54-5.

74. Since this dialogue took place, Israel and the Vatican, on December 30, 1993, signed an agreement that will lead to full diplomatic relations.

75. Joseph Kalir (1908-88), a professor of Jewish Studies at California State University, Fullerton. The quotation which follows is from his *Introduction to Judaism* (Lanham, MD: University Press of America, 1980), p. 109.

76. This was the last and most powerful Muslim empire that, at various times, ruled parts of Europe, Asia Minor, the Middle East and surrounding areas from 1326 to 1924. It became weak and finally ended with the abolition of the caliphate by Kamal Ataturk.

77. That is, the policy concerning the West Bank and Gaza of the Shamir government which was in office when this dialogue took place in fall, 1991.

78. The Susan and David Wilstein Institute of Policy Studies is an international research and policy studies center based at the University of Judaism in Los Angeles and Hebrew College in Boston.

79. At Israel's narrowest point, there are only about eight miles between the West Bank and the Mediterranean Sea.

80. George Bush who was, at the time of this dialogue, giving diplomatic support to Assad.

81. The conservative Likud party grouping has rejected territorial compromise as a means of achieving a peace settlement with the Arab states and the Palestinians.

82. The U.S. supported Iraq in the Iran-Iraq War of 1980-88.

83. Shimon Peres was Israel's prime minister briefly in the late 1980s and became foreign minister under Prime Minister Yitzhak Rabin in 1992.

84. Shortly before this dialogue session, in the fall of 1992, Hindus and Muslims clashed in several Indian cities because a mosque—which fundamentalist Hindus claimed had been the site of a temple to the god Rama centuries earlier—was destroyed by Hindu extremists.

85. Muslims comprise about 18 per cent of India's population.

86. These Berber Muslims from north Africa controlled parts of Spain from 1157 to 1223.

87. Daniel Ninburg, M.D., is Vice President for Institutional Affairs of the Academy for Judaic, Christian, and Islamic Studies.

88. Twice: in 1529 and 1683.

89. A leading Christian scholar of world religions and a specialist in Islam.

90. The Most Reverend Edward W. Scott, Primate of the Anglican Church of Canada (1971-86). Moderator of The Central Committee of The World Council of Churches (1975-84). An honorary president of the Academy for Judaic, Christian, and Islamic Studies.

91. *I and Thou* is the title of Buber's most famous book. (English translation: New York: Charles Scribner's Sons, 1970).

92. At the 1983 meeting in Vancouver, British Columbia.

93. A Presbyterian clergyman; professor at California State University, Fullerton; founding member and a Vice President of the Academy.

94. The Golden Age of the Umayyads in Spain between about 900 and 1200 C.E. when Jewish, Christian and Muslim cultures flourished together under tolerant Muslim rule.

INDEX

Printed in the United States
20412LVS00001B/175-216